D1104614

Constructing Socialism

Johns Hopkins Studies in the History of Technology

Merritt Roe Smith, *Series Editor*

Raymond G. Stokes

Constructing Socialism

Technology and Change in
East Germany 1945–1990

The Johns Hopkins University Press | Baltimore and London

© 2000 The Johns Hopkins University Press
All rights reserved. Published 2000
Printed in the United States of America on acid-free paper
9 8 7 6 5 4 3 2 1

The Johns Hopkins University Press
2715 North Charles Street
Baltimore, Maryland 21218-4363
www.press.jhu.edu

Library of Congress Cataloging-in-Publication Data
will be found at the end of this book.

A catalog record for this book is available from the
British Library.

ISBN 0-8018-6391-0

To the memory of Michael and Nora O'Shea

Contents

Acknowledgments ix

Introduction 1

Part I: Defining a Socialist System of Innovation in the GDR, 1945–1958 13

1 Technology in the Soviet Zone, 1945–1949 15

2 A First, Flawed Construction: Technology Planning and Practice through 1958 36

Part II: Socialist Technology at the Crossroads, 1958–1961 55

3 Metrics of Progress: Technological Tourism and Display 57

4 The High-Tech Hardware of Socialism 80

5 The Software of Socialism 110

Part III: From Fresh Start to Endgame, 1961–1990 129

6 The Controlled Experiment in Technological Development: Technology in the New Economic System 131

7 Substituting for Success, 1970–1989 153

8 Technological Tactics in the Endgame 177

Conclusion 195

List of Abbreviations 209

Notes 213

Bibliographic Essay 243

Index 253

Acknowledgments

At the end of the long process of research, writing, and rewriting, it is a pleasure to reflect briefly on the kindness, engagement, and encouragement of the numerous institutions and individuals who have helped me during the course of it.

Financial support for the project came from the German Marshall Fund of the United States, Rensselaer Polytechnic Institute, the Deutscher Akademischer Austauschdienst (DAAD), the University of Glasgow, the university's Department of Economic and Social History, and the Centre for Business History in Scotland. I am grateful for the generosity of all of these organizations. Rensselaer and the University of Glasgow were both also generous with another commodity in short supply, time, which I used for research and writing. Colleagues in my department at each institution were generous in yet a third way, with ideas and moral support, for which I am very grateful.

During the course of the project I enjoyed a productive year and part of an additional summer at the Free University of Berlin, for much of the time as a guest researcher in the Economics Department of the university's John F. Kennedy Institute. Professor Carl-Ludwig Holtfrerich, the head of the department, and Frau Barbara Spannagel, along with the other department members, made my family and me extremely welcome and provided a friendly, stimulating, and supportive working environment. I also enjoyed less formal, but still fruitful associations with the Economic History section of the Economics Department of the Humboldt University (under Professor Lothar Baar) and with the Institute for Economic and Social History of the Free University (under Professor Wolfram Fischer). Additional research time was spent at the Deutsches Museum. I thank Dr. Helmut Trischler, his family, and his staff, for making our time in Munich so enjoyable.

Much of my time in Germany was spent in archives. I would like to thank in particular the staff of the Bundesarchiv branches in the Berlin area, in Potsdam, in the Berlin city center, and eventually in Lichterfelde. Thanks, too, to Frau Prause of the Gauck Authority (responsible for the Stasi documents) in Berlin, who was enormously helpful in preparing documents for my inspection. The pictures used in the book came from two archives: the Bundesarchiv Bildstelle in Koblenz, and the Sammlung industrielle Formgestaltung in Berlin-Prenzlauer Berg. My thanks to these institutions for permission to reproduce the photographs. Thanks, too, in particular to Frau Lorenz for her accommodation to the needs of my schedule in selecting the photos at the Sammlung.

Although my project was generally a small-scale one for the most part, I had the good fortune to be associated with one larger project group directly, and indirectly with another. The Science under Socialism project, directed by Kristie Macrakis of Michigan State University and Dieter Hoffmann of the Max Planck Institute for the History of Science in Berlin, brought together a large group of American and German researchers interested in the history, science, and technology of the German Democratic Republic. The project was funded by the Alexander von Humboldt Foundation and Michigan State University. I benefited from comments by project participants on drafts of my paper on the East German chemical industry and from conferences associated with the project. In addition, I was pleased to be in contact with members of the Deutsche Forschungsgemeinschaft's large research project comparing innovation in the two German successor states between 1945 and 1990. They were even kind enough to invite me to one of their conferences, which was extremely helpful. In this context, I want to thank Stefan Unger in particular.

I presented papers based in part on the research for this book at the German Studies Association's 1995 annual meeting, two conferences of the Science under Socialism project, the Society for the History of Technology's 1996 annual meeting, the Free University of Berlin, the University of Glasgow, Cambridge University, the University of Strathclyde, the History of Science Society's 1998 annual meeting, the University of Cardiff, and the University of Bielefeld. Criticism and comments from discussants and participants have both enabled me to develop my ideas much further than I might otherwise have done and forced me to be more precise in thought and expression. Thank you to all. I also thank the editors and publishers of *German History* for allowing me to use, in chapter 5, substantial portions of my article "In Search of the Socialist

Artefact: Technology and Ideology in East Germany, 1945–1962," *German History* 15 (1997): 223–39.

My thinking has been shaped heavily by conversations with colleagues, and often as well by their comments on draft chapters and/or informal exchanges of ideas, sometimes long ago. I wish to thank them all, in particular Werner Abelshauser, Mike Allen, Mitch Ash, Johannes Bähr, Richard Bessel, Alan Beyerchen, Burghard Ciesla, John Connelly, Paul Erker, Dieter Hoffmann, Carl Holtfrerich, Paul Josephson, Matthias Judt, Rainer Karlsch, John Krige, Brian Linn, Kristie Macrakis, Cathy Olesko, Jörg Roesler, Harm Schröter, André Steiner, Anne Stokes, Agnes Tandler, and Helmut Trischler. I owe a particular debt of gratitude to Rainer Karlsch, who read and commented extensively and helpfully on the entire draft manuscript. Agnes Tandler also gave me useful feedback on the penultimate draft. Rainer Karlsch also provided some sources that were not easily available elsewhere, as did Agnes Tandler. Anne Stokes read through the penultimate draft of the manuscript, helping me enormously with style and clarity. Despite so much generous advice from so many capable people, errors undoubtedly remain; responsibility for those, of course, is mine alone.

As the book approached completion, I benefited from the encouragement of M. Roe Smith, the editor of this series, and of the history editor at the Johns Hopkins University Press, Bob Brugger. The anonymous reviewer for the press also provided useful comments.

Throughout the project, I have had frequent occasion to consider the more indirect, but still profound influence on my work of the ideas, insights, and wisdom of several of my teachers. I thank in particular William Berentz, Laszlo Deme, June Fullmer, and Alan Beyerchen.

My family have been very supportive during the research and writing, which sometimes involved extended absences from home. Anne, Jonathan, and Nik also sacrificed part of several holidays to "working vacations." Much more frequently, they somehow endured my endless distraction, which, I have to admit, is a major drawback of my writing technique.

This book is dedicated to the fond memory of my maternal grandparents, Michael O'Shea (1905–95) and Nora Stack O'Shea (1907–98), who exerted an enormous influence on both my personal and my professional development. I count it as a great blessing to have enjoyed that influence firsthand for so long.

Constructing Socialism

Introduction

With a cloud of blue smoke and a high-pitched whine, the Trabant, powered by its two-stroke engine, carried many an East German westward after the fall of the Berlin Wall in November 1989. The car's 1950s design, its obvious environmental incorrectness, and its all-plastic body had made it a symbol of the technological limitations of communism in the German Democratic Republic (GDR). The famous photographic image from the early 1990s of the rear of a "Trabi" (as they were called) protruding from a dumpster—however unfair and oversimplified—seemed to suggest that the car, like the system that had produced it, had been consigned to the dustbin of history.

The idea that things would end up this way would have come as a rude shock to East Germany's founders, and their apparently abject technological failure would have been especially galling. After all, Lenin had underscored the centrality of technology to the communist project in his oft-quoted slogan, "Communism equals Soviet power plus electrification of the whole country." East German leaders had tried from the first to realize the broader technological program behind these words. Nuclear power, sophisticated electronics, high-precision optical equipment and machine tools, together with plastics made from petrochemicals, were the high-prestige products favored by GDR planners and rulers. And high-technology projects associated with these and other industries were often touted as the solution to the country's persistent economic problems.

So what explains the communist deficiency, especially in this high-priority area of technology? For Soviet Russia and most other eastern European countries, the economic and technological backwardness of the areas the communists took over to conduct their grand experiment clearly played a major role in their ultimate failure. But this explanation does not hold for East Germany, where, starting in June 1945, Germans who were trained and supported by the Soviets could settle in the area

The first version of the Trabant leaving the factory in Zwickau in 1958.
Named after the first Sputnik, the Trabant, with its futuristic all-plastic body,
was admired in the West as well. *Bundesarchiv, Koblenz, Bildsammlung*

that would become the GDR to begin to conduct the communist experiment in an advanced industrial economy.

For the historian, the questions must be these: Why and when did this highly industrialized and highly innovative economy fall on such hard times? Were there opportunities for reform and resuscitation of its system of industry and innovation, or was it condemned from the start? If opportunities existed, when did they occur, and why were they not exploited? If they did not exist, how was the system able not only to survive, but even to convince outsiders that the GDR was outperforming many western industrialized nations through the 1980s? Finally, what best explains the maintenance of islands of technological excellence—which *did* exist, despite the general technological failure—in a generally second- or third-rate sea, from the beginning of the GDR's existence to its collapse?

In the following chapters, I examine these and other questions relating to the role of technology in East German history between 1945 and 1990.

My focus is on a relatively small country, and one that ultimately collapsed, yet the story I have to tell here is an important one. What is more, it can be told with the aid of an almost unbelievable abundance of archival evidence. East Germany's absorption into the Federal Republic of (West) Germany has opened up to historians the written record of the GDR regime from beginning to end. Official records of the dominant Socialist Unity Party (Sozialistische Einheitspartei, or SED) and the state it operated are a treasure trove, providing a fairly complete record of a historical era, in which the party and state controlled—or at least influenced and monitored—virtually every aspect of GDR society. The advantages of the centralized regime to the historian are obvious. The archival records provide an opportunity to investigate the development of technology policy by centralized institutions and its deployment in research institutes and factories. Secret-service records provide an unparalleled glimpse into the practice of technology transfer, legal and illegal, during the Cold War. The situation is as delightful as it is unprecedented.

These unusually favorable conditions provide the basis for a history of East German technology that embraces political, economic, and social factors, and covers the entire period of the country's existence. Consideration of the role of technology and innovation in the GDR's development will improve our understanding of post-1945 German history generally. It can also shed light on the role of science and technology in other socialist (or formerly socialist) countries, none of which can be investigated with anywhere near the same documentary range as the GDR. Such an investigation can also provide empirical evidence to help test more general theories about innovation and the process of economic development, the politics of technology, and the social shaping of technology. And finally—as many who have looked at the history, sociology, politics, and economics of technology have already documented—the study of "failure" can be as instructive as that of "success."[1] The case study presented here is a relatively modest one, but it has very general and important implications.

Faced with an embarrassment of riches, in the form of unprecedented access to enormous quantities of documents, the historian must distill them into a coherent tale. Large quantities of archival and other materials are a vocational hazard of those who investigate the post-1945 period for any industrialized country, and I have used time-honored techniques to render the subject and its documentation manageable. One way of doing this is to concentrate on a few themes especially well suited to the subject matter. Depending upon definition, for instance, *technology* in the GDR could be a very broad subject indeed, embracing everything from farm implements to microchips, from organizational psychology to management structures and procedures. It seemed sensible to limit the focus, so I have concentrated on technology-intensive industries of substantial importance for economic development and foreign trade. These include machine tools, optics, chemicals, and electronics. In investigating these industries, I have also emphasized several central themes related to them, such as German technological traditions, technology transfer, alleged Sovietization of technology, and the impact of ideology and planning on technological development.

I have also relied heavily on the work of other scholars and commentators to identify the kinds of questions that need to be answered. There seems, for instance, to be consensus among western scholars of the GDR that the primary explanation for its inefficiencies and relatively poor performance compared to its West German counterpart was the planning system.[2] One of the central issues explored throughout this book, then, is the question of whether systemic or other factors accounted for East Germany's relatively poor showing economically and technologically.

Scholars have also identified several issues concerning the specific role of technology in the GDR. Essentially, these boil down to the question of why the GDR was not able to innovate effectively (which in turn, of course, had a probable impact on economic performance). Speaking for many in the late 1970s, the German Institute for Economic Research contended that the causes behind the GDR's poor record of innovation were threefold: poor formulation of research tasks by industrial enterprises; weak links between research and production; and, most important, "the reluctance of the enterprises to accept innovations."[3]

More recent studies of management and technology in the GDR, completed in the aftermath of German unification and with the benefit of access to previously secret or inaccessible material, have reinforced these findings, but added some nuances of their own. Looking at research and development within the context of the industrial firm, for instance, Vincent Edwards and Peter Lawrence have pointed out that the GDR system discouraged new product development, instead favoring projects that facilitated the manufacture of existing products.[4] Raymond Bentley, in an in-depth economic analysis of research and technology in the GDR, identified several different problems, whose cause, he felt, was clear:

"obstacles to industrial innovation and diffusion . . . could not be overcome because they were endogenous to the system of central economic planning."[5] This brings us back full circle to the fundamental problem that most western analyses of the GDR economy identify. Johannes Bähr and Dietmar Petzina make a similar claim in their introduction to a long collection of case studies of specific industries and firms in East and West Germany. They argue that the individual cases lead to a general conclusion: although the GDR had a "bad start," its "bad run" was primarily responsible for its ultimate failure. The bad run, in turn, was caused by shortcomings in the system of planning and innovation itself.[6]

Common to such assessments is the implication that the system was a static one, predestined to failure from the outset. However, this seems unlikely on the face of it, and for that reason this study pays explicit attention to the analysis and assessment of GDR research culture as it changed over time. Assessment of the problems associated with the GDR system of innovation and their causes also figures prominently. Focus on the "high-tech" industries already mentioned (chemicals, machine tools, electronics, and optics) allows attention both to formulation of science and technology policy and to its implementation at individual factories and in particular technological systems. Such attention in turn permits a critical assessment of the notion that the GDR possessed a system of innovation that was at best ineffective, and at worst an outright failure.

In any case, the notion of a system of innovation in the GDR that was fundamentally flawed from the outset is a somewhat problematic one. The country, after all, had some major technological successes, as some of the most recent literature on individual technologies demonstrates. And these successes were not just in traditional technologies, such as printing machinery, but also in some of the most challenging, cutting-edge areas, such as laser technology and space optics.[7]

Several questions thus present themselves for further critical investigation: If the system itself was fundamentally flawed, how does one explain these successes under the very same system? How was it possible to succeed in some areas but fail in others? And if these successes were only a few exceptions that prove the rule, then why did the political, economic, social, and technological system in the GDR last as long as it did? Thus, while this book takes the work of other scholars into account, it starts from a completely different premise than is the norm. Instead of trying to explain failure—reasons for which abound—it seeks to explain success, or at least the maintenance of a system of innovation that was able to deliver some minimal level of technological excellence into GDR economy and industry, thus allowing the survival of the system as a whole for several decades. To do this, I start with the assumption that neither success nor failure was preordained. Instead, the development of technology in the GDR was contingent, shaping and being shaped by particular and ever changing political, social, and economic configurations in the country's forty-year existence.

Discussing the GDR's relative "success" or "failure" over time implies comparison with other countries, and this study makes frequent comparisons between GDR technology and technology developed elsewhere. But it has been far from self-evident which countries are best suited for such comparisons.

The most obvious point of comparison, and the one on which much of the now very large German scholarly output on the problem dwells, is "the other Germany."[8] This approach has much to recommend it, not least because it recognizes, at least implicitly, the existence of a common German technological culture, which began to unravel after 1945. Moreover, such a conceptualization makes it possible to investigate the factors shaping innovative behavior in a comparative and dynamic fashion. Some firms in East and West Germany, such as Zeiss and the successors of I. G. Farben, had actually been part of the same industrial corporation through 1945 and thus shared a common German technological culture as well as a common corporate culture. This fact makes such a mode of investigation even more intriguing and convincing.[9]

But there are problems with the German-German comparison, too. As most researchers who have adopted this approach have discovered, it is generally far easier to find differences than similarities between innovation patterns in the two countries, mainly because of the very different economic structures and international trading patterns of the two. And, on another level, the German-German comparison is not at all fair, because of the very real differences in geographic and demographic scale between the two German successor states. The West German Federal Republic was a medium-sized state with a substantial internal market of its own and considerable high-quality coal resources. The East German Democratic Republic was a relatively small state (on the order of one-fourth to one-third the size of West Germany in terms of population) with sizable quantities of relatively low-quality coal and of uranium ore, but few other natural resources.

One way of overcoming the problem of fundamental systemic difference inherent in the German-German comparison is to examine East German developments comparatively in the context of the eastern, Soviet-dominated bloc. Again, such comparisons seem valuable, not least because the Cold War produced an outpouring of literature by Sovietologists on technology under socialism.[10] This literature addresses the general problems and possibilities of innovation in the socialist planned economy, the importance and process of technology transfer both within the eastern bloc and between East and West, and the development of specific technologies under Soviet socialism.

But again, despite the systemic similarities between East Germany and other members of the eastern bloc, comparison between the GDR and its eastern neighbors has often been primarily an exercise in spotting differences rather than similarities. Most of the literature focuses on the Soviet Union itself. Certainly, issues of interest to the situation in the GDR do crop up in these studies, such as the coexistence of impressive innovation alongside astonishing backwardness, or the pronounced but often unexpected impact of state planning of the economy on technological change. But the USSR, even at the end of its existence, lay far behind the GDR in terms of development, whether measured technologically or economically (in terms of per-capita income). What is more, the problems of extreme differences in scale inherent in the German-German comparison are magnified several times in the USSR-GDR comparison. Czechoslovakia perhaps is the one country in the eastern bloc that may have been most comparable to the GDR in terms of level of economic and technological development, but the literature on the Czech case in western European languages is sparse, with virtually nothing on technology.

In brief, comparisons of the GDR with the "other Germany" and with other Soviet-bloc countries have their uses, but they also have their drawbacks. A more useful comparison would be with a country or countries that began the period after 1945 at a similar level of industrialization and that had, if not a fully planned economy, a heavily nationalized or state-directed one. Two candidates presented themselves to the East Germans in the late 1950s and the early 1960s: the United Kingdom and Japan. Clearly, there are problems in comparing the GDR with either or both of these, too. After all, systemic differences still stand out, and both Japan and the UK enjoyed much larger markets and populations than the GDR. Both, however, like East Germany, were also highly industrialized, with considerable scientific and technological capabilities.[11] They were likewise heavily dependent on foreign sources of raw materials and on foreign markets for their goods. And for the United Kingdom and Japan, centralized organization of government shaped crucial aspects of the economy and of technological change. For all these reasons, planners in the GDR thought they could serve as models and potential trading partners for commodities and technology.

The comparison with the UK is perhaps most intriguing if simultaneous comparisons are made between the two Germanies, on the one hand, and between the UK and the United States, on the other. Both sets of countries spoke the same language and shared extensive cultural traditions. In terms of population, both the GDR and the UK stood in approximately the same relationship to their "other" (a ratio of approximately 1:4). And, in each case a more planned and nationalized economy stood opposed to a more open economy, and a poorer record on innovation to relative technological dynamism.

Much more could be made of this comparison, which might make for a book in itself. Here I do not intend to pursue the comparison exhaustively, but instead wish to use it to make two points. First of all, the idea of comparison is useful in determining the extent to which the development of technology in the GDR conformed to or departed from broader trends in twentieth-century industrial societies. It also helps condition our historical imaginations, allowing us to think ourselves into the mindset of the East Germans. They, after all, thought in the very same comparative terms. Which brings me to my second point: like the East Germans of the time, I use such comparisons opportunistically throughout the book, highlighting them as they seem appropriate to the general discussion. Although East German technological development took place in an international context and although the East Germans were constantly comparing themselves to other countries, much of the story here is, like the history of all countries, *sui generis*. The primary focus has to be on internal developments within the GDR.

I have divided the chapters that follow into three parts, which deal roughly chronologically with the issues and themes outlined above. The beginning and end dates for each of the parts correspond to major political events, including the Soviet occupation of eastern Germany and the establishment of the GDR, the beginning of the Second Berlin Crisis, the construction of the Berlin Wall, the Ulbricht era, and the collapse of the GDR. But I argue that these political events had economic—and indeed, even more specifically, technological—causes and dimensions.

Part I, consisting of the first two chapters, deals with the early postwar years in the Soviet zone of occupation in Germany, the nascent GDR, and the first full-fledged attempts to establish a socialist system in the 1950s. The impact of war and defeat on technological traditions and trajectories, reparations and Soviet seizures of scientific and technological personnel, and initial attempts at reconstruction and Soviet-style reorganization of economy and society are key themes dealt with in these chapters. The mixture of misery, hope, and despair engendered by these events culminated in East Germany's first system failure, the uprising of 17 June 1953, one of the main causes of which was a dispute about work norms.

The period of stabilization and renewed crisis between 1953 and 1958 was when the first real attempts to create separate socialist technological traditions took place in East Germany. The return of major factories to East German control and their organization into People's Own Factories (Volkseigene Betriebe, or VEB) required the adaptation of old forms of research and development and the invention of new ones. More sophisticated planning had a similar effect. The return of German scientists from the Soviet Union and the continued hemorrhaging of qualified technical and scientific personnel to the West were two other major forces for change in the East German system of innovation during these years.

Part II, comprising chapters 3–5, addresses the issue of technology during the Second Berlin Crisis, between 1958 and 1961, a critical period in East German development. It was a time of extreme discouragement, as economic targets continued to elude the GDR and the outflow of qualified personnel continued. Yet cause for hope was seen in a series of new initiatives for development of new technologies, the successful launch of the first Sputnik by the Soviet Union, and opportunities for technological cooperation not just with the Soviets, but also with firms in the West.

The period 1958–61 therefore formed a crossroads for GDR decision-makers not just in political, but also in technological terms. Chapter 3 is concerned with the process of technology transfer during this critical period. Investigation of study visits to trade fairs in the West (focusing on the Hannover Trade Fair in spring 1959) and of attempts to devise ways of harnessing the Leipzig trade fair as a mechanism of technology transfer makes it possible to analyze the possibilities and problems of technological renewal in the GDR. This chapter also sheds light on the question of the extent to which East Germany developed its own distinct technological traditions and identity during these years, by contrasting its engineers, technology, and technological mentalities with those in West Germany and in other countries. East German technological culture, I argue, had already become very different from that in West Germany by the late 1950s. In other words, there was already a technological *Mauer im Kopf* ("wall in the head") between the two Germanies even before the construction of the Berlin Wall in August 1961. By the late 1950s there was a confusion of identity in East Germany that was engendered by a longing to form a separate and recognizably socialist technology, while at the same time being uncritically fascinated by capitalist machines and technological systems. This in turn led to early and pronounced differences between East German and West German technological culture.

Yet despite the existence of a technological *Mauer im Kopf* by the late 1950s, machines, their design, and their deployment remained in many ways quite similar in the two Germanies through the early 1960s. The rapid and—at least in technical terms—problem-free assimilation of young scientists and engineers from East Germany into West German industry attested to this, as did the continued respect through the 1950s for East German high-technology products, such as optics and machine tools. Analysis of technological decision-making during this period of crisis indicates that East German planners flirted with the possibilities of cooperation with the West, as the chapters on the "hardware" and "software" of socialism demonstrate. But there were also moves to tie East Germany more closely to the eastern bloc through technological artifacts, techniques of industrial organization, and technical and scientific standards. Essentially, I argue that the construction of a virtual wall in terms of technology preceded the construction of the concrete one. And after August 1961 the virtual wall reinforced the physical one and made it far more effective. Both had the same goal of trying to separate East Germany from the West, while simultaneously attaching it more firmly to the eastern bloc.

The construction of the Berlin Wall in August 1961 stabilized the East German system by halting the outflow of scientific and engineering personnel. It permitted the completion of a key stage in the construction of a virtual technological wall between East and West, and allowed the socialist system some breathing space within which to reform itself. The "second chance" for the GDR in the 1960s is the subject of part III, chapters 6–8, as is the subsequent endgame in which the GDR found itself by the late 1970s and 1980s. Walter Ulbricht's New Economic System, which began in 1963, foresaw a complete revamping of the economy, with a key role accorded to technology, and with major implications for it. Accompanied initially by a loosening of cultural constraints, the New Economic System appeared by the mid-1960s to be accomplishing its objectives, thus easing some of the bad feeling that had arisen from the construction of the Berlin Wall. But the late 1960s witnessed renewed crisis, which culminated in the removal of Walter Ulbricht as head of the SED in 1971 and his replacement by the GDR's second leader, Erich Honecker.

The crisis of the late 1960s had political and economic dimensions, but for the GDR a large part of the problem was technological. The country's resources and system of innovation had proven adequate—if sometimes barely so—in technologies that had been developed initially before 1945 and had matured in the postwar period. But they were generally not up to the task of innovation in key postwar high technologies, such as electronics and petrochemicals. Chapter 6 analyzes this failure of the system and assesses the role of the reforms of the New Economic System in it.

Chapters 7 and 8 examine the GDR's persistent crises and eventual endgame during the last two decades of its existence. The replacement of Ulbricht with Honecker in 1971 signaled a renewed commitment to consumer goods production, which, given the precarious financial status of the GDR regime, could only occur at the expense of high-technology development, especially in electronics, but also in chemicals and other areas. Increasingly, the GDR relied on substitutes for technological development rather than the real thing. Tactics included illicit copying of western technology, and such efforts were often supported in large part by spying. Espionage undertaken by the State Security Service (Staatssicherheitsdienst, or Stasi) had two aims. The first was the evasion of COCOM (the Coordinating Committee for East-West trade, which was responsible for western Allied technological sanctions against the eastern bloc) restrictions on trade in technology. The second was the acquisition of know-how from western firms, mostly West German ones.

During the 1970s and beyond autarky, or economic self-sufficiency, had even more of an impact on technological choice and change than before. It allowed unusual and exotic technological areas (such as acetylene chemistry) to flourish. It also promoted development of an extensive and generally successful recycling program (and associated technologies), the Secondary Raw Materials Office (Sekundärrohstoff, or Sero). These issues are also addressed in chapter 7.

Having virtually abandoned key high-technology research and development and investment, especially in the electronics sector, in the late 1960s and early 1970s, in favor of consumer goods production, the SED decided in 1976 that the GDR should develop indigenous capability in microelectronics technology and began to invest accordingly. Since internal political constraints determined that consumer production could not be scaled back to any significant degree, resources for the microelectronics industry had to come from neglect of other industries, such as chemicals. Raymond Bentley argues that this "mismatch between the GDR's research and development effort in various branches and the country's most important economic and social needs" was one of the main difficulties of the East German system of innovation in its final years.[12] Chapter 8 examines this contention. Finally, the conclusion revisits the themes sketched out in this introduction.

The book as a whole thus offers an interpretation of East German history as seen through the prism of the development of its technology and technology policy. I hasten to point out, however, that the focus on technology is not intended to exclude all else. Instead, the purpose here is to examine GDR technology as at once an important cause, and at the same time a key consequence, of the country's political, social, and economic development. It began to take on this dual role even before the country came into existence, in the immediate aftermath of World War II.

Part I | Defining a Socialist
System of Innovation
in the GDR, 1945–1958

| Technology in the
Soviet Zone, 1945–1949

As World War II drew to its spectacular conclusion in late spring of 1945, Allied military commanders ignored the postwar boundaries on which their governments had agreed. Strategic necessity, not the borders hammered out laboriously as political compromises, governed the movement of armies. The precise boundaries of the four Allied zones of occupation would be sorted out after the hostilities ceased. As a result, the Americans overshot their zone, moving well into those of their allies, including the Russians. When the Americans withdrew to the previously agreed borders in June 1945, more than a month after the conclusion of hostilities in Europe, the Soviet occupiers could survey their zone in its entirety. They were confronted with appalling levels of destruction to cities and industrial plants, within and between which roamed lost, displaced, and dispossessed people.

Because their own country was in even worse condition, from German invasion and occupation, the Soviets, even more than the Allies, focused on three main goals. First, they were keen to punish their vanquished foes and to make sure that they would never again foment war. Second, they wished to recast German society and political life in accordance with their notions of democracy. Finally, and perhaps most important for our present purposes, they wanted to use the material and intellectual resources of their zone for the reconstruction and economic and technological improvement of their own nation.[1]

Traditions and Locations

Germany had never been a stable area politically, and the end of World War II brought a renewed revision of its borders. The eastern parts of the old Reich, including East Prussia and Silesia, were hived off to Poland. The Soviet zone of occupation, later known as East Germany, had actually long been central Germany. It was a varied area. Generally far less densely populated than the western German zones that later formed the Federal Republic of Germany, the Soviet zone also had several large cities and industrial centers. The zone's industrial base was rich in tradition and in many cases technologically at the forefront of world developments. This industrial base was, of course, not uniform throughout the zone, but rather was divided into several different regions. Gary Herrigel, in *Industrial Constructions*, attempted to divide Germany into different regions based upon a typology of characteristics of industry and the economy. Herrigel provides a useful overview of what became East Germany, indicating that extensive portions of the regions making up the later GDR were highly industrialized and technologically very sophisticated.[2]

The northern half of the zone and most of the area surrounding the former German capital, Berlin, was primarily agricultural, and locations in these areas, such as Schwedt and Eisenhüttenstadt, later were the focus of East German regional development policies. But within this generally relatively backward area, Berlin itself featured very high levels of industrialization, with much of the industry located in the Soviet-controlled eastern sector of the city. In addition, there were major centers of industry to the south and west of Berlin. Dresden, Chemnitz (eventually renamed Karl-Marx-Stadt), Magdeburg, and Leipzig were all prominent industrial locations featuring a wide range of industries, but with particular strength in machine building and machine tools. Vital to every other industry, machine tools and machine building together constituted one of the most advanced industrial sectors in what would become East Germany. They were vital export industries for the country throughout its existence and were central to its technological development. Office machinery was another important industrial sector located in this area. Indeed, it is estimated that before World War II approximately 80 percent of Germany's office-machinery industry was situated in the area that would later become East Germany.[3] Postwar developments in these three industrial sectors also bring to light some of the hindrances to, and limits on, innovation in the GDR.

In addition to Berlin and its environs and the south and west of what became the GDR, two other sets of industrial locations were crucial for their technological tradition and potential. Some modern and very large chemical plants were located not far from Leipzig, in Wolfen, Bitterfeld, Schkopau, and Merseburg, in the so-called chemical triangle running northeast from Halle to Bitterfeld, southwest to Merseburg, and back northeast to Halle. Most of them—and all the important ones—had previously belonged to I. G. Farben, the giant German chemical concern of 1925–45.[4] Factories in Wolfen and Bitterfeld concentrated on dye and film manufacture. Schkopau was a major producer of synthetic rubber, or buna, while the Leuna factory in Merseburg had a sophisticated, technologically advanced plant producing a wide range of synthetic products. As the war ended in 1945, the Leuna plant was the largest chemical factory in Germany, in both capacity and number of workers.

Not far along the Saale River from Leuna stood Jena, center of a world-renowned optics and precision mechanics industry that also stretched to the north and west of the city. Jena's most prominent corporate citizen was the Carl Zeiss Works, an internationally respected producer of optical lenses and equipment. Zeiss was one of the major resources for the Soviet zone and, later, East Germany. It maintained a very high level of technological capability throughout the GDR's existence and was a major foreign-exchange earner for the often cash-strapped country. Other, less well-known firms performed similar yeoman service for the regime, including Zeiss Ikon in the camera industry, as well as others in the motor industry and industrial-design sector.

Despite this impressive legacy of earlier German industrialization and technological excellence, there were some inherent difficulties in the situation of the Soviet zone at war's end. First, although there were substantial damages to the industry of the area owing to the war and its aftermath, much of the physical plant that existed in the zone in mid-1945 had been built relatively recently. It therefore also bore the mark of the National Socialist orientation toward autarky, or domestic economic self-sufficiency, and war. Retooling of much of this plant and equipment would be necessary before it would be suitable for peacetime production.

Second, the zone suffered from a relative shortage of research and development (R&D) capacity that would be necessary for scientific and technological innovation. Berlin held some major research institutes of the former Reich, including the Physikalisch-Technische Reichsanstalt (PTR) and several of the major institutes of the Kaiser Wilhelm (later Max Planck) Society. Although some of them had been moved in the latter stages of the war to what would become the GDR, they were generally located in the western parts of the city, and most were therefore controlled by the western Allies.

Industrial R&D capacity, moreover, was also in short supply. Many of the plants located in the Soviet zone had been part of firms that were based in the western area of Germany, and R&D laboratories tended to be located in or near the corporate headquarters. One consequence of the occupation and later division of Germany was the complete loss of this capacity insofar as it was located in the West. There were some major exceptions: for instance, some machine manufacturers and the Zeiss Works retained substantial capability for research and development. But even there, the research capacity that did exist in what would become the GDR had, like the area's physical plant, been shaped by long years of isolation, autarky, and war, and would require major retrofitting for the postwar period. What is more, Zeiss's technological capability in the postwar period was hampered by the fact that eighty-four leading employees of the firm, drawn from a variety of commercial and scientific and technical fields, had been evacuated from the Soviet zone by the American occupation authorities when they withdrew in June 1945. Some of these émigrés went on to form the rival Zeiss concern in Oberkochen in western Germany.[5]

Third, the location of many corporate headquarters in the West meant that high-level managerial talent also tended to be located in the western areas. Plant-level managerial talent was plentiful in the Soviet zone, at least in 1945 (it would become less so later with the flow of emigration westward in the so-called "flight from the republic," or *Republikflucht*, of the 1950s). But as a result of the shortage of top-level managers, investment, financial decision-making, and long-range planning tended to be weak within factories in the Soviet zone. Again, there were major exceptions in some industries, such as machine building, machine tools, optics, and fine mechanics. But even here, difficulties arose from the preparations for the end of hostilities and for Soviet occupation that were made by many major corporations at the end of the war. In many cases, key firms simply relocated. So, for instance, the headquarters of the world-renowned Siemens corporation moved from Berlin to Munich toward the end of the war. A splinter group from the Zeiss corporation—composed mainly of those who had left Jena as the U.S. occupation troops withdrew in June 1945—eventually established a rival Zeiss corporation in Oberkochen, in Württemberg, West Germany.

The Technological Impact of the War

When they were sent to Germany in 1945 to assess the effects of strategic bombing on the German economy, the investigators of the U.S. Strategic Bombing Survey (USSBS) came up with surprising findings. Despite heavy bombing and considerable ground fighting at the end of the war, much of German industrial capacity was still intact. Damage to buildings far exceeded that to machinery, and even that was astonishingly limited. The final collapse of the German war economy was indeed caused primarily by bombing, but it was the oil industry (and related industries) and vital infrastructure systems, such as rail lines, water and sewage facilities, and the like, that were most affected.[6]

Despite these overall conclusions, it was also clear that there were considerable differences in the extent of damage by region and by individual factory. One might have expected that the area that would become the Soviet zone of occupation would have been especially hard hit. It contained a heavy concentration of war-related industries, and the chemical industry—which was located in the Soviet zone in the area around Halle and had extensive synthetic oil and rubber production capacity— was a favorite target of Allied bombers. In the final weeks of the war, moreover, the future Soviet zone had also experienced intensive ground fighting in and around Berlin, which was also a major industrial center.

GDR historical literature eventually relied on these facts to contend that war-related damage to industry in the Soviet zone was especially pronounced. But the contention is simply not true. War-related damages to the industrial basis of the future GDR were on average no greater, and probably far less, than those in the future West Germany.[7] Rainer Karlsch, who has done the most extensive study of war damages, reparations, and dismantling in the Soviet zone, gives an estimate of total war damages to industry in the future GDR of 15 percent of the capacity that had existed in the area in 1944. Damages to industry in the future Federal Republic and West Berlin reached 22 percent. In both the future GDR and the future Federal Republic, the damages to buildings were far higher than to productive plant capacity. The result for the Soviet zone, like all the other zones of occupation, was that "most of the large-scale factories were in the position to take up their usual activities again only a few weeks after the end of the war" (see table 1).[8]

Again, though, these global figures need to be treated with some caution. Individual plants experienced the bombing and the end of the war very differently: some were hardly damaged at all, while others were nearly completely destroyed. What is more, there was a general tendency for factories in more research-intensive industries to be more seriously affected by the fighting than those in more traditional industries, mainly because they were frequently the targets of Allied bombing raids. Ma-

Table 1. Capacity Losses of Selected Industrial Branches in the Soviet Zone of Occupation Owing to War and Dismantling, in Percent (as of August 1946)

Branch	War-Related Losses	Dismantling	Remaining Capacity
Metallurgy	10	64	26
Machine-building	24	53	23
Vehicle manufacture	21	54	25
Electrical goods	20	60	20
Fine mechanics and optics	15	65	22
Chemicals: soda		80	20
Gypsum industry	5	35	60
Artificial fibers	5	30	65
Textiles	10	15	75
Shoe manufacture	5	15	80

Source: Adapted from Rainer Karlsch, *Allein bezahlt?* (Berlin: Ch. Links, 1993), 282.

chine building, the electrical industry, and the vehicles industry all lost more than one-fifth of their 1944 capacity through war damages.[9] But there were also exceptions to this general tendency. The Zeiss main and south works, for instance, suffered a total of about RM 3.91 million worth of damage through the fighting, of which damage to premises (buildings and grounds) made up about 41 percent. In relation to the total value of the plant and assets of the two facilities, however, the damages were minuscule, amounting to just 2.43 percent.[10]

In assessing the impact of war damages on German industrial capacity in all zones of occupation, we also need to take into account that these figures are based on capacity in 1944—in other words after the German war economy had grown considerably. Karlsch reckons that industrial capacity in 1944 was nearly 50 percent greater than it had been in 1936, the last relatively "normal" year for the German economy. (By 1936 the economy had recovered from the Depression, but had not yet been skewed substantially through war production.) As we would expect, relatively high-technology industries, such as machine and vehicle building, electrical goods, chemicals, and precision goods and optics, increased their production and capacity more substantially on average than those in more traditional industries.[11]

These findings have several implications for assessing the technological level of industry in the future GDR. In terms of physical plant, the Soviet zone was relatively no worse off, and probably far better off, than the western zones as the war came to an end. Much of the plant capacity was intact, and much of it was of relatively recent vintage. Investment and production during the war, moreover, had focused above all on relatively research-intensive industries. But much of the relatively new, relatively high-technology plant in the future GDR was designed for war production, which diminished its usefulness, at least potentially, for the postwar period. It had also been used heavily during the war, so that wear and tear was substantial. Thus, although the Soviet zone retained a high level of intact and very sophisticated technology, replacement and retooling would soon be needed.

In terms of war damages, then, the Soviet zone in summer 1945 faced exactly the same problems and prospects as did the other zones, although with marginally better artifactual resources. Still, the zone suffered several technological disadvantages compared to its western counterparts. First of all, the breakdown of traditional regional relationships in Germany through the division of the country into four zones had a greater impact on the Soviet zone than on the western zones. Second, as already noted, high-level managerial talent was in relatively short supply in the Soviet zone compared to other zones, and the zone had insufficient capacity for research and development. Probably the most important factor shaping technological development in the future GDR, however, was the presence of the Soviet occupiers, whose actions changed fundamentally the material basis of their section of Germany.

The Soviet Occupation and Its Technological Effects

The Soviet occupation, which began in the late spring and early summer of 1945, had three major effects on technology in the area that would become the GDR.[12] First, the Soviets had a critical impact on the *hardware* available in their zone. They dismantled substantial amounts of machinery and plant, either as reparations or as part of programs to demilitarize the German economy. Second, they adopted policies that affected the technological *software* (people and ideas) available in their area of occupation. Like the western Allies, they seized vast amounts of technological and scientific information for use in their own science and industry. Unlike the western Allies, they also forced large numbers of engineers and scientists to move to the Soviet Union to work on R&D projects there. Finally, they altered fundamentally the institutional *context* within which industrial innovation took place by changing ownership structures.

Seizures of plant and machinery were the most obvious impact of the Soviet occupation. Dismantling, much of it for reparations, took place on a scale unknown in the other zones of occupation and dramatically decreased industrial capacity in the Soviet zone. In general, the loss of capacity through dismantling was far greater than what was lost through bombing or ground fighting during the war itself (see table 1). Numerous factories that were still intact at the end of the war were dismantled and taken away to the Soviet Union as early as the summer of 1946. Aluminum and magnesium capacity, for instance, was intact at war's end, but stood at zero in September 1946. The same was true for some parts of the chemical industry. Magnesium-oxide capacity was removed entirely. Ninety-five percent of automobile tire production plant was dismantled. Eighty percent of soda capacity disappeared. All of these were sectors that had survived the war intact.

For other important areas of industry, the dismantling, coming on top of war damages, severely curtailed production capability. The metallurgical industry, diminished by about 10 percent by the war, saw more than 60 percent more of its capacity disappear, leaving just over 25 percent in 1944. The machine-tool industry, which was about 25 percent destroyed in the fighting, saw a further loss of 53 percent. The electrical industry lost about 20 percent during the war and about 60 percent more in its aftermath, leaving just 20 percent of its capacity in 1944 intact. And the fine mechanical and optical industry lost 15 percent of its capacity in the fighting, and a further 65 percent through Soviet dismantling.[13]

When confronted with such astonishing statistics, one cannot help but recognize that the area that became the GDR had severely diminished economic and technological capacity by the late 1940s, compared to a decade earlier. But it is also necessary to recognize that East German industry could perhaps afford to lose considerable capacity after the war without significant effect—at least in principle—on its ability to produce for the postwar period. The capacity of German industry in general was running about 50 percent higher in 1944 than in 1936, the last year during which the German economy was oriented toward peacetime production. Moreover, the industries that held the most interest for the Soviets were generally high-technology industries that had seen the largest increases during the build-up to war and during the fighting. Capacity in these industries had by and large grown more than 50 percent between 1936 and 1944. To generalize, we may say that all other things being equal, we should have expected the Soviet zone to have lost at least one-third of industrial capacity across the board, and even more in research-intensive and war-related industries, and still be able to produce at 1936 peacetime levels.

It is equally important to stress that loss of machinery does not necessarily mean diminished technological capability. In fact, it can have the opposite effect. In this context, we may recall that much of the machinery and equipment that lay in the Soviet zone of occupation in mid-1945 had been designed for wartime needs and war-related production. At the very best, the machines themselves or the technological systems within which they operated would in any case have had to be reconfigured for peacetime production; at worst, they would have had to be completely revamped or else discarded. The same might be said concerning another characteristic of much of the Soviet zone's technological basis—that it was often heavily worn. Even if machinery and equipment could be easily reconfigured for peacetime needs and were relatively lightly worn, in many research-intensive industries the pace of technological change meant that they would have had to be replaced soon in any case.

The implication of this line of argument is that the Soviets were not necessarily doing irreparable harm to the East Germans by removing irrelevant, worn-out, or obsolescent technologies. The East Germans were forced to replace such machinery sooner than expected, and the dismantling and removals (along with seizures of patents and know-how) may therefore be seen, with some allowance for exaggeration, as a potential force for innovation for postwar German industry.[14]

Keeping in mind both the statistics on war damages and removals and the mitigating circumstances of those removals, we come to an accurate, nuanced picture of the impact of dismantling and reparations on East German technology. Removal of "excess" plant and equipment was not at all pleasant for the works affected, at least in the short term, but it had a potential positive impact in the longer term through stimulation of technological innovation, especially in research-intensive industries. Still, because the scale of the dismantling effort went well beyond removal of "excess" capacity, the East Germans started the postwar period severely hampered in vital industrial and technological sectors. Furthermore, they had a severely diminished capability of mustering the capital investment necessary to reconstruct them and a curtailed capacity for research and development both in terms of personnel and organizations. Shortages of high-ranking managers made things more problematic. To make matters even worse for the East Germans, the Soviets were not yet finished with their dismantling, removals, and general exploitation in their zone in 1946. It is clear, therefore, that East Germany was affected considerably by the Soviet removals in the aftermath of the war, although not unambiguously.

But what are we to make of the impact of this process on the receiving country, the Soviet Union? Although this is not a question that can be answered completely here, it is worth considering briefly because it speaks to debates on the alleged Sovietization of the East German economy.[15] The third volume of Anthony Sutton's massive study, *Western Technology and Soviet Economic Development*, indicates that Soviet dismantling and removals in its zone of Germany were central to Soviet technological development in the postwar period. Contrary to the usual picture that commentators paint of dismantled German machinery rusting on railway sidings and plants reconstructed but still inoperable owing to German sabotage or inadequate know-how, Sutton claims that German machinery was actually put to good use in the Soviet Union after the war. The Soviets, Sutton notes, were especially good at dismantling, having had extensive practice beforehand, unlike the western Allies. They worked carefully, quickly, and effectively, selecting their targets deliberately.

> The Soviets concentrated on plants containing equipment and machines that could be safely transported. Close comparison of removals in Manchuria and East Germany indicates that almost 100 percent of removals had high salvage value and were easily removed and transported, i.e., machine tools, precision instruments, and small items of equipment *not* made of fabricated sheet metal. On the other hand, the Western Allies in Europe appear to have concentrated their removals on plants with relatively low salvage value. One cannot, for example, satisfactorily remove an iron and steel plant to another location, which is exactly what the Allies tried to do.[16]

By focusing on individual machines rather than on technological systems, the Soviets were able to transport them safely and to deploy them within their own technological context. In this sense, Soviet technological capability was enhanced by the arrival of German machines and ideas, but that technology did not change the Soviet system fundamentally. Still, much of this seized German machinery continued to produce for the Soviet economy for years. These machines also served as templates for other machines. Thus there was bound to be some "Germanization" of Soviet technological systems. Sutton gives an indication of the effect of this on the Soviet electrical industry: he suggests that "current [early 1970s] backwardness in control instrumentation and computers" might be traced back to "the technical nature of the transfers from the German electrical industry at the end of World War II."[17]

Sutton's arguments, which were developed in the context of the Cold War using materials available at the Hoover Institution, require some revisiting now that the Cold War has ended and former Soviet archives have become more readily available. But his work and that of others suggest that German influence on Soviet technological development was considerable.[18] The interaction between the two technological styles, which had begun in the 1920s, changed character through time with evolving power relationships and historical context. But the fact of long-term interaction is important, and recognition of it may well help us to understand the later process by which East German technological culture was allegedly Sovietized.[19]

The impact of Soviet occupation practice on the "software" of East German technology and science has only recently been studied in any detail, but the effects were probably much more far-reaching for both the East Germans and the Soviets than in the case of material transfers. Like the western Allies, the Soviets investigated scientific and technological developments that had taken place in Germany during the Third Reich.[20] This effort involved systematic visits of specialist scientists and engineers to laboratories and factories; during these visits technical documentation was seized and/or microfilmed, and leading scientific and technological personnel were interviewed. In the West, an extensive series of reports based on this information was made widely available to Allied companies and individuals, who could order them from government printing offices. Those interested could also gain access to microfilms of much of the original technical documentation. It is not clear how this knowledge was disseminated within the Soviet Union, but it is likely that parallel efforts were made to inform state-owned companies of the progress of German science and technology during the war.

Both sides also engaged in seizure of German scientific and technological personnel, but the western seizures occurred at a different time and had a different character from those by the Soviets. Much has been made of the contribution of German "rocket scientists" and aeronautical engineers to the development of airplane and missile technology in the immediate postwar period and, even more important, to the burgeoning U.S. space program.[21] These men were gathered together very quickly as the war came to an end, and most were already in the United States by the summer of 1945. German atomic scientists were also seized and incarcerated at Farm Hall, where their conversations were secretly monitored. These men, unlike many of those associated with the V-2 program and the air force, returned to West Germany by January 1946.[22]

In the immediate aftermath of World War II, the Soviets made similar seizures of German scientists and engineers in the fields of aeronautical engineering and nuclear physics and engineering. Both groups made contributions to Soviet aeronautical technology and the atomic bomb project, although the atomic and hydrogen bombs and the successful Soviet intercontinental rockets, all of which were functioning by the late 1950s, owed as much to Soviet as to German research and design.[23] Western and eastern Allied policy and practice diverged during 1946, by which time forced (or governmentally enticed) migration of scientists and engineers from Germany to the West had ceased. The Soviets, in contrast, redoubled their efforts to recruit German scientists and engineers (largely involuntarily) in autumn 1946 and in a second, smaller action in February 1947.

The Soviet Operation Ossawakim to collect and deport German scientists, undertaken in October 1946, far exceeded anything undertaken by the western Allies, both in the numbers seized and in the breadth of their fields. The effect of the action was magnified by the relatively small size of the Soviet zone of occupation compared to the western zones. The Soviets also departed from previous Allied practice, which had emphasized individual, and generally extremely well-known, scientists and engineers; had privileged theoreticians; and had favored war-related science and technology. Instead, the operation in October 1946 transported entire teams working on specific, often civilian-oriented projects in chemistry, electronics, and other fields. These teams included not just scientists and engineers, but also their assistants, laboratory personnel, technicians, and skilled workers.[24] Machines and laboratory equipment frequently accompanied them on the journey eastward. In all, the action in autumn 1946 affected approximately 3,000 specialists who, together with their families, were transported to the Soviet Union. They worked in a variety of fields, including nuclear research, chemistry, aeronautics, rocket technology, and optics. Some of them began returning home in 1949, although most returned between 1952 and 1956. A few were detained until 1958.[25]

Clearly, the loss of so much technological talent was especially damaging to the Soviet zone of occupation and the GDR, where the need for reconstruction and technological modernization was so great. It must be noted, of course, that owing to Allied restrictions on war-related research and development, which lasted into the mid-1950s, not all the specialists could have pursued work in their fields unimpeded even if they had remained in East Germany. They might have been forced to apply their talents elsewhere, as occurred in the parallel case of Japan. Allied restrictions on the activities of Japanese aeronautical engineers led many of them to migrate to the automobile industry. There they introduced sophisticated practices of manufacturing and planning—an indication of the potential positive economic and technological impact of such forced reorientation. But this did not happen in East Germany, primarily because of the Soviet action. Furthermore, the Soviet seizures may have had a subtle, but even more nefarious effect on the technological basis of their zone. As Karlsch points out, one of the key indirect effects of Operation Ossawakim was to make the technical intelligentsia in the Soviet zone fundamentally insecure about their positions.[26] Many worried about the potential for similar actions in future. All of them understood the operation as the end to the previous regime in which scientists working for the Soviets often had better working and living conditions than did those employed by the western Allies. This can only have increased the general tendency during the 1950s for leading East German scientists and engineers to take up offers of employment from West German universities, laboratories, and industry.

One of the major points made in the main study of the German specialists resident in the Soviet Union after 1945 reinforces the point made above with regard to physical reparations. Ulrich Albrecht and his collaborators argue that there were important aspects of continuity in the German-Soviet technological relationship stretching back to the 1920s, when there was extensive cooperation in the armaments industry. This tradition was revisited briefly during the Nazi period between the signing of the nonaggression pact in August 1939 and the invasion of the USSR in June 1941. They contend that "the use of German 'specialists' in the Soviet Union beginning in 1945 also built upon experiences which had been made already in the 1920s and 1930s." But even though the German specialists resided in the Soviet Union for a considerable amount of time (over a decade in some cases), there were limits to their impact on Soviet technology. They did not, as is frequently alleged, build the Soviet atomic bomb, nor did they provide more than the basis for Soviet missile and rocket projects. In fact, German specialists made substantial contributions only to jet engine technology. They "functioned . . . mostly as givers of ideas, as ideal competitors in the development of variants for optimization, and as practical trainers of Soviet scientists and engineers, who were supposed to acquire the 'German style,' the renowned accuracy and capability in experimental innovation."[27]

It is therefore difficult to argue that there was a total Germanization of Soviet scientists and engineers in the aftermath of World War II. Still, as was the case with physical reparations, intellectual and nonmaterial reparations after 1945 gave a German inflection to Soviet technological culture. This inflection may in turn have facilitated the subsequent Sovietization of East German technology during the 1950s and beyond.

Besides having an impact on the hardware and software of East German technology, the Soviet occupiers also affected the context within which East German technological systems functioned and innovation occurred. They did this primarily by fundamentally changing ownership structures and by introducing planning. Both changes had an impact on how technology was deployed and innovation carried out in the Soviet zone of occupation.

Within months of the start of the occupation, the Soviet Military Administration in Germany (SMAD) had ordered a land reform, which eliminated most large landowners and took the first steps toward socialization of agriculture. This action was followed, beginning in 1946, with a series of measures to change the ownership structure of industries. Most large enterprises and those whose proprietors were politically tainted were nationalized. SMAD consolidated the largest of the large enterprises into twenty-five Soviet Joint-Stock Companies (Sowjetische Aktiengesellschaften, or SAGs). The SAGs accounted for about one-third (and possibly somewhat more) of the zone's industrial output and comprised much of its high-technology industry, including all of the chemical industry, much of the machine-tool industry, and much of the optics industry. They remained under Soviet control and ownership until 1953, when they were turned over (at a cost of over 2.5 billion marks!) to the East Germans. They subsequently became People's Own Enterprises (Volkseigene Betriebe, or VEBs), thus remaining in the public sector.[28]

The primary effect of the establishment of the SAGs was to halt dismantling of large-scale industry in the Soviet zone, and in this sense they mitigated the impacts described above regarding transfer of German hardware to the USSR. However, the primary motivation for the establishment of the SAGs was to provide for more effective transfer of goods and services from the GDR to the USSR—essentially by not killing the goose that laid the golden egg. Thus, one of the major impacts of the formation of the SAGs was to deny the fruits of a significant part of the productive capability of Soviet-zone industry to the Soviet zone. Although the SAG factories remained on German soil, they essentially were part of the Soviet economy and society.

The precise impact of these changes in ownership structures on technology is not clear. Although the factories were owned by the Soviet Ministry of Foreign Trade and various Soviet industrial ministries, they employed German workers and German managers to carry out production. In a sense, therefore, the SAGs may have promoted continuity to an even greater degree than in other zones (and especially the U.S. zone) because "the Soviet directors paid little attention to the denazification of their factories. . . . [T]he SAGs brought back the old Nazi factory directors and chief engineers to run the factories."[29] Such continuity in personnel, it would seem, could only have helped maintain, rather than alter, previous German technological traditions within Soviet-owned factories.

Joachim Radkau, in a thought-provoking article on technology in the GDR, claims otherwise. He argues that the SAGs "anchored . . . structures of Russian applications of technology in the production apparatus of the GDR." These "structures" included a tendency to design artifacts and technologies that were "wasteful of resources and far too large in scale."[30] This is a fascinating thesis and one that, if true, would provide evidence for an additional mechanism through which Sovietization of East German technological culture may have occurred. But demonstrating it conclusively would require extensive research into the day-to-day operations of one or more of the SAG factories, research that has thus far not been carried out.

In the meantime an alternative thesis seems more convincing: that Sovietization of GDR technological culture by means of the SAGs was slight. It did occur, but primarily indirectly, because the enterprises were forced to produce and invest based on the needs of the Soviet economy and the Soviet market, and not those of the East German economy or its traditional foreign markets. Although GDR and Soviet technology remained different in many respects from 1945 through 1990, there was a gradual convergence. However, this was not solely related to the SAGs. As Radkau indicates, the most persistent damage from the Soviets to East German technology may have come not through dismantling and unequal trade treaties, which made things difficult for the GDR, "but rather through that which made the GDR all too comfortable: through the [Soviet] purchase [from the GDR] of superannuated machines which had no chance on western markets."[31] But this contention gets us ahead of our story somewhat, and will be revisited in later chapters.

Introduction of Soviet-style planning in the Soviet zone also had a limited influence on GDR technological development at first. Ultimately, however, planning proved a very important shaper of GDR innovative capability. In the initial occupation period all the Allied occupiers retained some key institutions and regulations for controlling and directing the German economy that had been put in place during the Nazi period. The Russians were no exception. The main difference came later: while the western zones began to dismantle such controls and institutions by 1948, the Soviets were expanding them. In 1947 the German Economic Commission (Deutsche Wirtschaftskommission, or DWK) was established. It had responsibility for devising plans for the zone's economy, and its decisions had the force of law. Eventually the DWK became the basis for the government of the GDR, which was established in October 1949, and its planning functions were eventually turned over to the State Planning Commission (Staatliche Plankommission, or SPK), which was set up in 1950.

The main initial task of the DWK during the second half of 1948 was to devise a Two-Year Plan for the economy. The short time frame would allow the establishment of procedures and techniques for planning and would also synchronize GDR planning with that of the other countries in the eastern bloc. Initially, however, several factors limited the impact of planning. First of all, the Soviet zone, even more than the other zones of occupation, was still in a state of flux during 1948 and 1949. Therefore, "planning" essentially boiled down to organizing industrial production at a very basic level, ensuring that the population was supplied with basic needs, and making certain that reparations targets were met. Only during the first Five-Year Plan (1951–55) were rudimentary techniques of planning developed into a sort of template, which would be developed and improved in following years.[32] Another factor limiting the impact of planning during the occupation period was that less than half of the economic enterprises in the zone, and probably only about 30 percent of industrial enterprises, were under direct central control.[33] Lastly, initial planning in the Soviet zone/GDR did not focus on innovation directly or to any great degree, which limited its direct impact on GDR technologi-

cal development and indeed guaranteed at first a certain degree of auton-
omy for science and technology.[34] Still, the techniques and procedures
for planning developed in these years had an indirect impact on the GDR
system of innovation, making it more like the Soviet system in how
resources were deployed and incentives given. And they provided the
basis for later development of extensive planning of GDR science and
technology beginning in the early 1950s.

The Beginnings of an Alternative System of Innovation

The system of industrial innovation in the Soviet zone of occupation
was composed primarily of people, machines, and institutions that had
emerged from German history through 1945.[35] Thus, despite the changes
in hardware, software, and context noted above, the East German system
remained in many ways quite (prewar) German. It was in the 1950s and
later that more fundamental changes took place owing to generational
change, the impact of ideology, and the altered political-economic system. Nevertheless, these changes began during the occupation period, as
new institutions were formed and old ones redefined.

The topmost institution for science in the GDR was the German Academy of Sciences (Deutsche Akademie der Wissenschaften zu Berlin, or
DAW), which was founded under the auspices of the Soviet occupiers in
summer 1946 as a successor to the Prussian Academy of Sciences. Although it drew some of its membership and much of its tradition from
the older Prussian institution, the DAW had some new elements, such as
having its own research institutes, and over time it became even more
different from its predecessor. From the beginning there was a certain
tension in the definition of the DAW's role. On the one hand, it was
supposed to be an all-German institution; on the other, it was supposed
to become a "socialist research academy." This tension was heightened
by the criteria for membership in the academy, which were implemented
by 1949: one was "professional quality"; another was "suitability for the
fulfillment of state duties," which meant, among other things, "offering
scientific help to the people's owned industry of the eastern zone." Essentially, then, the DAW became a peculiarly East German institution—
one that, by taking over functions previously exercised by Kaiser Wilhelm Institutes and state-run laboratories, operated a vast network of
research establishments and attracted to its employ many of the GDR's
best scientists and engineers (and also, incidentally, social scientists and

scholars from the humanities). The pan-German function was largely lost.[36]

Again, these changes came to fruition only during and after the 1950s, but they were implicit in the constitution of the DAW. One of the main innovations here was the explicit linking of elite science to applied science and technology, the economy, and society, although there were certain linkages of this sort in German scientific tradition.[37] Another, even more dramatic break with the German past was the mobilization (and control) through the DAW of much of the East German scientific and engineering establishment within the confines of a single institution.

Although the full impact of these changes would again be felt only later, during the 1950s, it is clear that the establishment of the DAW, along with the concentration of industry into SAGs (and subsequently VEBs), had a pronounced effect on the structure of East German science and technology. Under Soviet tutelage and control, the East Germans began to develop much more centralized structures to replace the relatively decentralized and flexible system of innovation traditional to Germany. As these relatively centralized institutions developed and became more effective, they permitted a higher level of planning of science and technology policy and strategy, which began to occur from the early 1950s onward.

In the shorter run, during the actual occupation period, the constraints on scientific and technological development were such as to prevent anything more than the most primitive measures. The war and the long-term isolation of Germany from international scientific and engineering best practice meant that the country had fallen behind its rivals in many fields. Seizures of plant, information, and personnel only exacerbated these difficulties, and they were especially bad in the Soviet zone. Funding for science and technology was in short supply. Yet the Soviet zone, like those in the West, needed desperately to improve productivity. Since the usual sources of productivity increases, science and technology, were unable to deliver, more desperate measures were undertaken.

Essentially, in this situation, East Germans were told to work harder and faster in order to produce more, and the efforts were personified by a coal miner, Adolf Hennecke, leading to the so-called Hennecke movement. On 13 October 1948 the forty-three-year-old Hennecke mined nearly four times his normal quota of coal in a single shift. Little different from the Stakhanovite movement of the 1930s in the USSR, the Hennecke movement was based on an artificial "accomplishment" achieved

Adolf Hennecke (1905–75), pictured in October 1948. Aided by extensive preparation and support, Hennecke mined nearly four times his normal quota of coal in a single shift in October 1948. The resulting "Hennecke movement," which encouraged workers simply to work harder and faster, indicated the bankruptcy of innovation policy in the Soviet-controlled zone in the early postwar period. *Bundesarchiv, Koblenz, Bildsammlung Bild 183/W0514/301*

through extensive preparation. It was also politically inspired and mercilessly propagandized in the aftermath. The movement spread to all industries in the Soviet zone of occupation, causing widespread resistance to what was in fact a socialist, and corrupted, version of Frederick Winslow Taylor's scientific management. Such toying with quotas and work norms eventually culminated in the workers' uprising of June 1953.[38]

During the Soviet occupation the area that would later become the GDR faced enormous difficulties. There were severe disruptions to the Soviet zone's system of innovation owing to war, occupation, German division, and new political and economic institutions. But did these disruptions and developments during the occupation period throttle the area's ability to innovate from the outset? Or, as the editors of a recent collection of studies of East German innovation put it, given that we know East Germany ultimately failed technologically, was that failure a result of a "bad start or a bad run"?[39]

To some degree, this question begs a more fundamental one. When did the start occur? One might argue that it occurred in 1945, during the "zero hour" of German history. But alternatively, one might argue that it happened in 1948, when the currency reform took place, the First Berlin Crisis began, and the DWK began its planning work. Rainer Karlsch, for instance, seems to locate the origins of the GDR's problems with innovation around this time in "the Stalinist social system which was establishing itself." After smashing the democratic façade in the Soviet zone, that system began "to hamper increasingly the innovative forces of the society."[40] A third possibility would be to place the start date in 1949, with the founding of the GDR.

Regardless of when precisely the start of the GDR is deemed to have occurred, it is clear that the conditions in 1949, as the initial Soviet occupation period came to an end, were very bad indeed. It is just as clear that the GDR at its official founding was not all that far behind the Federal Republic in technological terms, was still competitive in key industries, and was still very good in science and engineering education and practice. Therefore, the proximate causes of the ultimate failure of the GDR system of innovation must be placed later than the occupation period, at the very earliest in the 1950s. But there is also a need to explain the country's continued ability to innovate, both during the 1950s and, to a lesser degree, beyond. Even if the GDR was falling behind technologically relative to the capitalist West, it was still very respectable in international terms and was the envy of the eastern bloc.

This tension between the looming specter of failure on the one hand and the grudging recognition of both success and enormous potential on the other is a key theme in GDR history, lying at the heart of its development from its very origins. The tension grew more acute as the occupation period drew to a close and the nascent GDR regime took over increasing control of its own affairs.

Still, it must not be forgotten that the Hennecke movement, one of the few concrete measures actually implemented to increase productivity in the Soviet-occupied area, was a pathetic demonstration of the real weaknesses of East German science and technology. It was also a premonition of the country's inability to function effectively in this vital area. At the same time, however, it is important to keep in mind that the changes that had taken place were not irrevocable. Despite war damages and removals of equipment and personnel, East Germany retained an imposing technological and scientific capacity compared to virtually every country that surrounded it, even the Federal Republic. The relative decline of East German science and technology, the increased divergence from German traditions of organization and deployment of science and technology, and the frequent failures of the East German system of innovation lay largely in the future.

Chapter 2 | A First, Flawed Construction

Technology Planning and Practice through 1958

Shortly after the founding of the Federal Republic of Germany (FRG), the East German Democratic Republic was established, in October 1949. Both successor states to the formerly united Germany set about creating the institutions and traditions required by any nation. From autumn of 1949 they regained a considerable amount of control over their internal political, social, and economic affairs, but both continued to labor under severe restrictions on their sovereignty. Neither, for instance, was invited to take part in the proceedings of the newly created United Nations (and indeed the two did not become full members of the UN until 1973). Nor were they initially welcomed into other international organizations, such as the International Standards Organization (ISO). Berlin, the former capital, remained an occupied city in which the four former Allies had the ultimate say. The Federal Republic's actions continued to be overseen by representatives of the western Allies in the form of the Allied High Commission, while the Soviets retained crucial aspects of political control in the East.

Despite these similarities, it is clear that the constraints on decision-making were greater in the GDR than in the FRG, especially in the areas of science, technology, and the economy. Some of the constraints were the indirect results of the war and Soviet policy and practice. For instance, infrastructure problems affected all aspects of life in the GDR well into the 1950s, the result of wartime destruction and Soviet rapacity. GDR industry and science suffered from the severing or loosening of links with counterparts in the West. Other constraints were much more direct. The GDR, for example, continued to be plagued by a shortage of scientific and technical talent, exacerbated by the Soviet seizure of scientists and engineers in 1946. The experts began to return in the early 1950s, but they were not all back until the middle of the decade. More important, in the context of the late 1940s and early 1950s, the Soviets constrained economic and technological decision-making at virtually all the major factories in the GDR. The SAGs controlled most of the largest concerns in the GDR until the beginning of 1954 and eventually accounted for around 30 percent or more of the GDR's industrial output. They produced for the needs of the Soviet economy, not for those of the GDR, and decisions on investment, expansion, and technological research and development were made on that basis.

But even had all these constraints, deliberate and otherwise, been removed, the GDR would still have been faced with a major task at the beginning of its existence. As a new state, it lacked both the institutions and the links between them through which to sustain delivery of high-quality products of science and technology. To use more recent technology, it needed to create the institutions and practices for establishing a "national system of innovation."[1] In this, the GDR could draw for inspiration upon the many distinguished and successful models and traditions of the pre-1945 German system of innovation.[2] But at the same time, the leadership most surely did not wish to re-create the institutions and practices of united Germany; in fact, they wished consciously to break with them. During the 1950s, therefore, they jettisoned key aspects of tried and true German practice, centralizing scientific institutions on the Soviet model, nationalizing the means of production, and engaging eventually in detailed planning, not just for production and consumption, but also for research, development, and innovation.

The leadership's commitment to science and technology was demonstrated dramatically at the beginning of the decade: expenditures for research and development increased by 474 percent between 1949 and 1950, from under 20 million to 90 million marks. The vastly increased sum still represented only a tiny proportion of GDR national income, just one-half of one percent in 1950. But that proportion grew steadily throughout the decade, reaching an average of just under 2 percent of national income by the early 1960s.[3] In attaining this level of spending, the East Germans were not far out of line with their West German counterparts. In fact, the public and the industrial sectors in the Federal Republic spent just under one and one-quarter percent of the country's GNP on research and development in 1962, with the figure rising to 2 percent only in the late 1960s. Of course, it must be kept in mind that the two countries differed in their definition of what constituted research and development. More important, although West Germany spent proportionally slightly less of its GNP on research and development than did the GDR in the early 1960s, the GNP was much larger and growing faster. Thus, in absolute terms, West German spending far exceeded that of East Germany.[4]

The GDR's first attempts to create a new, socialist national system of innovation during the 1950s entailed dependence upon people, organizations, and technologies from the German past. But by 1957–58 a very different set of institutions and practices had been created—one more centralized, planned, and regimented than at any time before in German history. To be sure, the efforts ended in severe disappointment, as the new system of innovation failed to deliver on its promises, at least as compared to the performance of the rival and thrusting West German system of innovation. But compared to the outlook at the beginning of the 1950s, when GDR managers and bureaucrats started their task, the situation in 1957–58, though facing frequent crises, was relatively favorable. The decade had begun in almost unimaginable conditions as the GDR leadership, armed with very little besides their ideological zeal, began to cobble together a new socialist world.

Lurching toward the First System Crisis, 1949–1953

Rudimentary planning for the economy had begun in 1948 under the auspices of the nascent government of the GDR, the German Economic Commission (DWK). During 1948 and 1949 a large number of R&D facilities in fields ranging from basic research in physics, chemistry, and biology to economics and applied research came under the formal control of the DWK, which established a Main Section for Science and Technology (Hauptabteilung Wissenschaft und Technik) to oversee them. Officially, the DWK gave research assignments to each of the 453 laboratories under its formal control, supervised their activities, and provided some of the funding.[5] As might be expected, the heaviest concentration of facilities was in the areas in which German industry was strongest. Approximately 20 percent were in the machine-building and machine-tool industry, for instance, and about 10 percent each in applied chemistry, precision mechanics and optics, and the electrical industry.[6] During 1949, as reconstruction began in earnest, new attempts were made to harness research and development for the GDR's economy. In January 1949 the DWK's responsibilities for funding of and planning for the facilities were placed under the auspices of the Plan for Research.

Simultaneously, moves were made to establish a patent system of the GDR to succeed that of unified Germany. German patents had been seized during the war by the Allied governments, and an agreement reached in London in July 1946 made them available without cost to signatories.[7] This was something of a blow to both German successor states, as the patents were undoubtedly extremely valuable.[8] But the agreement also provided a basis for establishing a new patent system once the two successor states were formed. The FRG set about doing this first with the establishment of the German Patent Office in Munich in October 1949. The GDR passed its patent law in January 1950 and established its patent office in Berlin on 1 October 1950.[9]

Despite these energetic efforts to begin to gain control over the R&D system within its borders, the GDR government faced real limits to its power in this area. Shortcomings of the planning system itself were partly responsible. There were not enough planners to tackle this complex task, and they lacked adequate tools (both information and machines to process data). At times, they did not carefully define the tasks that needed to be accomplished, and sometimes they did not pay enough attention to the relationship between the costs of research and the benefits derived from it.[10] But the power of GDR planners to harness their R&D system to the benefit of the economy was limited much more severely by the fact that a huge part of the R&D establishment—especially in the area of applied research—was entirely outside their control. Most of the R&D work undertaken in the early years of the GDR took place, after all, within the confines of the SAGs and the other factories of the nationalized sector, the VEBs.

Almost immediately after the end of the war, the factories that later became the SAGs and VEBs began to develop processes that would allow them to make better use of their existing facilities, and they continued with this task through the early 1950s. In addition, they created new laboratories for factories that had previously depended upon research done in the western part of Germany. The Zeitz Hydrogenation Works, for instance, had been part of the state-directed Braunkohlenbenzin AG (BRABAG) and had had no need for its own laboratory facilities through 1945. A lab was established, however, when the permanence of the separation from the West became apparent. One of the key areas of research for both existing and new laboratory facilities was the development of new products, or new uses for old ones, to enable the GDR to manufacture materials to substitute for those previously supplied from the West. In other words, the German tradition of autarky, or economic self-sufficiency, continued in the GDR. Aspects of this tradition continued in the West as well—for instance, in the chemical industry, where traditional coal-based chemistry continued to dominate into the 1960s.[11] But while the traditions gradually disappeared in the FRG, they actually gathered new force in the GDR during the 1950s and beyond. Through all these efforts, the GDR was able to return to some semblance of the German traditions of technological excellence in the chemical and machine-tool sectors by the early 1950s.[12]

There were clearly crucial limits to the ability of the SAGs in particular to pursue clear, coherent, and successful R&D programs well into the mid-1950s. The same was true to a lesser degree for the VEBs. For one thing, as noted earlier, SAGs produced primarily for the Soviet market and were not very sensitive to the needs of the GDR itself. In addition, the leadership of both the SAGs and the VEBs needed to focus almost entirely on the immediate and pressing need to increase production rather than on R&D planning, which was a longer term consideration. Constant reorganization of the means of production during the first decade after the war also led to problems with R&D within the SAGs and VEBs, since this necessarily involved a "splitting up of research and development capacity."[13]

The case of a major camera manufacturer, the VEB Zeiss-Ikon works at Niedersedlitz, illustrates these and other problems facing East German industry in the first decade after the war. Zeiss-Ikon's cameras had attained international renown through the 1930s, and it seemed reasonable to expect that they would regain some of their market position in the postwar world. That did happen for the East German Zeiss-Ikon group as a whole, but not for the Niedersedlitz works in particular, in part because of intense competition from the West German Zeiss-Ikon group.[14] Like other rival groups set up in the wake of German defeat and division, such as Agfa and Zeiss, West German Zeiss-Ikon challenged its East German counterpart for market share. In this somewhat unusual case the challenge was ultimately unsuccessful, since the West German group went into receivership in the mid-1960s.

But Niedersedlitz faced other problems than just West German competition. Part of the difficulty in regaining market share in international markets undoubtedly had to do with poor quality. Between 1945 and 1952, Zeiss-Ikon's works at Niedersedlitz produced cameras, but with a staggering rate of defects. At times during this period, up to 98 percent of production had to be discarded! Attempts to overcome the problem were hindered by such factors as frequently changing leadership, emigration of skilled workers and engineers to the West, and organizational uncertainty. The last of these had important implications for attempts to improve quality and product development. Placed initially in the Union of VEBs (Verein Volkseigene Betriebe, or VVB) for the Mechanical Industry, the VEB Zeiss-Ikon was cut off from its suppliers and from crucial networks of technological information. It did not begin to reestablish these contacts until it was moved to the VVB Optics in 1950.

Finally, the VEB Zeiss-Ikon at Niedersedlitz suffered from two related difficulties: reaping reasonable returns on its R&D investment, and translating the results of R&D into production. These difficulties plagued the GDR system of innovation in general to a greater or lesser degree throughout its existence. In the case of Zeiss-Ikon Niedersedlitz, the company spent considerable sums on R&D during the period 1945–52, but with disappointing results. Management of research was poor, as were facilities, and there was instability in the work force. Even when satisfactory results were obtained, the Niedersedlitz factory had enormous difficulty mobilizing funding for investment, which often came late, if at all.[15]

A study undertaken during 1959 in the Ministry for Machine Building indicates that the experience of the VEB Zeiss-Ikon Niedersedlitz factory was in many ways fairly typical. The study was intended to give an overview of major R&D projects undertaken in the heavy machinery, general machine-building, and electro-technical sectors of the GDR economy between 1950 and 1958, all of which had failed to be introduced into production. Altogether 722 projects were placed under scrutiny, for which nearly 60 million marks had been spent (see table 2). The main reason given for the failure to introduce R&D results into production was the rather nebulous category of "other reasons." A further 9.4 percent of the projects were going to be implemented soon, which indicated some progress. But the figures suggest strongly that the GDR system of innovation was not at all effective. Some of the reasons given clearly represent a failure of the system to link R&D expenditure to production. In all, cases of "abandonment," uselessness, outdatedness, and inadequacy accounted for 43.3 percent of all R&D projects that were not introduced into production in these vital sectors of the GDR economy.[16]

Clearly, although the GDR experienced some successes as it struggled to build a new set of organizations and traditions to foster innovation, there were many more failures. This was true even in some areas of former German technological excellence. What could be done to over-

Table 2. Reasons for Nonintroduction into Production of Results of R&D Efforts in the GDR Machine-Building and Electrotechnical Sectors, 1950–58 (% of total projects; N = 722)

Partially used	10.9
No useable solution*	15.7
Technically surpassed*	8.0
Difficulties with suppliers	1.5
Difficulties introducing into production	3.2
No one wishes to use*	17.1
Abandonment by those initially interested*	2.4
Development for own needs	0.1
Negligence on the part of the ministry or other state organizations*	0.1
Implementation currently being prepared	9.4
Standardization	0.1
International agreement	3.5
Other reasons	26.5

Note: Asterisk indicates reasons that represent failure of the system to link R&D expenditure to production.

Source: Calculated on the basis of figures in "Zusammenfassung nutzbarer Ergebnisse abgeschlossener Forschungs- und Entwicklungsarbeiten, die nicht in die Produktion eingeführt wurden, im Zeitraum 1950–1958," n.d. (ca. 1959), 5, BAP DE1/2299.

come these severe difficulties in scientific and technological development, which had such massive impacts on economic recovery and development? One of the first actions undertaken by the GDR regime was to try to identify the problems at hand and to rank them in order of urgency for solution.

Two sets of problems stood out above all others in this regard. The first—true to form for the bureaucrats of the new state, who were zealous planners—was to identify shortcomings in the planning process. In particular, they pointed out, GDR industry suffered from lack of "perspective," focusing on a single year rather than on any long-term vision.[17] This tendency toward short-term thinking was endemic to GDR industry, even the sectors at the forefront of high technology, such as optics and electrical goods. Planning for and investment in research and development tended, therefore, to be neglected. The first Five-Year Plan, launched on 1 January 1951, was meant to help overcome this tendency, although planning still remained very rudimentary and, in the area of science and technology, policy was restricted primarily to education and training.[18] Not until the later 1950s, in the context of vastly improved and stable political and economic conditions, did the tools become available to commit more heavily to planning and investment in science and technology, and the planners responded with the adoption of perspective planning and a Seven-Year Plan. It was later still, in the 1960s, that planning of science and technology became fully functional in the GDR, in part owing to a perception of growing backwardness and an awareness of sinking exports, and in part as a response to the rise of science policy in the West.[19]

The other main difficulty was the tendency for larger and larger numbers of technically and scientifically trained personnel to flee the country. This problem appeared amenable to more immediate solution. It was also far more important in the short term, since if enough scientists and engineers fled, the game was up before it began for GDR industry.

Fleeing the GDR eventually became an officially recognized crime, *Republikflucht* ("flight from the republic"), but the official legal response lagged considerably behind other short-term measures meant to stem the growing problem. The borders between West and East Germany had been fixed based on Allied decisions made during the war, and from the beginning of the successor states' existence, there were some difficulties in crossing them. Yet there were no controls at all in Berlin, and people routinely crossed the border between East and West Berlin, as well as the longer border between the "mainland" of East and West Germany, to go to work or to visit relatives. The main stretch of border between the two countries was already effectively sealed by the early 1950s, partly in response to a growing problem of more permanent emigration from East to West, but the Berlin border remained open into the early 1960s.

One figure makes clear the extent of the problem: between 1949 and 1961, when the Berlin Wall went up, an estimated 3.5 million East Germans emigrated to the West. There they were entitled to a West German passport, "welcome money" (a one-time payment to emigrants from the GDR), and the right to all the assistance of the growing welfare state. About half a million people emigrated in the reverse direction, yielding a net emigration from the GDR of about 3 million people.[20] For a country short of workers, such as the GDR, this constituted a major problem indeed. In general, the rate of emigration increased during the 1950s, but it was a recognized problem from the beginning of the GDR. Moreover, a considerable proportion of the emigrants were young and/or scientifically or technically trained. The blow to the East German economy was thus quite severe.

This much has long been generally known about emigration from the GDR before the construction of the Berlin Wall. Now that archival materials have become available, it is possible to paint a more nuanced and complete picture of the process of emigration and of its impact, in particular on technology. One study of the problem undertaken by the chemical industry indicated that well over 10,000 workers from the "centrally administered factories" had fled between 1955 and 1958, with most of them absconding in the period 1955–57. Of those who left during 1958, just under 1,800 in all, more than 75 percent were workers, while just 1 percent were "leading white-collar workers" and just over 6 percent were members of the "intelligentsia" (scientists and engineers). The remainder were clerks of various sorts, and low- and mid-level managers.[21]

These figures do not appear to support the usual interpretation of the effects of emigration from the GDR to the FRG on East German science, technology, and industry. But the report on the chemical industry, as well as reports on illegal emigration from other industrial sectors during the 1950s, give some additional information that restores to some extent the validity of that interpretation. They note the tendency for many of those who left industrial employment either to return or to be replaced by incomers from the West. The 1,370 workers who left the East German chemical industry for the West in 1958, for instance, were offset by 1,073 workers going the other way (termed in the report "population movement from West Germany"). But only 5 of the 115 members of the "intelligentsia" who emigrated were replaced by incomers from the West. The report noted further that older, more established chemists and engineers were overrepresented among the emigrants, as were those who had been taken to the Soviet Union during the late 1940s. In fact, nearly half of the 55 specialists who had gone to the USSR from the major chemical works in Bitterfeld had left for West Germany by 1959.[22]

In other words, scientists and engineers who joined the ranks of the emigrants did so in much smaller numbers than did workers. But they were far more likely to stay abroad and not to be replaced by similarly qualified people from the West. Furthermore, the most experienced and talented segments of the group—those who had worked for I. G. Farben or had been deemed by the Soviets to be of sufficient caliber to be brought to work in the USSR in the late 1940s—were most likely to leave the GDR permanently. The impact of this pattern of emigration on GDR science, technology, and industry was therefore profound, with the effects far exceeding what the raw numbers of emigrants might indicate.

The challenge was to come up with a way to stop the outward flow of the GDR's population toward the West. Westward emigration was a problem with which the GDR bureaucracy grappled, in increasingly draconian ways, until the construction of the Berlin Wall. But in the early 1950s the country's leadership resorted to more conventional sticks and carrots.

The primary stick was a tightening of the rules for crossing the borders with the West and an increase in the fines and penalties for doing so illegally. This process was more difficult than it sounds. Studying the problem in 1950, the GDR Ministry of Justice and the attorney general came to the conclusion that since the German-German border did not represent a "state border," the Passport Penal Decree of 27 May 1950 could not come into force. Those who engaged in *Republikflucht* (the term was used in official correspondence beginning in 1953) were therefore to be punished, when possible, for crimes against the economy, primarily sabotage. It was not until the alteration of passport legislation in late 1957 that *Republikflucht* became an official crime, subject to severe fines and up to three years' imprisonment. Even preparations for, or attempts at, flight were subject to this legislation, although those who were caught were often tried for espionage as well. This gave the state the opportunity to impose even more severe penalties.[23]

Various carrots were intended to entice scientifically and technically qualified personnel to stay in the GDR. The most important of these, undertaken in the early 1950s, was the improvement of pay and working conditions—as, for instance, in the Ordinance on the Increase of Salaries for Engineering and Technical Personnel of 28 June 1952. Later in the 1950s, as the problem grew more acute, the GDR leaders also gave scientists and engineers a bigger say and stake in the formulation of technological and economic policy and practice in the GDR at the highest levels. They did this through the formation of the Research Council (Forschungsrat).

In the short term, the attempts to win over the intelligentsia through pay increases for engineers and scientists did not work at any level. Technically trained personnel continued to leave the country, and in fact the numbers increased as the mid-1950s approached. Furthermore, the pay increases for technically trained personnel had the effect of further alienating workers, who were already frustrated by government policy. In particular, they quarreled with the government's imposition, by official edict on 28 May 1953, of what was essentially a Hennecke-type policy for increasing "productivity" (read production) through requiring workers to work harder and longer under the cover of "technically determined work norms" (TAN).

Nothing indicated more clearly the paucity of ideas for workable solutions to the problems faced by the GDR system of innovation than this raising of requirements for the output of individual workers. Planning innovation, encouraging registration of new patents, retaining and fostering scientists and engineers: these may have been the aims of policy-makers, but the leaders were unable to implement them in the early 1950s and instead resorted once again to the most primitive measures to increase production. And the measures backfired, with workers in a variety of industries engaging in wildcat strikes beginning shortly after the announcement of the edict. Protests culminated in massive work stoppages by mid-June and in broad-based demonstrations in Berlin and elsewhere on 17 June 1953, which had to be quashed by the Soviets and their tanks. The regime backed off hastily from its heightened work norms. Somewhat chastened, and in the context of even greater Soviet support, a greater degree of sovereignty, and a slightly more relaxed Cold War climate, it was finally able to formulate ideas and institutions that would become the long-term basis of the GDR national system of innovation.

Relative Stability and the Creation of a GDR National System of Innovation, 1953–1957

As Eckart Förtsch and Clemens Burrichter, two long-time analysts of East German science and technology, point out, the GDR had no science and technology policy "as an institutionalized state sector, as programmatic planning and control," until the 1950s. And it was the middle of the decade before "the state laid down its objectives and criteria of relevance. Technology was from now on supposed to contribute to rationalizing the economy of the GDR and to promote the country's prestige in international competition."[24] The two key factors in this change were increased levels of sovereignty for the GDR and more sophisticated planning practices.

Like the FRG, the GDR gradually gained sovereignty back from the

Allied occupiers during the first half of the 1950s. East Germany became a full-fledged member of the Council for Mutual Economic Cooperation, or COMECON, in September 1950, while trade agreements with the USSR and other eastern bloc countries, and an agreement on scientific and technological cooperation with the Soviets were concluded a year later. In May 1953 the Soviet Control Commission in Germany was disbanded, officially ending the occupation, while on 25 January 1955 the state of war between the USSR and Germany was finally declared by Moscow to be ended. Later that same year the GDR joined the Warsaw Pact, the eastern bloc's military counterfoil to NATO.

With this gradual regaining of some measure of political sovereignty, the GDR also gained more and more control over its economy and its scientific and technological development. Reparations ended officially with the disbanding of the reparations office in Berlin in January 1954. At the same time, the last of the SAG enterprises were returned to East German control and joined the ranks of the other state-owned enterprises, or VEBs. The Soviet market continued to dominate the thoughts of GDR planners and managers in making decisions about investment, as did the needs of the developing world and other COMECON countries.[25] But the fact that virtually all large-scale industrial establishments were brought under the control of the GDR state marked a fundamental change in the potential for planning and coordinating production, investment, and R&D for most sectors of East German industry.

The GDR began to realize this potential through developing better methods of collection and analysis of information on the economy. Provision of foodstuffs and other goods to consumers was on the increase, while the GDR at the same time reconstructed many of its key industries. Other sectors, such as heavy machine tools, which had been located exclusively in western Germany before 1945, were developed from scratch. In all, manufacturing industry's contribution to the total GDR economy rose from just under 56 percent to 66.5 percent between 1950 and 1960.[26]

Much of this growth, of course, came from older industries, or from growth in relatively low-technology ones. Steel production, for instance, increased dramatically through the development of the EKO combine in Eisenhüttenstadt during the decade.[27] But the SED felt confident enough in its achievements and in its potential for still better performance to commit the country to a higher technological plane in formulating the Second Five-Year Plan. The plan, which began in 1956, called for the intensification of basic research, as well as solution of key scientific and technological tasks central to economic development. The funds committed to research and development rose by 270 percent compared to the First Five-Year Plan, and training of scientific and technical personnel was to rise to unprecedented levels.[28]

The new emphasis on high-technology development was reinforced with considerable fanfare at the Third SED Party Conference in March 1956. The Second Five-Year Plan, which the conference endorsed, was full of references to "scientific-technological progress" and "socialist reconstruction." More specifically, Ulbricht and the party faithful were committed to an "industrial transformation" of the GDR based on rationalization, mechanization, automation, and nuclear power. Clearly, the country's machine-tool, machine-building, and electrical-goods sectors (both individually and jointly) would be crucial in achieving these ambitious goals. The ultimate objective was a very high one indeed: to "catch up with and surpass capitalism in terms of technology."[29]

The ambitious aims announced at the Third Party Conference were by and large not achieved, regardless of industry. Productivity in the machine-tool branch, for instance, declined severely during the 1950s. Its 1957 level was 93.5 percent of the 1950 level, mainly because of continuing overreliance on designs dating from before 1945, insufficient attention to new automation technologies, and overinvestment in development of a heavy-machine sector. The level improved only slightly during the rest of the decade, reaching 111 percent of the 1950 level in 1959.[30]

But there were some achievements as well. For example, the late 1950s saw renewed and sustained attention to the development of a domestic semiconductor industry and heavy commitment to the traditional source of German technological strength, the chemical industry. In addition, the first nuclear reactor in East Germany came on line in Rossendorf, near Dresden, in December 1957. The reactor's design and construction was Soviet, but it was to be used by East German researchers at the Institute for Nuclear Physics to develop domestic capability for producing atomic power. Moreover, the GDR was able to bring a new line of automobile, the Trabant, into production in 1958; the car's futuristic design and all-plastic body attracted worldwide attention. All in all, although the GDR clearly remained well behind the West in economic and technological development in the latter part of the decade, just as it had earlier, there appeared to be grounds for optimism. A technological euphoria seized the whole of the eastern bloc with the launch of the first Sputnik by the Soviets on 4 October 1957; in fact, it was Sputnik that inspired the name Trabant, or "satellite."[31]

These technological achievements may have lagged behind those of the West in many areas, but they were impressive nonetheless. They were made possible by the GDR's national system of innovation, the main elements of which were in place by the late 1950s. The system was a complex one, and only its most important aspects are sketched here. The system had three basic institutional elements. The first, centered primarily on the universities, and especially on the German Academy of Sciences (Deutsche Akademie der Wissenschaften, or AdW), focused heavily on basic scientific and technical research (as well as research in the social sciences and humanities). The second, centered primarily in large-scale industry, concentrated on development tasks associated with turning basic research into production. The third consisted of several state organizations for providing support and coordination of the first two.[32]

One of the main difficulties of the GDR system of innovation in the early 1950s was insufficient coordination and communication between basic researchers and production teams. For this reason, the results of research were frequently not transferred into production, or else they were transferred only with considerable delay. Planners in the GDR believed that part of the problem was that many scientists and engineers were inattentive to the needs of industry. To improve links between research and the economy, a system of contract research was developed. VEBs directly commissioned laboratories associated with the AdW and other organizations to conduct research of interest to them, a practice that became widespread in 1958.[33]

The change in practice accompanied a shift in official ideology, as the party moved science and technology from the base to the superstructure. Like other fundamental economic forces, science became a "force of production," a view popularized by Gerhard Kosel's 1957 book, *Produktivkraft Wissenschaft*. After considerable discussion and general acceptance, it was made into official communist dogma at the twenty-second congress of the Communist Party of the Soviet Union in 1961.[34] In 1958 Ulbricht himself underscored this new ideological direction and the scientists' and engineers' responsibilities under it: "The socialist style of work in the area of science and technological progress expresses itself above all in the idea that *scientists dedicate themselves in their work, in correspondence with societal interests, above all to significant economic questions.*"[35]

These organizational improvements and ideological changes were discussed at length and devised at the highest levels of GDR politics and society, in particular in the party's Central Committee during 1957. By 1958 the Fifth Party Congress agreed that the "economic main task" for the GDR was to demonstrate within just a few years the superiority of the socialist system over the capitalist one (and specifically of the GDR over the FRG) in terms of per-capita consumption. This, of course, could only be attained through an increase in productivity on the basis of science and technology.

According to the new version of the "economic main task," all high-technology industries were to be fostered. But in November of the same year the chemical industry was singled out for special attention at a conference of the party's Central Committee and the SPK at Leuna. Between 1958 and 1965 chemical production in the GDR was to double. Manufacture of petrochemical feedstocks, plastics, and synthetic fibers—the newest and most demanding areas of chemical production and technology—were at the center of this ambitious aim. It could only be achieved through increased spending on research and development; construction and expansion of the Schwedt petroleum refinery for processing Soviet oil into petrochemical feedstocks; and increased commitment to coal-based acetylene chemistry at the large Buna factory at Schkopau. (Petrochemicals and the expansion of the Schwedt facility are dealt with at greater length in a later chapter.) Worth emphasizing here is that although the GDR was planning to participate in the highest technology areas of the expanding chemical industry, it would do so partly on the basis of coal-based technologies, which the rest of the world was in the process of abandoning. The chemical program of 1958 therefore represented both an ambitious (some might say overambitious) gambit to regain a place at the forefront of international technological development and a concession to the reality that the GDR would have to depend upon domestic brown coal reserves in its chemical production.[36]

The chemical program's peculiar combination of *Flucht nach vorn* and retreat to the tried and true was characteristic of the GDR leadership's decision-making in the late 1950s. And it was symptomatic of the crisis in which the leadership found itself. The economy in the Federal Republic was developing faster than that in the GDR, and West German technology was clearly superior in most areas. Scientifically and technically trained personnel in the GDR, seeing this, were deserting East Germany in droves. Those who remained were frequently dispirited, not just at this state of affairs, but also because they felt that they did not participate fully enough in the decision-making about scientific, technological, and economic development. To overcome this morale problem, the GDR engaged in a further series of organizational reforms beginning in the second half of 1957.

Within the state bureaucracy, a secretariat for research and technology was established (Staatssekretariat für Forschung und Technik) under the leadership of Dr. Alfred Baumbach. This was part of the upgrading of the bureaucratic position of research and development that culminated in the formation of the Ministry for Science and Technology in 1967. In conjunction with the state secretariat, an Advisory Council for Scientific and Technical Research and Development (Beirat für naturwissenschaftlich-technische Forschung und Entwicklung), was also formed in late August 1957. The Forschungsrat, or Research Council, as it came to be known, was attached to the GDR Council of Ministers and had responsibility for advising the government on science and technology policy, providing evaluations and assessments of science and technology, and writing draft directives for perspective planning on science and technology. Initially it consisted of forty-seven scientists, engineers, and leading functionaries from the state apparatus, but its numbers and influence were expanded considerably during the 1960s: staff support for the Research Council from the state apparatus was made available as the organization's official role grew.[37]

The leadership of the Research Council represented the older, established intelligentsia, and its formation was motivated by the desire to coopt this group, and in particular those specialists returning from the Soviet Union. It was chaired by Professor Peter-Adolf Thiessen, a physical chemist born in 1899. Thiessen had been an early member of the National Socialist Party, joining in 1926, and had a distinguished career during the Nazi period as professor of physical chemistry at the University of Münster and subsequently as director of the Kaiser Wilhelm Institute for Physical Chemistry and Electrochemistry in Berlin between 1935 and 1945. He was one of the many specialists taken to the Soviet Union in 1945 and 1946, and he remained in the USSR working on the Soviet nuclear program into 1956. To retain his services in the GDR, the leadership appointed Thiessen, upon his return, director of the Institute for Physical Chemistry, professor at the Humboldt University, and member of the Academy of Sciences. The chairmanship of the Research Council provided him with a direct means of influencing formation and implementation of policy. He was joined by other well-established figures from the intelligentsia, including Buna's Professor Johannes Nelles, a renowned specialist in rubber synthesis who had been in a leadership position at the plant since 1941, and whom the Soviets had appointed works director in 1945.[38]

The Research Council gave scientists and engineers a forum within which to influence GDR science and technology policy at the fundamental level. In a sense, then, since it represented a corresponding decrease in the power of state bureaucrats, it was a radical response to the economic and technological problems facing the GDR in the late 1950s. It was therefore both symptomatic of the severity of the crisis in which the country found itself and yet another instance of the tendency to embrace strategies of *Flucht nach vorn* (in this case *through* retreat to the tried and true) to deal with it.

In 1949–50 the GDR was in desperate straits, with small numbers of planners dashing madly about trying to resuscitate the economy. They lacked the necessary tools, and even if they had had them, they lacked the authority to apply their plans to large swathes of industry. As sovereignty was devolved from the Soviet occupiers to the GDR state, more and more of the country's industrial capacity came under its control. Additional planners used improved techniques to coordinate and develop the economy. By 1957–58, on this basis, the main organizational structures of the GDR's first real attempt at a national system of innovation had emerged, including institutions for pursuing basic research, applied research, and production, and for planning and coordinating these three areas.

As might have been expected, given the communist political system, the GDR system of innovation was characterized by extensive state ownership of the means of production and a profound and extensive intervention of the state in all aspects of economic development. Other features of the system—which emerged in part from German traditions, in part from communist ideology, and in part from the position in which the GDR found itself during the 1950s—included shared responsibility for planning and implementing science and technology policy, between state bureaucrats and the intelligentsia; attempts (usually frustrated through the late 1950s) at cooperation with the Soviet Union and other eastern bloc countries; and an emphasis on high-technology development above all else. Science, as a force of production and in its most refined forms in automation, precision machinery, electronics, organic chemicals, and nuclear power, would allow the GDR to achieve its aim of overtaking and surpassing the capitalist system during the coming decade.

We know, of course, that this did not come to pass. But from the perspective of the late 1950s, the dream of demonstrating the superiority of socialism over capitalism seemed attainable, if perhaps also extremely ambitious and optimistic. The Second Berlin Crisis—the attempt between 1958 and 1961 by the GDR with the support of the Soviets to regularize and resolve Berlin's ambiguous status—lent a sense of urgency to the proceedings. The GDR scrambled to identify, develop, and implement additional organizational structures and technologies it would need to carry out its "main task." German technological traditions, which allowed it to link effectively with developments in the West, combined with Soviet technological prowess, as demonstrated by Sputnik and in a host of other, less spectacular areas, to make the task seem doable despite the GDR's current difficulties. In short, the GDR was coming to a crossroads during the period 1958–61. But would it be able to maintain its position between the two blocs in terms of technological tradition? Would it be able to jumpstart its national system of innovation to provide the high-technology products and processes its leaders believed it needed to promote strong and self-sustaining economic growth? Or would the leaders be defeated, not by the GDR's inability to produce high-technology wares, but rather by the inability to provide "the thousand objects of everyday need," which they neglected in large part because of their concentration on leading-edge technology?[39]

Part II | Socialist Technology
at the Crossroads,
1958–1961

Chapter 3 | Metrics of Progress
Technological Tourism and Display

During the 1950s, before the construction of the Berlin Wall, East and West Germany had already grown far apart in terms of economic policy and practice. Yet there remained close links between them, not just in terms of language, but also in terms of business and technological culture. Most managers and engineers in East Germany had come of age professionally within the same corporations as their West German counterparts. They used the same machines, employed similar production practices, and shared assumptions about the design and construction of implements and processes. They represented a common German management and technological culture. This culture, however, was weakening in the period after 1945, although it is not entirely clear when and how the process of cultural division took place. It is certain, however, that the process was far advanced by the late 1950s.

Technological Tourism and Cultural Misunderstanding: The Hannover Trade Fair

Since technology is apparently value neutral and independent of political system, one might expect that there could be little misunderstanding in this area, especially in newly divided Germany, with its long traditions of management of technological change and its shared and distinguished development of particular technologies. Nonetheless, such misunderstandings did occur between East and West Germans, even at this relatively early date.

The task of identifying such misunderstanding, assessing its significance, and evaluating how deeply it ran entails close reading and interpretation of materials that are generally incomplete and somewhat impressionistic. Here I use firsthand accounts written by East German visitors to West German industrial exhibitions in the late 1950s, to establish and analyze the depth of cultural misunderstanding between the two German successor states—a cultural misunderstanding that had already emerged in the first decade of their existence. These sources, written by engineers and managers for bureaucrats in the SPK, are particularly valuable, since they offer frank criticisms and insights into cultural assumptions that were either caricatured, papered over, or expunged from higher level official reports produced by the SPK, the East German state, and the SED. My discussion makes use of the notion of "technological tourism," which captures some dimensions of the process of cultural division that might otherwise be lost. The main focus is on the Hannover Trade Fair of April 1959, which some East German engineers and managers attended.

The Bus Trip

In the midst of the Second Berlin Crisis, on 26 April 1959, about a hundred managers and engineers from several different industrial sectors in the GDR boarded three buses in East Berlin and set off for a five-day study visit to the Hannover Trade Fair in West Germany.[1] Their objective was to observe systematically the technological artifacts on offer at the trade fair from around the world—and especially from the capitalist countries. They were in effect "technological tourists," in terms of their economic significance in West Germany (short-term visitors rather than permanent residents), their social role there (outsiders), and their own view of themselves and their purpose (observers who would be somehow edified by contact with the foreign culture).[2]

These tourists, however, were different from many others on account of their ambiguous status. Were they from another part of the same country or from abroad? After all, they spoke the same language as their hosts. That in itself is not such an unusual experience for tourists: English-speaking North Americans frequently visit Britain, for instance. But these men had been citizens of the same country just a few years before, and many of them had worked for the same companies as their West German counterparts. Furthermore, although their government sought to differentiate itself from that of their hosts, official West German government policy did not recognize their government diplomatically and still considered East Germans to be citizens of the Federal Republic.

Their means of transport to the trade fair reflected this ambiguity. They traveled, not in long-distance tour buses, but rather in city buses without any luggage compartments or specially padded seats. This must have resulted in an extremely uncomfortable journey. Every seat, even the folding ones, was occupied. The men held their luggage on their lap during the long hours of the journey. There are many possible explanations for why city buses were chosen for this group, but in any case the choice reflected the close physical proximity of East Berlin and Hannover.

Like other tourists, the East German engineers had to have accommodation during their stay abroad. Their luck was not good, and although the exact cause is not clear, security concerns apparently played some role. For this reason, those organizing the trip attempted to keep all the hundred-odd GDR participants together in a single group during the hours when the delegates were not attending the fair itself, by locating them in a single hotel. The problem was that no hotel in Hannover could offer enough rooms for the entire delegation when it arrived. Almost all the East German delegates therefore ended up spending their first two nights in a hotel in Bad Harzburg, 92 kilometers away from Hannover. They spent five hours of each of their first two days traveling by city bus between Bad Harzburg and the trade fair. Security concerns eventually yielded to the protests of the GDR representatives, however, and in the end their leaders arranged for lodgings closer to Hannover.

At least one of the participants in the trip, a designer from Zeiss Works by the name of Söldner, saw the bad luck with the allocation of rooms as symptomatic of a deeper menace: "What happened to us was that the rooms which had been allocated to us had been given away privately. At least 50 people stood in front of the travel agency offering rooms on the black market."[3] According to Söldner, then, what happened was not mere accident, but was rather systemic and compared unfavorably to what would be the case in the GDR. He claimed that "the population of H[annover], unlike that of Leipzig, is not heart and soul at the trade fair . . . Here everything is commercialized."[4]

Attending the Hannover Trade Fair, April 1959

Söldner's evident distaste for West German capitalism pervaded his report, and the same was true of many other GDR visitors to Hannover that year. Many of the reporters took the opportunity in their account of the trip to suggest that, although the technology on display in Hannover may have been superior to that in the East, the organization of the trade fair revealed the fundamental weaknesses of capitalism. By implication, this weakness would ultimately and inevitably undermine capitalism's ability to produce world-class technology. One representative from the electronics industry, for example, said he had been impressed by the lack of standardization in electronic components, something he saw as symptomatic of capitalism: "Electrical and electronic components are available in all possible variations and designs. Close examination leads the observer to recognize immediately the great advantages which are possible in the planned economy."[5]

The overall report of the electrical/electronics delegation made a similar point:

> It is very difficult to get an overview of the offerings in the exhibition spaces [of the Hannover Trade Fair], and this expresses the fragmentation of capitalist, and especially West German industry, compared to the clarity of the Leipzig Trade Fair.
>
> The flow from one section to another, which moves so pleasantly for the visitor to the Leipzig fair, is missing here, something that is determined by the mammoth booths of the great concerns with their extensive production programs on the one hand, and by the unwonted number of small (and even tiny) exhibition booths on the other.[6]

The tone and content of these selections warrants a more critical examination. After all, expressing a distaste for capitalism's lack of direction and "fragmentation" (*Zersplitterung*) might simply have been something that was de rigeur in such narratives, a ritual that perhaps showed one's passionate commitment to socialism. Certainly this was a typical characteristic of the "socialist style" of nonfiction writing in the later years of the GDR. But on the basis of these reports and other archival evidence, this characterization does not seem to apply to the 1950s. For one thing, not every report criticizes capitalism; many criticize socialism—at least as practiced in the GDR—far more savagely. Although the delegation members in general clearly believed (or at least many of them said they believed) that the GDR could still hope at some time in the future to catch up with international technological best practice, they were painfully aware that their homeland was lagging behind the West. In their summary report, for instance, members of the delegation from the electrical and electronics sector stated clearly that "the [1959] Hannover Industrial [Trade] Fair demonstrates that we have serious deficiencies in certain areas." One area of the sector after another was singled out in the report to be raked over the coals. Design and performance of high-voltage apparatus and low-voltage switches were severely wanting, primarily because of "the much too long, and in part cumbersome development work as well as the deficient implementation of lightweight construction." There were also "deficiencies in the procurement of small and miniature [electronic] components of appropriate quality," which resulted from

the frequently deficient, but above all fluctuating quality of materials. A certain insecurity results from this among those responsible for development and design. An additional factor is technological processes, which are not applied or mastered fast enough, with the result that frequently years pass before their introduction into production. Through this sort of development, we have the greatest delays in manufacture of devices and plant installations in all areas, for example, in commercial telecommunications, small radio receivers, and measurement apparatus.

The quantity and scope of ideas for construction and design in East Germany came up short in international comparison, especially in electrical household apparatus, and there was also "insufficient attention to new product development, especially in radio broadcasting and recording technology."[7]

Those representing the office-machinery industry found that in conventional technology GDR industry was still quite competitive, but in technology involving application of electronics, "backwardness is still to be noted."[8] This must certainly have troubled the representatives of this branch of GDR industry, who had already in the early 1950s recognized and begun work on applying electronics to the office-machinery industry.[9]

But if some accounts of the trip criticize socialism, these are not necessarily the same ones that also criticize capitalism. This is yet another reason why the reports should be taken seriously. In these unsanitized reports, written only for the eyes of government bureaucrats, rancor and criticism of all sorts flowed freely, and it is reasonable to believe that many of the GDR's representatives felt an aesthetic as well as principled revulsion to capitalism as experienced in Hannover, and that they expressed it in their accounts of the fair.

Revulsion toward capitalism is perhaps an expected response, but it is helpful to know that it was probably genuine. One might imagine that such deeply held views would have a significant impact on communication between the German visitors and their German hosts. Although this is a difficult issue to assess, the reports generated by the East German

Tape recorder from 1957 showing the pronounced capability of East German designers. Unfortunately, it was frequently not possible to translate their ideas into mass production of goods. Delegates to the Hannover Trade Fair in 1959 detected technical deficiencies in GDR electronic equipment, including tape recorders, compared to the products of capitalist countries. *Sammlung industrielle Formgestaltung, Berlin*

participants in the visit to Hannover in 1959 allow some conclusions, if only by indirection.

One of the most striking things about these reports is how seldom they mention contact with West Germans. In this respect one report, which contrasts the ease of obtaining information and even price lists from representatives of West German firms in Hannover in 1959 with the difficulty in doing so just two years earlier, stands out.[10] For the most part, the reports simply describe the machines the GDR representatives saw on display.

Now one way to explain this would be to point out that these were, after all, engineers, more interested in machines than in other people. Another way would be to recognize that, given the political climate of the day, it may have been considered wise not to mention personal contact with West Germans.

There is probably something to each of these interpretations, neither is sufficient. For one thing, we must remember that the GDR representatives did travel and lodge together as a group; judging from the reports, even during marathon visits to the fair itself (generally eight or nine hours a day without breaks), the tendency was for four to six representatives from the same industrial sector to look around together. Like other tourists, then, the GDR engineers probably spent far more time with one another than they did with those whose country they were visiting. Moreover, even when they did interact with West Germans, there were often other East Germans around.

It is also likely that the East German engineers engaged in social activities to a much greater degree than their reports indicate. The systematic neglect of such socializing in the reports, however, is less likely a function of fear of reprisals than an acceptance of conventions followed by engineers and scientists in all countries: what was important was to expunge the human element from the narrative, the social and political context within which all science and engineering knowledge is created.[11] Instead, the focus was on the machines.

When they were looking at machines, the East German engineers and managers were actually observing displays deliberately designed to mislead—or to put it another way, to project an image.[12] It was, after all, not a representative sample of capitalist production on display in Hannover, but rather the best the participating firms had to offer, displayed in the best possible light. In this regard it is far less striking that virtually all the reports speak glowingly about capitalist technological capability than that none of them shows any critical awareness about the propaganda to which they were being subjected.

Although physical artifacts allegedly are the focal point of the proceedings at a trade fair, they actually play a relatively modest role. In the complex dance between representatives of various competing and cooperating institutions and countries that constitutes the trade fair, intangibles are of the utmost moment. Competence, shrewdness, hard work, dependability, reasonableness, toughness, intelligence: any combination of these qualities or their opposites can form the basis for a decision about whether to enter into negotiations for sales or purchases or technology transfer with a firm. The intangibles are communicated from one party to another by means of symbols, including, for the exhibitors, the physical objects they have on display, but also the brochures they offer, the lighting and design of their booth, the dress of their representatives and their manners and sociability, the hotels they stay in, the food they eat, and so on. The medium is the message. But the GDR representatives seemed much more conscious of the physical artifact than of its presentation and symbolic importance, at least when it came to the representation of capitalist technology at the fair.

In direct contrast, some representatives showed extreme sensitivity in assessing the image they themselves were projecting in Hannover. Engineers, businessmen, and government bureaucrats from the GDR in the 1950s were, of course, engaged in creating an alternative society that would differ in important ways from that of capitalism. They contrasted the chaos of capitalist production and lack of standardization with the rationality of the planned economy, as we have seen. But they did not extend their analysis of the differences between capitalism and socialism to trade fairs themselves except superficially and in passing. As a result (and probably in any case), representatives of the socialist GDR who attended trade fairs, like the 1959 event at Hannover, generally accepted the same symbols and values as their capitalist counterparts.

In this, there was no question: the GDR looked bad. The country's representatives traveled in large and unwieldy groups in buses, and they all stayed in the same hotel miles away from the fair. They had limited means at their disposal, and they suffered from poor organizational and logistical support. In a sense, it was the least of their worries that their technology was sometimes inferior to that of the West. Even when a particular machine or process was not in the least inferior (there were many cases of this in the late 1950s, and a few later), the main problems were that the East Germans could not produce enough of them, or the machines were unattractive, or they were produced, sold, or serviced by people who suffered from poor organizational and logistical support.

Undoubtedly, those who intimated such fears in their reports on their trip were correct, at least in part. To the extent that we know about western reaction to the GDR, its technology, and its economic capability, the visitors to Hannover undoubtedly confirmed broadly held preconceptions. However, this is less interesting than the suggestions that a few of the East German participants made as ways of correcting these false impressions, for here we get to the heart of the confusion and ambiguity that characterized the image GDR representatives were trying to project.

In general, the reports show that GDR representatives to the Hannover Trade Fair found aspects of their own system—at least as it showed its face to the outside (western) world—especially unsettling. Surely it is important that virtually every account mentions the bus journey and the accommodation in critical terms. Both appeared in the eyes of many to be the result of poor organization and therefore correctable in the future. But some saw deeper symbolic importance to such errors, and could intuit the extent to which it would therefore be difficult to correct them. The delegation's arrival in buses in a single group appeared to one of the representatives to "make us appear uniform and is spoken about in that way by various outsiders." (He might have made a similar comment regarding the lodging.) But he also suggested an alternative form of transport that would have a different meaning: "Travel with a private automobile, which almost every participant possesses, would require less foreign currency and would demonstrate a higher standard of living."[13]

The point about saving foreign exchange may be debatable (although it certainly was true that savings would come in the case of those living close to the West German border, who might purchase their fuel in the GDR and drive directly to and from Hannover rather than embarking on the long trip to Berlin only to return by bus), but I think that this particular passage shows especially clearly the ways in which the East German visitors to the West were in an especially ambiguous position. The members of the *Reisekader*, the elite engineers who were allowed to travel to the West, enjoyed a standard of living such that they could afford private automobiles, and they realized that demonstrating this might be of value at a trade fair. Yet they were also in the process of creating a completely different type of state and society from that in the West, which suggested some different kind of strategy, and perhaps the group bus tour might better serve that aim. There are, of course, other interpretations. On a more mundane, but perhaps more important, level, there were elements of East German behavior that were dictated by the particular historical circumstances in which the young country found itself: it was struggling to keep its technical and scientific elites from emigrating en masse to the West, and allowing transport by automobile would have undermined centralized control. Yet here, too, the downside of the decision to adopt a strategy of group-based rather than individualized technological tourism was that it tended to undermine the prestige and negotiating power of the GDR in the West.

Some Preliminary Conclusions

The story of the East German delegation's visit to the Hannover Trade Fair in 1959 conveys a lot about the way East Germans engineers viewed themselves and the process through which they were becoming different from their West German counterparts. It is, of course, just one set of stories from one particular point in time, but similar accounts crop up in reports of visits by GDR representatives to other trade fairs in the same year and to Hannover and to other western trade fairs in other years.[14]

For this reason, the unusually rich and frank collection of travelers' reports from Hannover in 1959 is instructive. They indicate that the "wall in the head" (*Mauer im Kopf*) was firmly in place well before the construction of the actual Berlin Wall. This is perhaps not surprising, given the extent of governmental and other changes after 1945 in East Germany. But it is surprising among engineers who spoke the same language, and often came out of the same traditions and corporate and engineering culture, as their West German counterparts.

A fundamental tension was expressed in many of the reports. As committed socialists, the authors wished to play their part in creating a new society; this meant critiquing capitalism, but also suggesting ways in which socialist technology would be different from its capitalist counterpart. At the same time, as engineers who had grown up in, and for the most part been trained within, a capitalist (or fascist-capitalist) system, they accepted many of the same tenets for design and performance of artifacts as did engineers in West Germany.

Being the same as, and yet at the same time very different in background and outlook from, those they were visiting in Hannover meant that the GDR engineers, many of whom saw themselves as relatively close to home spatially and culturally, functioned as foreign rather than domestic tourists. Like other tourists visiting foreign countries, they tended to stick to themselves and to have little contact with the local population. They also tended, like other technological tourists abroad, to see not necessarily what was there, but rather what they wanted to see.[15] Thus, they generally accepted capitalist technology without criticism, while criticizing other aspects of capitalism without any deep consideration.

Miscommunication was endemic in this situation. Although ostensibly clear in many respects, the party line could not help the visiting engineers resolve the tension. They were unable, therefore, either to receive or to send information clearly to those whom they were visiting, whom they were trying to impress, and with whom they wished to cooperate. Already by 1959 GDR engineers and industrialists as a group had become strangers in a strange land when visiting the Federal Republic. In part for this reason, they tried at about this same time to build up their "home-court advantage" at their own internationally known trade fair in Leipzig.

Exploiting the Leipzig Trade Fair through the Early 1960s

Sending trained personnel to trade and technology fairs in the capitalist West was one way of making sure that the GDR was kept abreast of the latest technologies in the nonsocialist world. But the strategy had drawbacks, two of which were particularly important. First of all, it required the use of foreign exchange. For trips to the FRG, especially to a place like Hannover near the German-German border, the amounts involved were not enormous. Nevertheless, the hard currency required to pay for fuel, lodging, and meals for a group of GDR visitors could quickly add up.

When the destination was further afield—to London, Rome, or Paris, for instance—the sums were even greater. There were, then, natural limits to the number of trade fairs that could be visited in a given year, and to the number of delegates who could be sent to each of them. The second problem with sending GDR personnel to the capitalist West throughout the country's existence, but particularly in the 1950s, was the possibility that the visitors would seize this opportunity to emigrate. Close supervision, both at home and at the trade fair, and careful selection of *Reisekader* (officially vetted travel cadres) kept this problem in check to some degree. But even so there were often at least one or two who remained in the West. Here, the desirability of West Germany as a destination, from the point of view of common language and of limiting expenditures of foreign exchange, was offset by the fact that East German defectors could immediately claim their right to West German citizenship.

The challenge, then, was to gain knowledge of developments abroad without at the same time incurring the expenses and risks of travel to the capitalist West. In this area, the East Germans were fortunate to have within their borders the city of Leipzig, which had a long and distinguished heritage of trade and technology fairs. From the beginning of the GDR's existence, the East German leadership saw the Leipzig fairs as a means of displaying the accomplishments of socialism. But from the early 1950s it was clear that they did not want to limit it to that: by showing off the accomplishments of socialism, "the Leipzig Trade Fair in no way loses its significance for the economies of the capitalist and economically underdeveloped countries. Just the opposite. The Leipzig Trade Fair is capable through this [i.e., the demonstration of the accomplishments of socialism] of fulfilling a great new mission, which is the promotion of trade of goods between the capitalist countries and the world economic system of the socialist states."[16] By the late 1950s this function of the fair was portrayed more simply and directly in the slogan "Center for East-West Trade."[17]

As the 1950s progressed, planners saw these expanding functions of the trade fair at Leipzig as an unprecedented opportunity to carry out what amounted to industrial espionage with a home-court advantage and virtually unrestricted resources.

Leipzig: Symbol and Meaning

In Leipzig the GDR inherited one of the most distinguished trading cities in Europe and the world. Its fairs, which occurred twice annually, in spring and fall, dated from at least the thirteenth century and were some of the oldest in the German area. By the late fifteenth century the Leipzig fair had expanded its influence from local and regional to national and international. Occasional outbreaks of piracy and political unrest in the Mediterranean guaranteed the city's continued prominence even during the eighteenth century, when other central European trading cities and their fairs declined in importance. The Leipzig spring and autumn fairs emerged as a venue at which western and eastern, southern and northern markets met.[18]

By the twentieth century an annual technical fair had joined the two traditional fairs, while other, more specialized fairs occurred throughout the year. At these events exhibitors from around the world displayed their best new wares, companies struck commercial deals and technological cooperation agreements, and the German state engaged in political posturing and demonstrations of economic might. This last function of the fair was especially important during the peacetime years of the Nazi period, of course, although it was far from unknown under previous German governments.

Small wonder, then, that the new regime moved quickly after the end of World War II to restore the fair to its former prominence. Little wonder, too, that West Germany soon established a rival fair for trade, technology, and industry in Hannover. Understandably, given the importance of the Leipzig fair and the competition with Hannover, the East Germans engaged in constant comparisons. Initially the predominant attitude of East German planners, managers, and engineers toward Leipzig's competitors ranged from condescending to unconcerned, although one early commentator noted that the quality of goods on display at Hannover meant it was "to be taken seriously as a competitor."[19]

By the late 1950s, however, the comparisons were less flattering to Leipzig, especially when the writer of a report was a member of the *Reisekader* who had just returned from a visit to the West. Milan, for instance, was singled out for the "design of the sales kiosks and fast-food shops." Commenting on fast-food operations may not seem especially significant on its own, but the author in this case went on to speculate about the probable effects on a foreign visitor of "the wooden shacks of the trade organization and of the cooperatives at the Leipzig Technical Fair," a speculation he found "embarrassing for me."[20] Hannover, however, was clearly the main competitor, and its rise was not just for culinary or aesthetic reasons. By 1957 Hannover was displaying relatively more items from the capitalist world, noted one major observer from the SPK's Central Office for Research and Technology.[21] Returning from a trip to Hannover in April 1959, an engineer from the Zeiss Works, one of the most technologically advanced companies in East Germany, reported that "this trade fair stands at a very high level and can be compared in every way with our Leipzig trade fair."[22]

Such tidings were not good. If Leipzig were to continue to fulfill its functions as a showpiece for socialist technology and a link between East and West, it would have to do much better. And if it could, this would allow it also to perform a vital new function, as a resource for industrial espionage and technology transfer.

Exploiting Leipzig as a Resource

The idea of exploiting a trade fair to gain vital intelligence on the state of technological development of competing firms and countries was not, of course, the invention of the East Germans. Indeed, this was one of the major reasons for having trade fairs in the first place. What was different in East Germany in the 1950s was not the notion of gathering technical intelligence through hosting or attending trade fairs, but rather the method by which it was to be accomplished. The scale of the GDR effort was also unusual. Broad-based scientific assessment of exhibited wares would allow precise identification of the leader in a particular field of technology and—depending on who was in the lead—a precise measure of how far behind the East German technology might be. Such evaluation would be of enormous practical value in developing strategies for maintaining technological leads or overcoming technological lags. But it also conformed nicely to the general ethos of scientific socialism as practiced in the GDR.

The task, then, was to move beyond the impressionistic evaluation of individual machines and vague notions of international standing in a particular area of technology to a rigorous and reproducible ranking based on unambiguous criteria. The desire to accomplish this led to a growing obsession, among technical and scientific circles in the GDR, with the notion of measuring *Weltniveau*, or world-class technology. GDR engineers and bureaucrats discussed at length different ways of accomplishing this. By 1957 the technical journal *Maschinenbautechnik* reported that a reliable method had been developed to assess the technological level of complex machine tools, one of the key bases of technological achievement in any industrial society, and one of the strengths of the GDR in particular. This method would allow identification of the leader and of the extent to which the GDR was currently producing goods to match the leader's accomplishments. Like previous, more holistic and impressionistic assessments, the new method was meant to be deployed by well-informed experts in a given field. Five separate criteria were to be used in the evaluation:

1. Exterior design, especially of the machine stand and the main components
2. Workmanship, i.e., precision in manufacture and quality of surfaces
3. Performance capability of the machine (in terms of quality and volume)
4. Input of materials (in relation to output)
5. Safety technology, i.e., cultivation of devices for prevention of accidents

In passing, it might be noted that if such criteria had been developed by a group of engineers in a capitalist country, the list would have looked much the same. Data on these points were to be entered in detail onto an index card along with comments on especially advantageous characteristics of the design and any technical novelties. The aim was "to recognize without any additional effort . . . in what manner further development of one's own products would have to move forward." The cards, taken together, would provide a clear picture of the international technological state of play for machine-tool manufacturing. Calculations of the level of GDR technological development would provide a measure of the extent of backwardness and an unambiguous indication of the goal for attaining world technological levels. It would, of course, be necessary to update the index cards constantly and to maintain them in the documentation center of a factory's R&D laboratory along with patent and other vital reference information.[23] By 1960 exactly this same sort of "scientific" determination of *Weltniveau* was advocated prominently in *Einheit*, the main SED ideological journal. The article claimed that "the *main method* for investigating and continuously following the *Weltniveau* is through scientific and technical documentation and information" and suggested the need for one "document and information specialist" for every ten scientists or engineers.[24]

The implementation of such an ambitious project depended upon availability of vast resources of personnel and effort. But ultimately it depended upon access to and examination of machines that were designed and produced abroad, as well as those manufactured domestically. Using trade fairs to gain such access was clearly the most efficient means to this end, and a pilot project for technological assessment along the lines suggested in the article was applied during 1957 and 1958. The focus was on the assessment of displays of heavy-machine-building technology—an area in which the GDR had only recently developed domestic capability—in Leipzig. On the basis of this experience, the SPK's Research and Technology Section was charged with developing a plan to carry this out for all industries. The plan was put together in summer 1958 in consultation with the highest levels of the party apparatus as well as the recently created, elite Research Council (Forschungsrat). It was to be implemented at all trade fairs attended by GDR delegations, but especially the Leipzig fair. The plans completed and resources marshaled, the first major trial occurred at the Leipzig spring fair of 1959.[25]

The effort to prepare for the fair was enormous. Armed with the support of the Politburo and its Economics Commission, the SPK began planning well in advance. Each Union of People's Own Factories (Verein Volkseigene Betriebe, or VVB) set up a study group composed of highly qualified scientists and engineers who would study the exhibits in Leipzig. In all, 215 of these groups were formed, and they joined representatives from the Central Office for Research and Technology, the Office for Standardization, and others in descending upon the fair. For the machine-building sector alone, the number of specialists assigned to the trade fair in 1959 was 290. In all, probably around 1,800 technically trained personnel were involved.[26]

The results of these ambitious and massive assessment efforts were in turn assessed in detail by the Politburo's Economics Commission. By and large, the commission was happy with these first trials, which produced "correct and also important accounts of technical details." But there were many problems. Many of the study groups did not actually compare GDR exhibits with foreign ones, missing entirely the point of the exercise. The report criticized one local representative of the Chamber of Technology for his statement that he had appreciated being told to go to Leipzig since it forced him to attend the fair for the first time since 1945. Many of the study groups, moreover, had not taken up the offer of the Research Council for cooperation in planning and evaluating the work of the study groups, although there was a major exception in the area of measurement and regulation technology, where Professor Kienast and Dr. Herbert Kortum made a thorough and detailed report of their findings.[27]

The report presented an overview of the findings of some of the key study groups. Machine-tool development was in general terms quite satisfactory: "most of its products reached world class." Automation, standardization, and the introduction of the modular system (*Baukastensystem*) were critical areas of scientific and technical advancement, and the Institute for Machine Tools was instrumental in maintaining a strong presence in these areas for the GDR. Thus, although there were noticeable lags compared to foreign machines in some fields, such as cutting and shaping machinery and electrical hand tools, the GDR was relatively well placed within the machine industry.

The situation with regard to electrical and electronics technology was far less satisfactory. In critical fields such as high-frequency and communications technology and semiconductors, the GDR's lag compared to its competitors was "very serious." The same was true in the area of measurement and regulation technology, in which, despite some products at the cutting edge, the GDR generally lagged considerably behind world technological levels. Optics technology, on the other hand, was still very advanced, but competitors from abroad were catching up in areas such as 35 mm single-lens reflex cameras. Consumer durables was one field in which the GDR was quite far behind. Even Yugoslavia outperformed the GDR in the design of electric kitchen stoves.[28]

The report concluded with the observation that the results of the investigations were gratifying in two ways. First of all, they confirmed that the GDR had reached international levels in many areas of technology and that there was a solid basis for building upon this achievement. Second, they provided ideas and motivations for improvements in technology and organization, which would allow this process to continue. The idea of using large numbers of GDR personnel to investigate the Leipzig trade fair to evaluate the state of world technology was viewed as one that should be continued, improved, and extended.[29]

The measures undertaken by the GDR in 1959 to gather and digest information on foreign technology through study of exhibits at the Leipzig trade fair involved a massive and unprecedented commitment of resources, and the country clearly expected a suitable payoff for this large investment. Although the East Germans did gain some insights into the state of foreign technology and ideas for improving their own, it soon became clear that the payoff would be extremely disappointing. For just as the GDR geared up to implement this strategy, the Leipzig trade fair was becoming less significant, having already reached a peak in both quantitative and qualitative terms.

The number of visitors to and exhibitors at the Leipzig spring trade fair grew substantially following the fair's reinstatement in 1946; growth was especially pronounced during the 1950s.[30] The total number of visitors grew from 172,400 in 1946 to over 450,000 in 1950. Although the numbers fluctuated somewhat in the following years, they were invariably well over half a million during the last half of the 1950s. Visitor numbers reached a high of 629,200 in 1961 before dropping significantly to 520,300 following the construction of the Berlin Wall. Interestingly enough, the drop in visitors occurred across the board between 1961 and 1962, with the relative proportions of East Germans, citizens of other socialist countries, and citizens of capitalist countries in attendance remaining approximately the same. The overall figures went up again by the mid-1960s, although the proportion from other socialist countries increased somewhat. A new overall peak of 735,200 was reached in 1965 before tumbling again to under 600,000 by 1968 and 1969.

Throughout the period from 1946 until 1969, about 90 percent of the visitors were East Germans, although this fluctuated between about 86 percent and about 95 percent depending upon year. There was a dip to slightly below 90 percent in 1964, and a further drop in the late 1960s to about 86–87 percent. But much of this could be explained by increases in the numbers of visitors from other socialist countries in the late 1950s and after the construction of the wall, rising to about 5 percent of the total. The number of visitors from capitalist countries overall was generally around 7–8 percent, with about three-fourths of these from the FRG and West Berlin.

Other quantitative indicators of the strength of the Leipzig spring trade fair behaved similarly. The total amount of space devoted to exhibitions grew feverishly during the 1950s, rising by more than ten times between the resumption of the fair in the aftermath of the war and the construction of the Berlin Wall. Exhibition space grew from 26,400 square meters in 1946 to just under 300,000 by the early 1960s. After the construction of the wall, however, the growth slowed considerably, and during the late 1960s exhibitor space had stabilized at about 350,000 square meters. Around 70 percent of that was occupied by East German firms. The other 30 percent varied through time, but was approximately equally divided between exhibitions drawn from other socialist countries, from West Germany and Berlin, and from non-German capitalist countries.

The variation of another indicator, the total number of exhibitors, is perhaps more telling. This figure also increased markedly during the late 1940s and 1950s before stagnating in the 1960s. The number of exhibitors grew from 2,771 in 1946 to 9,472 in 1960. Thereafter, the numbers fell to well under 9,000 during the early 1960s. The statistics indicate a healthy rebound beginning in 1965, to more than 10,000 per year through 1968, followed by another decline, to 9,811 in 1969. However, these global figures conceal significant developments in statistics gathering: virtually all of the increase in numbers was due to a change in the way that exhibitors from socialist countries were counted. Through 1964 the statistics counted the number of foreign trade companies (*Außenhandelsgesellschaften*, which represented the actual manufacturing companies in socialist countries) represented at the fair. Beginning in 1965, however, the number of factories that had items on exhibit was counted instead. The result was a hefty increase in the number of exhibitors from socialist countries in a single year, from 294 in 1964 to 2,425 in 1965—this while exhibition space increased only slightly, from 41,000 to 43,000 square meters. In the meantime, the number of exhibitors from the capitalist world remained about the same, although there had been a dip in participation by West German and West Berlin firms between 1962 and 1964. Most significant, however, the number of exhibitors from the GDR actually *decreased* beginning in the mid-1950s, from a peak of over 7,000. By 1960 that number had fallen to 6,241, by 1965 to 4,636, and by 1969 to 4,230. Some of this decline from the mid-1950s through the late 1960s was no doubt due to continued concentration of GDR industry. Nevertheless, this must have been a worrying development for East German authorities.

The quantitative measures all indicate rapid growth in the size and significance of the Leipzig spring trade fair from the end of World War II through the late 1950s. The reaction of exhibitors and visitors from abroad to the construction of the Berlin Wall caused some decline in numbers, but attendance had recovered by 1964–65. Nevertheless, on the basis of the statistics, it is difficult to argue against the idea that the fair had reached the limits of its growth, and that it was stagnating. The renewed confidence in the aftermath of the Berlin Wall and the recovery in numbers attending the fair that was already in progress were probably the main reasons that official statistics on the fair appeared in the *Statistisches Jahrbuch der DDR* beginning in 1963. The increasingly apparent stagnation of the fair in the late 1960s, combined with the change in political leadership during the early 1970s, probably explains the disappearance of these figures from the *Statistisches Jahrbuch* by 1972.

The quantitative evidence indicates an end to growth of the size and coverage of the Leipzig spring trade fair. This finding in turn could be used to support a thesis that the fair was either in stasis or in relative decline. Qualitative evidence, however, clearly supports the contention that the Leipzig trade fair was declining considerably in significance at precisely the same time the GDR was seeking to rely upon it more as an instrument of technology policy.

Even as the technical personnel at the Leipzig spring trade fair in 1959 swarmed over the exhibits from abroad, some sensed that all was not as it should be. One report trumpeted that "foreign countries in general are bringing themselves into line with the continuously rising technical level of the Leipzig Trade Fair," but also noted "a certain hesitation among exhibitors from the capitalist countries, and especially West Germany, to show their latest products." This tendency, the author claimed, was especially pronounced in the area of pharmaceuticals, because of the forthcoming exhibition in Karlsruhe, and in machine building because of the industry fair in Hannover.[31] The full implications of the reluctance on the part of capitalist manufacturers to show their most advanced technology were not explicitly addressed in most of the reports on the 1959 trade fair. Still, one study group came directly to the depressing conclusion that the scientific basis of the assessment effort was suspect. Every specialist report of the high-voltage apparatus study group used the very same formulation to indicate just how hopeless the situation was. In effect, the exhibits allowed the technical personnel little opportunity to make comparisons, except insofar as they were based on evidence other than the exhibits themselves: "We were forced to realize that only a few exhibits are on display, so that a comparison of the items exhibited is only possible to a limited extent, from which comparison the technical state of the particular country or company can in no way be deduced. . . . The report consequently cannot always refer to the exhibited goods, but rather had to be expanded to that which was not exhibited, and had in part to be based on what those writing the report already knew."[32]

After the massive effort in 1959, things only got worse. In 1960 the general report on the technical assessment effort at the spring trade fair noted that not only did foreign exhibitors refuse to show their newest technology, they also showed a less varied collection of wares. Furthermore, some of the foreign exhibitors showed only items they deemed appropriate to the socialist marketplace—essentially a skewed sample of products not necessarily of the highest technological level (which was in stark contrast to the skewed sample on display in Hannover). It appears that the nearly two thousand specialists recruited to examine the foreign artifacts were left without enough to do. Because of the unsatisfactory representation of exhibits from abroad, the specialists were assigned to undertake additionally "a comprehensive assessment of the level of technical development of *our* products."[33]

At the autumn trade fair in 1960 the problems not only continued, but actually worsened. Most of the study groups could not do proper comparisons of machines or products in their own specialized areas because their foreign counterparts did not exhibit them. The problem was not restricted to any single area, but affected all sophisticated technologies—for example, electro-technical apparatus, household appliances, control technology, optics, instrument building, and chemicals. It was clear that "an exact estimation of world level . . . [can] be undertaken only in conjunction with assessment of other foreign trade fairs."[34] But, as we have seen, this option was already closing off because of the Second Berlin Crisis, continued problems with *Republikflucht* among engineers and scientists, and a host of other difficulties.

The construction of the Berlin Wall only intensified the tendency among exhibitors from the capitalist countries to show fewer and older wares. Although the numbers of socialist visitors and exhibitors to the Leipzig Trade Fair increased, they also were to deliver a blow to the fair's prestige and its prospects as a tool for technical assessment. After a visit to the 1962 spring fair in Leipzig, one member of the SPK stated baldly that "an exact estimation of scientific and technical development of the *socialist* countries using the items on exhibit at the trade fair is not possible." The reason was that the eastern bloc countries reserved their most sophisticated technological novelties for their own trade fairs; Czechoslovakia was seen as "especially crass" in this regard.[35] The attempt to use the Leipzig Trade Fair as a forum at which to evaluate scientifically and precisely relative world technological levels had failed utterly, not just with regard to capitalist technology, but even in terms of socialist technology.

With the end of World War II and Germany's subsequent division into two separate countries with vastly different socioeconomic and political systems, both German successor states vied for leadership in a variety of areas, including display of technology through trade fairs. For the far smaller German Democratic Republic, the fairs marked an opportunity to gain access to technical knowledge relatively cheaply and efficiently.

For this reason, the GDR engaged in a policy of sending large groups of trusted engineers to Hannover during the 1950s, while at the same time trying to exploit its own, more established Leipzig Trade Fair. Traveling to Hannover, though, became a less and less viable option owing to the rising costs of participation, both in terms of foreign currency, which was in increasingly short supply, and in terms of potential loss of talent through flight of qualified engineers, scientists, and managers from the GDR. Leipzig therefore rapidly emerged as the focus for resources and effort.

The Leipzig Trade Fair, for centuries one of the most important in the world and since the dawn of industrialization a key venue for display of leading technology, was an extremely valuable inheritance for the Soviet zone of occupation and later the GDR. Thus, East German leaders, encouraged by the Soviet occupiers, scurried to reestablish the fair in the aftermath of World War II, mounting a preliminary exhibition in October 1945 and resuming the spring trade fair in 1946. They saw the fair as a vital resource, and that perception only strengthened with time. Although they wished to change their society fundamentally, East German leaders were in many ways traditionalists who were proud of Leipzig and its past. They saw it as a major demonstration of East Germany's prestige in the area of technology, as a means of displaying East German accomplishments while also keeping a finger on the pulse of international technological activity. It would serve a central political purpose as well, maintaining lines of technological and commercial communication during the vagaries of the Cold War. East German engineers, scientists, and managers who actually put on and attended the fair saw it as a way of socializing with their counterparts from abroad (some of whom were former colleagues in West Germany) and of keeping abreast of technological novelties. The tangible artifacts on display at Leipzig and conversations with the people there provided a crucial complement to articles and advertisements in trade and professional journals.

The idea of using this resource more effectively by developing and implementing a program for scientific assessment of items on display at Leipzig followed naturally from these perceptions. It also fit in well with the worldview of East Germany's communist leadership. Scientific socialism could develop scientific techniques for harnessing science and technology for the improvement of the only workers' and peasants' state on German soil. Leipzig would provide an ideal venue for this project, for it was growing in importance during the 1950s. And the government could marshal an army of specialists to take advantage of this growing significance. Furthermore, this could be accomplished at minimal cost and free of foreign exchange outlays. The objective was to study foreign technology intently, systematically, and precisely with an eye toward improving technology in East Germany across the board. It seemed a wonderful idea. Why did it not work out? Was the project unrealistic from the start, or were there other reasons for its failure?

Clearly, there were factors beyond the control of the East Germans that hindered the success of the undertaking. The difficult years of the early 1950s made it virtually impossible to contemplate anything like this. The East German state only came into existence in 1949, it was wracked with difficulties from the start, and organization on this scale was one of the most difficult challenges it faced. One indicator of this was that the GDR was only able to produce its first statistical yearbook in 1955. Certainly this was a larger project than investigation of the Leipzig Trade Fair, but it was also fundamental to the operation of a modern state and of necessity had to proceed first. Organizing a massive technical assessment exercise was a luxury that could only be afforded in the late 1950s.

By that time, of course, COCOM restrictions were well in place and the Second Berlin Crisis had begun. Thus, although there was growing interest in the fair at Leipzig from both East and West, there was also considerable reluctance to invest it with the importance that the East Germans would have preferred. Other governments in the eastern bloc feared the technological might of GDR. Quite possibly they also feared the ideological and political contamination of associating with East Germans who might have designs on a dash through the still porous Berlin border toward a West German passport and employment in burgeoning West German industry. Western capitalist firms were interested in developing business and technological contacts with the eastern bloc. But they were also wary of potential political instability and, in the area of high technology, of the wrath of their own government (or at least of the U.S. government) because of infractions of COCOM restrictions. Such anxieties led necessarily to a situation in which exhibitors, whether from the West or the eastern bloc, became more conservative, showing products and processes that were far from the technological cutting edge.

In this sense, the East Germans were simply unlucky with the timing of their great project for scientific study of the Leipzig Trade Fair. Despite pleasing growth in the numbers of visitors to and exhibitors at the trade fair, the political events of the late 1950s combined with socialist rivalries to diminish its importance. From their historical vantage point, the East Germans could not have known the long-term implications of these developments, which are obvious only in retrospect.

Still, there is a sense in which the East German hopes and dreams for the investigation of the Leipzig Trade Fair were unrealistic in ways that should have been anticipated. There exists an air of lack of engagement with reality, which also pervaded the effort to study technology on display in Hannover. Essentially, the East Germans made several naive assumptions as they formulated their plans. First of all, they appear to have assumed that the goods on display at Hannover represented not the best, but rather the *typical* level of technological proficiency of the capitalist world. Second, they seem to have believed that the Leipzig Trade Fair served primarily technical rather than commercial functions. This may have been because planning was left primarily in the hands of engineers and technocrats. It is difficult to see how the planners could have overlooked this, but they did. Third, they assumed that foreign firms would simply comply with their wishes, both in Hannover and Leipzig, not recognizing that these firms had different interests. Finally, as became clear through the experience of Leipzig, the very idea that it would be possible to identify, on the basis of exhibited objects, the precise extent to which the GDR was ahead or behind potential competitors should have been suspect. A precise equivalent of a machine produced at home was seldom found represented by firms from abroad. And even if one had been found, the complexity of the evaluation process made it virtually impossible to contemplate scientifically verifiable and reproducible figures for each of the machines produced domestically compared to those produced abroad.

The efforts to investigate and evaluate the Hannover and Leipzig Trade Fairs failed in part for reasons outside the control of the GDR. Yet the mere idea should have been suspect to begin with. That it was not is significant in itself, for it indicates the power of the scientific and engineering establishment within East Germany: they were able to implement their politically naive ideas in part because of the faith of the political establishment in science and engineering. Such faith was clearly ill-placed, as the fate of high-technology industries in the GDR made clear.

Visits to trade fairs abroad were one means of gauging the extent to which technology in the GDR conformed to international best practice. The visits also facilitated transfer of technology from the capitalist West to the GDR, although this function was clearly subsidiary to that of benchmarking. There was a much more direct and important means of technology transfer, not only from the West to the GDR, but also within the eastern bloc: the actual exchange of physical artifacts, designs, and blueprints. This took place in a variety of industries, but was perhaps most important in the development of two key postwar technologies, petrochemicals and semiconductors. Both industries were in the throes of explosive technological change and production growth. Both drove economic growth and—through their impact on a wide range of other industries and products—societal change during the same period.

Like the gradual intellectual alienation of East German from West German engineers and scientists, a process of movement away from the West and toward the East took place in the physical realm in the late 1950s, a process most prominent in petrochemicals and semiconductors. East German planners faced difficult choices about these technologies and their development: unable to develop them domestically to full maturity, as they would have preferred, planners at first tried to import them from the West before turning to the Soviet Union for assistance. The eventual result was a sort of Sovietization of East German technology in the artifactual realm.[1]

Petrochemicals in the GDR

The modern organic chemicals industry may have had its origins in Britain and France, but it achieved its first full flowering in Germany. By the eve of World War I, German ability to produce organic chemicals, such as dyes and pharmaceuticals, as well as more sophisticated high-pressure products, was unsurpassed. The war itself disrupted international trade in chemicals and allied products, especially supplies of intermediates and finished products from Germany to overseas markets. Because the country was responsible for nearly 90 percent of world trade in organic chemicals, this disruption had major consequences. All the major industrialized nations threw resources into the development of the industry. Great Britain and (even more so) the United States were spectacularly successful in this regard from the 1920s on.[2]

Yet despite unprecedented challenges in international markets from companies based abroad, the German chemical industry remained very strong, especially after the consolidation of its major firms into I. G. Farbenindustrie A. G. in late 1925. I. G. Farben was the largest chemical firm in Europe and one of the largest industrial corporations in the world. Its technological capability, maintained in well-equipped and well-staffed industrial laboratories with close connections to academic chemistry, continued to flourish during and after the late 1920s. The company developed new processes for producing synthetic fuel and rubber, as well as a host of other chemicals. Because many of these items were so important to German self-sufficiency, I. G. Farben was supported by the late Weimar German state as it tried to deal with the effects of the Depression. Similar concerns about economic self-sufficiency and the additional impetus of active preparation for war conditioned the relationship between I. G. Farben and the National Socialist state as well. The company and the Nazis did not have identical interests and indeed frequently came into conflict. Still, the interests of the firm in developing its technologies, investing in new plant and equipment, selling its products, and making large profits generally fit in well with the aims of the Nazi regime. The company's collusion with it led the occupying powers in Germany after 1945 to agree on the need for breaking up the firm.[3]

The breakup of I. G. Farben, especially its components in West Germany, has been described more fully elsewhere.[4] The main concern here is with the I. G. Farben successor factories in the Soviet zone of occupation. The breakup left what later became East Germany with some of the largest and most modern production facilities previously owned by I. G. Farben. There were also many engineers, scientists, and technicians who understood and could operate the demanding technologies deployed in the plants. Yet most of I. G. Farben's R&D capability lay in the other zones of occupation, and consequently was lost to the East German successor factories. The same was true for most of the company's highest level managerial capability. War-related damage to East German factories was substantial, although probably not all that different from that in the West globally, but dismantling affected the Soviet zone facilities far more than those in the West. In addition, many scientists and engineers were forcibly removed from the Soviet zone in October 1946 and taken to the Soviet Union to work on projects there. Although these individuals began to return to East Germany in the early 1950s, their services were lost for several crucial years.[5]

Although the East German successors to I. G. Farben were clearly at something of a disadvantage compared to those in the western zones of occupation, they retained formidable technological and productive capability. In both West and East Germany this capability was almost exclusively coal-based, continuing the German tradition of turning the country's one major natural resource into a vast palette of dyes, drugs, and plastics.

Coal was not the only starting material from which to synthesize the building blocks of organic chemical production, called feedstocks. In principle, virtually all organic chemicals can be produced using any of the major sources of carbon chains as a starting material. These sources include coal, alcohol, natural gas, and petroleum. Although the end product may be the same regardless of ultimate hydrocarbon source, the processes and equipment for making it may differ substantially. Alcohol was the least common starting material for industrial processes, although its technology was often lighter in weight and less capital-intensive than those based on coal, natural gas, or oil. Coal-based technology for producing organic chemicals in general differed considerably from petroleum-based production, both in the reaction process itself and, even more important, in the scale of the reaction.

The rise of petrochemical technology occurred at the same time as the rise of motorization, so that the United States became the first major producer of petrochemicals and hence the first major employer of a new kind of professional, the chemical engineer. By World War II the industry was beginning to boom, not least because petrochemicals were particularly suitable for large-scale production of key plastics and synthetic rubber, which had applications as substitute materials for military needs. They were also critical for use as insulation in electronic components and electrical apparatus. But, despite these uses, little attention was paid to the development of petrochemicals in Germany before 1945. The Germans were able to use coal-based feedstocks to produce small quantities of plastics, such as polyethylene, for military use. (Large-scale production of polyethylene required petroleum-based feedstocks.) Furthermore, the relatively slow pace of motorization in Germany during the 1920s and 1930s, combined with the Depression and the war, gave little opportunity for moving into this new technology.

Two things were clear as the war came to an end. First, to regain competitiveness, especially with regard to British and American firms, the German chemical industry would have to move into petrochemical technology. Second, it appeared that this process could take place gradually, since most specialists agreed that there would always be a place for coal-based chemistry. At that time coal-based chemistry was moving in a promising new direction, that of acetylene chemistry, which held the possibility of producing as broad a range of plastics and other materials as could be manufactured using petroleum-based feedstocks. Furthermore, coal-based chemistry could produce some products for which as yet no appropriate or workable petrochemical processes existed.

East Germany developed its chemical industry in this international context in the 1950s.[6] Its scientists and engineers recognized early on the need to develop petrochemicals. Discussions about future directions in the emerging technology took place at the major chemical facility in the GDR, the Leuna Works in Merseburg, by late 1947. Similar discussions had taken place for the first time in the West at BASF only a year earlier.[7] By 1951 the East Germans had embarked upon a research program to develop the capability of producing polyethylene in large quantities using petroleum-based feedstocks. They were not far behind their West German counterparts in recognizing the importance of this work or in setting up an active program of development. But the GDR had difficulties in two areas, which caused the country to fall behind during the 1950s.

First, the chemical industry was unable to come up with adequate technological processes or equipment for producing high-quality petrochemical products. Small-scale apparatus for the manufacture of polyethylene was in place at the Leuna Works by 1953, but it had faulty seals and was unable to maintain a proper operating temperature—a clear indication of the GDR's lack of an industrial sector for manufacturing heavy-duty chemical apparatus. A redesign of the apparatus led to some experimental production in 1954, but yields were extremely low and the product was unsatisfactory. A year later a pilot plant was in place, but the product continued to be of poor quality, and Soviet consultants indicated that the problem was the level of throughput for ethylene gas at the plant. These and other difficulties were gradually overcome, and in 1958, despite frequent breakdowns in operations, the facility for manufacturing low-density polyethylene at Leuna produced 1 ton of usable product, a definite improvement. But production capacity elsewhere puts this in perspective. The Soviets, for instance, could produce 1,000 tons per year in 1955, while the Rheinische Olefinenwerke plant in West Germany, jointly owned by BASF and Shell, had an annual capacity of 35,000 tons in 1956. Despite large commitment of resources to developing this and other petrochemical technologies during the 1950s, the GDR, largely left to its own devices, was plagued with enormous difficulties.

But even if these technological problems had been overcome more rapidly and more satisfactorily, the GDR faced a second, fundamental problem. Petrochemical production depended ultimately upon availability of sufficient quantities of petroleum, to which the GDR did not have access through the mid-1950s. Despite heroic, if clearly misplaced, efforts to find petroleum under its own soil, the GDR lacked sufficient domestic stocks of this vital raw material.[8] In fact, it had almost none. Procuring petroleum in large quantities from the West was out of the question, owing to foreign exchange difficulties and political tensions during the 1950s, and until the late 1950s the Soviets were reluctant to supply petroleum to their German satellite in the quantities needed.

By the late 1950s, then, GDR planners, scientists, and engineers in the chemical industry recognized that they faced severe difficulties. The petrochemical sector and its technology had grown and improved far more rapidly than anyone in the GDR or elsewhere had anticipated. Domestic development of the industry, while deemed necessary for various reasons during the first part of the decade, was proving unworkable. The GDR now needed to look abroad for help in three major areas: supply of crude oil; assistance in developing petrochemical feedstock technologies; and aid in developing technologies for manufacturing chemical products on the basis of petrochemical feedstocks. Because of political and foreign exchange considerations, the Soviet Union was the unquestionable answer for the first two problems. The actions of the GDR in the late 1950s and early 1960s with regard to the last area, which was much more technologically demanding than the others, were more ambiguous.

The effort to improve GDR technology and productivity in the chemical industry in the late 1950s occurred under the auspices of the so-called chemicalization program, sketched out by Walter Ulbricht in 1958. Issued under the slogan "Chemistry gives bread, beauty, and prosperity!" the program was approved in general terms at the Fifth Party Congress of the SED in July, and Ulbricht announced the details in November at a special conference at the Leuna Works.⁹ He identified three crucial areas of development for the industry. First, plastics and synthetic materials would be high on the agenda, and they would be produced using petroleum-based feedstocks. Second, R&D efforts in the area of chemical technology would have to be redoubled in the GDR. Finally, the GDR would concentrate on building up its capacity for producing acetylene from coal for use in the chemical industry. Ulbricht announced with some fanfare that *"the VEB Chemische Werke Buna will become the largest producer of carbide* [made from coal, and from which acetylene is made] *in the world."*¹⁰

Essentially, Ulbricht promised that the GDR would buck world trends by making renewed commitments to coal-based technologies at the same time as it moved into new petrochemical technologies. He also indicated that the previous efforts to develop new chemical technologies domestically would continue. He stated, however, that the GDR would turn increasingly to the Soviet Union for assistance in supply of raw materials and technology. In the event, the East Germans found that, the more demanding the technology, the less help the Soviet Union could supply. The GDR therefore continued to pursue the possibility of purchasing licenses and equipment from the West, in particular for plastics production, and especially from France and Great Britain.

Drilling, pumping, and transporting crude oil are technically demanding procedures. But the technical expertise was required primarily in geology, machine building, pumping, steel-pipe construction, and welding, rather than chemistry proper. These were all areas in which the Soviet Union and/or its eastern bloc neighbors were competent, and they excelled in some of them. Building a pipeline to carry crude from near the Ural Mountains to the East German border was therefore a major project, but one the Soviets and their allies were well able to carry out. The success of the effort depended primarily not on the ability to construct a pipeline to supply the countries of the Soviet bloc, or on the ability to pump sufficient oil out of the ground, but rather upon the political will of the Soviets to use their oil to fill the pipeline once built. The key issue was whether the ties of alliance against the capitalist world in the context of the Cold War would be strong enough to overcome the allure of hard currency for the Soviet economy.

In the late 1950s, at the height of the Second Berlin Crisis and with

Sputnik demonstrating the potential of socialist scientific and technological power, the ties of alliance were especially strong. The Soviets were therefore pleased to support their German satellite in supply of crude oil. Planning for construction of a pipeline, dubbed Friendship, began at about the same time as the announcement of the chemicalization program, and it came into operation to supply the East German facility at Schwedt on 18 December 1963.[11] It carried crude that had been lightly processed at the oil fields to remove most salt and water, and to guarantee that it contained only hydrocarbon chains with at least five carbon atoms. The pipeline stretched from the Urals to the Ukraine, where it split to carry crude northwest to Poland and East Germany and westward to Hungary and Poland.[12]

The Soviets promised to deliver 4.8 million tons of crude per year to the GDR by 1965, and the amounts actually delivered increased steadily from the late 1950s to the early 1960s. Following a massive increase in imports of oil—nearly 40 percent between 1958 and 1959, mostly owing to supplies from the Soviet Union—GDR oil imports continued to rise by well over 20 percent a year between 1959 and 1966. During this period, between 93 percent and 96 percent of total oil imports came from the USSR. True to form, the Soviets overfulfilled their target by 1965, exporting just over 4.9 million tons of petroleum to the GDR through the Friendship pipeline.[13]

Because of the pipeline and because limited foreign exchange made purchase of crude from the West very difficult, the East Germans were beholden to the Soviet Union for continued fulfillment of its promises. But the stabilization of East Germany following the construction of the Berlin Wall made supplying the GDR a less pressing priority for the Soviets, and the attraction of earning foreign exchange through sales to the West proved impossible to resist. Already in 1962 the Moscow embassy of the GDR reported that a key Communist Party official saw "the development of the GDR's energy basis [as] insufficient." The official also criticized the GDR for not developing its own oil production capacity fast enough, comparing East German efforts unfavorably to those in West Germany.[14]

Some East Germans undoubtedly saw this as an omen of problems to come, and they would have been correct in their intuition. The minister of the chemical industry of the GDR, G. Wyschofsky, accompanying a high-ranking Soviet delegation touring the chemical exhibits at the Leipzig Trade Fair in March 1964, reported disquieting evidence of growing

Soviet reluctance to supply its ally with petroleum. His memo was passed on directly to Erich Apel, the man in the Politburo with primary responsibility for the GDR economy, who in turn passed it on to Walter Ulbricht himself. Both men read the memo carefully, marking particular passages in colored ink.[15]

Wyschofsky reported that a member of the Soviet delegation had examined the exhibits at the 1964 Leipzig Trade Fair that were designed to show East German progress in refinery construction and petrochemical manufacture. The Soviet representative then took the East German aside to tell him that the GDR should really be overcoming its energy deficit on its own—indeed, through use of brown coal. Despite Wyschofsky's sharp objection to this line of argument, the Soviet official had continued on the same tack. He had noted that brown coal was very cheap and that it was being used more and more heavily in West Germany. Ulbricht marked this passage of the memo with a large question mark in the margin. Again, Wyschofsky had objected to the general drift of the Soviet delegate's conversation, but the train of thought continued. The Soviet official—who, in Wyschofsky's view, did not speak just for himself but for the whole of his delegation—had claimed that the East Germans "had to have some understanding of the fact that crude oil had to be sold by the Soviet Union to capitalist countries, even if there were deficits in the GDR." That the West Germans were already refining 45 million tons of crude oil per year and would increase this to 70 million tons by 1970 was, according to the Soviet official, due entirely to the fact "that they simply could afford it."

The conversation summarized in the memo from Wyschofsky did not bode well for the future of oil refining in the GDR. Although the increases in exports of petroleum by the Soviets to the GDR appeared very generous indeed on a percentage basis, the big problem for East Germany was that it had started from such a small base. With about one-third the population of West Germany, the GDR was only refining one-tenth the amount of petroleum per year. Furthermore, the West Germans also imported substantial quantities of finished products from petroleum refining, while the East Germans generally did not. In fact, West Germany's considerable refining capacity covered only about 80–85 percent of its demand for oil products during many years in the 1950s and 1960s, with the remaining 15–20 percent of demand being made up with imports of finished petroleum products.[16]

The GDR desperately needed large infusions of cheap oil from the

USSR, but it appeared in the mid-1960s that these would not be forth-coming. In January 1964 Ulbricht met with a Soviet delegation of experts on questions related to oil and natural gas. During the meeting, he under-scored the discrepancy between East and West Germany in terms of oil refining and emphasized the importance of oil to competitiveness. The Soviets, he said, had been most helpful with suggestions about rational-ization and savings here and there, but had said nothing about the key question: where would additional supplies of petroleum come from? Warming to his subject, Ulbricht noted that it would, of course, be possi-ble to live within the current oil budget of the GDR if living standards simultaneously fell, although this was not his vision for the GDR:

> We are capable of organizing an economic crisis exactly like the one in Czechoslovakia within six months. It can be done quite easily in six months. It requires no real talent. We only need to sink the standard of living and implement the kind of measures that have been undertaken there. But we have a different economic policy from other peoples' democracies. . . . Our starting point is the struggle to increase productivity and the attainment of the highest scientific-technological level.[17]

Other speakers from the GDR reinforced Ulbricht's point. They high-lighted the difficulties encountered in mining brown coal, arguing force-fully that coal was not, and never could be, as economical as petroleum. They aired the possibility of using hard currency to purchase petroleum from other countries than the Soviet Union, such as Egypt. And they stated in no uncertain terms that a turning point had been reached. Erich Apel finished his contribution to the discussion with a dramatic state-ment of the centrality of petroleum to the GDR's future: "We must, to be able to progress at all in the development of a national economy, build up a modern chemistry, a petroleum-based chemistry. We have no other path to follow; there is no other way."[18]

Later that same year, in October 1964, Walter Ulbricht wrote directly to Khrushchev. The eight-page letter was a long plea for additional deliv-eries from the Soviets. Ulbricht pointed out the economic significance of such supplies, not only for the further development of chemical technol-ogy, but also for other key industrial branches in the GDR. He noted, "We are forced to introduce new chemical materials, such as high-quality plastics and synthetic fibers, especially for the development of a modern machine-building industry. In order to do this, we must use more crude oil and natural gas." The GDR, Ulbricht stressed, had tried desperately to find petroleum under its own soil, but this effort had so far been largely unsuccessful. There was thus a real need for additional imports from the Soviet Union.[19]

Ulbricht's importunings were effective insofar as they led to increases in total imports of crude oil of 21 percent and 26 percent respectively in 1964–65 and 1965–66. But the Soviets were clearly eyeing the international market and its hard currency, a move that would have severe consequences for the GDR. In 1965 the head of the Soviet State Planning Commission stated explicitly that, owing to the USSR's relatively high burden of supplying raw materials and energy supplies to, and military protection for, its allies, economic relationships within the Soviet bloc would have to be rethought. New targets for exports of petroleum and chemical intermediates to the GDR agreed upon in October 1964 had stretched the USSR to its limits. *"An additional [increased] delivery would not be possible until 1970 [at the earliest]."*[20] Soviet negotiators suggested that the GDR try its luck with Algeria and Iraq.[21]

The Soviets, as it turned out, kept their word. There was a clear break in the previous pattern of increases in deliveries between 1966 and 1967, when imports of petroleum by the GDR increased by a mere 3.1 percent and the Soviet contribution to the GDR actually decreased slightly for the first time. There were some additional increases in supplies from the Soviet Union between 1969 and 1971, but in general, in the years leading up to the first oil crisis, the GDR was falling further and further behind most other industrialized countries in terms of petroleum consumption, and brown coal continued to meet nearly 90 percent of the country's energy needs.[22] Even as late as 1984, oil accounted for just over one-tenth of energy consumption, with brown coal accounting for three-fourths. In contrast, oil covered more than half (55 percent) of West Germany's energy needs by 1973.[23]

The pattern with regard to chemical feedstocks was similar to that for energy. Although the GDR moved slowly into petrochemicals production through the late 1960s, coal continued to provide a substantial proportion of its feedstocks. For instance, a 1965 projection of the "demand of the chemical industry for the most important organic basic chemicals" for the years 1966–70 indicated that the biggest single source of starting materials would continue to be "acetylene for chemical uses," produced from coal. In addition, the report predicted that "the proportion of organic basic chemicals made from petroleum in the GDR, reckoned on the basis of carbon content, is supposed to reach 35 percent of total consumption of the chemical industry in 1970."[24] In contrast, the West German organic chemicals industry had reached this level by 1958–59, and by 1961 over half of all organic chemicals in West Germany were produced using petroleum-based feedstocks.[25]

It was one thing to purchase crude oil from abroad, which the GDR was able to do despite disappointments and shortfalls; it was another to refine crude oil in such a way as to optimize its usefulness to the GDR economy. To do this, East Germany had to develop a domestic capability in oil-refining technology. Rather than proceeding on its own, however, the GDR turned once again to the Soviet Union for assistance. In this case, the Soviets were quite willing to help their ally. They expressed their willingness by the mid-1950s, in conjunction with the discussions on supply of petroleum, and signed an official agreement with the GDR on 22 October 1958 that called for close cooperation in this crucial area. In return for a substantial amount of cash, the Soviets would supply the GDR with refining equipment and blueprints to aid in the design of the facility. They would also train East German personnel in the USSR to operate the plant.[26]

The East Germans chose a site near the Polish border, Schwedt, for the construction of the new facility. There were several reasons for the choice. The most obvious, of course, was that the Friendship oil pipeline ended there, although it would have been a relatively straightforward matter to continue the pipeline within East Germany. But the GDR leadership was also concerned with regional development and other issues. Located in a largely agricultural and relatively lightly industrialized region, Schwedt, like Eisenhüttenstadt for steel and Frankfurt (Oder) for semiconductors, offered the chance to "set aside the backwardness left over from the period of capitalism." Large supplies of frequently underemployed, underskilled, yet highly trainable labor constituted another point in Schwedt's favor. Located on the Oder River, the town was also well situated from the standpoint of availability of water for both transport and plant operations. The site, moreover, had substantial room for expansion. When construction of the refinery began in November 1960, it was designed to start production in 1964 at the rate of 2 million tons per year. Capacity would rise to 4 million tons in 1966, eventually reaching an annual throughput of 8 million tons of crude oil by the late 1960s.[27]

Although funds were available, a site had been found, and Soviet assistance secured, the construction of the Schwedt plant was not a simple matter. Soviet technology had to be adapted, sometimes radically, to fit the needs of the GDR. Already in January 1959, shortly after the signing of the official agreement on Soviet aid, one of the key state officials responsible for the chemical industry outlined in a presentation to the East German Research Council (Forschungsrat) some of the difficulties involved in technology transfer from the USSR to the GDR.[28] Soviet refineries, he noted, processed vastly larger quantities of petroleum than Schwedt ever would. Refining in such volume in turn ensured adequate provision of the "higher fractions" that could be used most readily as petrochemical feedstocks. These higher fractions, including olefins and aromatics, were generally the by-products of the refining of gasoline and diesel fuel, and normally constituted only a tiny proportion of the range of products manufactured in a particular refinery. Schwedt's relatively small throughput meant that engineers and scientists in the GDR would have to adapt the Soviet technology to substantially increase the yield of higher fractions.[29] Furthermore, over one-third of the petroleum deployed in the projected plant would be thick residues of the distillation process, again unlike Soviet plants and requiring somewhat different technology. Petroleum pyrolysis technology, initially deployed at the Leuna Works, would therefore have to be further developed at Schwedt to maximize the yields of olefins. And other processes would have to maximize output of aromatics, something neither the Soviets nor western countries were able to accomplish satisfactorily. All in all, the GDR would have to supplement and adapt the influx of Soviet technology. This would involve bringing up to industrial scale processes for platforming, re-forming, hydroforming, cracking, and fluidized-bed coking of petroleum, processes that had been developed domestically in the GDR.[30]

Although the deployment of Soviet technology at Schwedt required enormous effort to adapt it to conditions in the GDR, Soviet assistance was absolutely essential to construction and operation of the plant. Besides importing from the USSR equipment worth some 45 million East German marks to be used at Schwedt, the GDR requested technical assistance in the form of thirty-seven different sets of blueprints and licenses for processes. It was agreed as well that sixty specialists from Schwedt were to be sent for training to plants in the USSR, with most of the training, blueprints, and processes coming from the large Soviet plant at Kuibyschev.[31] By and large, cooperation with, and assistance from, the Soviets in developing refining technology at Schwedt was successful, and by 1961 it appeared that the plant's first stage of construction would be completed as scheduled, by the mid-1960s. The project was recognized and trumpeted for what it was: politics conducted through technology. Large in scale, Schwedt was "the most recent project in the series of large-scale construction projects of socialism in our Republic" and thus fit into the Soviet socialist style of gigantic projects.[32] Its connection to the pipeline and extensive deployment of Soviet equipment and technology created a network insulating the GDR from the West and integrating it into the East.[33] It was therefore a deliberate realization of the desire to decouple East Germany from the West and to link it artifactually to the eastern bloc.

Despite the warm feelings engendered by the successful cooperation with the Soviets at Schwedt, the GDR had less luck in obtaining Soviet aid in the more demanding area of chemical process technology and in the construction of chemical apparatus. Both of these areas had been represented primarily in western Germany through 1945, and they were virtually nonexistent in East Germany until the onset of the chemicalization program. Early in 1960 the GDR complained that Soviet–East German cooperation in chemical technology worked only in the case of Schwedt and in other specific areas in which there was official agreement at the government level. "Every other topic, however, that was transferred in the form of individual questions to the partner outside of the agreement, [was] dealt with so slowly, that the German section intervened and sent in the ambassador [among others]." Despite this, the results were disappointing. The Soviets, for instance, simply ignored requests for East German study of Soviet processes for making hydrogen peroxide, methanol, PVC, and other products.[34] Thus, the tradition of looking westward for assistance remained in many areas despite the conscious decision to Sovietize East German chemical technology.

Dissatisfaction with Soviet assistance in this area and the tradition of westward orientation maintained by the managers of key chemical works in the GDR (most of whom had come of age professionally within I. G. Farben) led in the late 1950s to negotiations with the French and the British for equipment and assistance.[35] The British connection was by far the more important. In early 1961, as the Second Berlin Crisis was reaching its height, the regime reluctantly approved agreements to purchase licenses and equipment from England for the production of polystyrene, polyethylene, ethylene, and acetate. Contracts for purchase of chemical technology constituted the largest single item by far in the budget for purchasing technology abroad, and the contracts with Britain amounted to more than 9 million marks in foreign exchange, a vast sum for a cash-strapped country.[36]

The connection with Britain in the area of chemical process technology continued even after the construction of the Berlin Wall. British technology and equipment obtained by means of an agreement of April 1961 from Imperial Chemical Industries (ICI) and the engineering firm Simon-Carves were critical to overcoming difficulties in producing low-density polyethylene (LDPE) at the Leuna Works. By 30 November 1965, thanks to outside help, three LDPE production lines were in place, but technical problems remained. The end of December, however, saw the first manufacture of ethylene of sufficient purity for LDPE production, and during January 1966 full-fledged production finally commenced.[37] The East Germans, with western assistance and Soviet raw materials, had graduated to the petrochemical age, but only after a series of critical delays that left them more than a decade behind their West German counterparts.

The story of the development of petrochemicals technology illustrates some key themes in East Germany's high-technology development in the context of the Second Berlin Crisis. Torn between political loyalty to the Soviet Union and technological affinities with the West, the East Germans sought to resolve the tension by cooperating with the Soviets in areas in which the larger country excelled. One of these was petroleum refining, especially for the purpose of producing petrochemical feedstocks, and there was an undeniable Sovietization of East German technology in this vital area by the early 1960s. Soviet assistance was less desirable for more demanding chemical process technologies, and the East Germans were therefore reluctantly forced into cooperation with the West, in particular with Great Britain.

Semiconductors

Besides petrochemicals, the other key high-technology development in the late 1950s and 1960s was semiconductor technology. This field offers many parallels to the case of petrochemicals, but there are also key differences.

In the case of the petrochemical industry, there are recognizable precursors from before World War II. And it is clear that many in the industry in the 1950s thought—probably wrongly—that petrochemicals did not represent a new technology, but a continuation of the old chemical industry by means of another feedstock.[38] However, the semiconductor industry was clearly something new. There may have been prewar precursors in traditional vacuum-tube technology that could perform the same sort of functions as the new semiconductors. But from the beginnings of the industry in the early 1950s, there was no question that the speed, reliability, and size of semiconductors had revolutionary implications for the electrical and electronics industry, even if the technical problems they posed in their infancy allowed ample space for continued use of traditional tube technology for some time as well.[39]

The most important and revolutionary breakthrough in this technology was the development of the germanium transistor. Bell Labs (the research arm of AT&T), where the transistor was invented in December 1947, was the first to produce transistors commercially beginning in 1951–52, and this marked the start of explosive growth and technological change in the electronic component industry. In the years that followed, Bell Labs continued to be a major player in this area, along with General Electric and other American firms, and the United States invariably led the way in development of new components and new materials (such as silicon). But some British and European firms followed fairly closely behind the Americans. Like the petrochemical industry, the semiconductor industry benefited enormously from the postwar expansion in international technology transfer within the western world economy.[40]

Although the GDR, like all other industrialized countries, followed the U.S. lead in semiconductors, it did not lag far behind. Again the parallels with petrochemical development are striking. Already in 1952, in an effort to catch up with the West, development work on semiconductors began in the VEB Works for Electrical Components for Communications Technology (VEB Werk für Bauelemente der Nachrichtentechnik "Carl von Ossietzky," or WBN) in Teltow, near Berlin. Professor Martin Falter led a team of three scientists and ten engineers and technicians, a group that within the next five years grew to include twenty scientists and forty engineers and technicians.[41] By the beginning of the 1960s, when the development lab at WBN was transformed into the Institute for Semiconductor Technology, the group had grown to 74 engineers and scientists among a total of 625 employees.[42] Although this represented considerable growth over a relatively short period, the numbers of R&D personnel were still insufficient for any sort of leadership role in the semiconductor industry. Bell Labs alone, for example, had a total nearly 6,000 employees in the late 1940s, of whom over 2,000 were highly qualified scientists, engineers, and managers.[43] But if leadership was out of the question, the GDR's researchers, exclusively dedicated to problems related to semiconductor technology, could as followers at least theoretically have done much more with fewer people.

In practice, however, the WBN facility's spheres of development activity expanded even more rapidly than its numbers of workers, engineers, and scientists. Responsible for broad-based R&D work in the area of semiconductors, it moved quickly by the mid-1950s into actual production as well, and the breadth of the technological tasks facing the relatively small staff taxed it severely. Production grew, but in comparison to the needs of the economy and compared to other countries, the growth was disappointing. In 1955 WBN was able to produce only 25,000 germanium diodes and 700 transistors for use in development laboratories in the electrical equipment industry.[44] According to a 1958 report on output prepared for the SPK, production by that date had increased to about 100,000 each of diodes, rectifiers, and transistors.[45] During 1959 there was no growth in production at all, but by 1960 manufacturing output had risen to about 250,000 of each type of semiconductor component. Production continued to increase, to 550,000 of each in 1961, 900,000 each in 1962, and about 2 million each in 1963.[46] Such growth seems impressive treated in isolation, but compared unfavorably, both in absolute and in relative terms, with most other major industrialized countries. The distance behind the world leader, the United States, was several orders of magnitude. In 1957 alone U.S. output of transistors was 27.8 million units, and this number increased by nearly five times by 1960, to over 131 million units.[47]

What accounted for WBN's relatively poor performance? One key factor, of course, was that many fewer personnel were allocated than were needed to attack this broad and complex new technology. But there were other problems besides the clearly inadequate resources available to the WBN facility. One commentator noted in 1959 that the research laboratory of WBN had never enjoyed the full support of management, and especially of its head accountant.[48] There seems to have been something to this. In late 1958 an investigative team composed of one member each of the SPK, the Central Office for Research and Technology, the Ministry of Finance, and a central banking institution reported that the biggest problem facing Teltow and its subsidiaries was "deficient technical understanding [on the part of the administration] for the requirements [of semiconductor production]." The principal director of the Association of People's Own Factories for the Electronic Component and Vacuum Technology Industries (VVB RFT Bauelemente und Vakuumtechnik), to which Teltow belonged, did not consult Professor Falter, the head of Teltow, or his associates when making plans for expansion of production capacity. Furthermore, the main works administration was just as apt to ignore their wishes. Local administrators, for example, did not seem to see any difficulty with dumping hot ashes directly in front of a factory window behind which the pilot production of semiconductor elements was taking place. They thus ruined the semiconductors themselves, and also made it impossible to set reliable production parameters for the projected full-scale plant. Again, the chief accountant denied a request for an allocation for felt slippers for production workers, even though they were needed to prevent build-up of static electricity during the production process.[49]

Even before the critical report that resulted from the 1958 inspection was written—indeed, already in 1956—the performance of the WBN in semiconductors attracted interest and eventually criticism from the highest levels in GDR politics. At the Third Party Conference of the Socialist Unity Party, held in Berlin in March of that year, the party ratified a "Directive for the Second Five-Year Plan for the Development of the Economy of the German Democratic Republic 1956–60." The directive placed heavy emphasis on technology as a means of economic development, and Ulbricht himself called for an "industrial transformation" based on mechanization, automation, and nuclear power. The ultimate aim was to "catch up with and surpass capitalism in terms of technology."[50] Semiconductor development and manufacture were vital to this vision, and the industry therefore received higher priorities in planning and allocation of resources.[51]

By 1957 this renewed effort to develop semiconductors more rapidly involved various plans to expand production capacity at or near Teltow, but the plans were not realized, because of technical problems and the difficulties in finding a suitable site for the new plant. At this point the district leadership of Frankfurt on the Oder approached Helmut Wunderlich (in 1957, minister for general machine building and shortly afterward responsible for machine building in the SPK) with a proposal to build the new plant there. The Frankfurt area offered fresh air relatively free of pollutants, proximity to raw materials and water, and a large labor force. Furthermore, because of limited skill levels, the work force was

Frankfurt Semiconductor Works, 1964. Although it was plagued with difficulties, the Frankfurt semiconductor works eventually produced in large quantities using Soviet-based technology. *Bundesarchiv, Koblenz, Bildsammlung Bild 183/L10121/18/2*

highly trainable. Not far from Teltow, the Frankfurt area was made more attractive still by the district leadership's promise to build new accommodations for the laborers, scientists, and technicians.[52] By 1958 the final decision had been made to establish a new, state-of-the-art semiconductor manufacturing facility at Frankfurt.[53] Initially at least, the VEB Semiconductor Works Frankfurt (Oder) was to be "a branch factory of the development institute in Teltow."[54]

Clearly, concerns about regional development were significant in decision making in the semiconductor industry, just as in the petrochemical industry. It is no accident that both the Frankfurt plant for semiconductors and the Schwedt facility for petrochemical feedstocks were built in part to industrialize a previously backward area in the GDR. It is evident, too, that in semiconductor development, as in petrochemical development, the GDR was not far behind other industrialized countries in recognizing the significance of the new technology. Nor did the GDR lag especially far behind in the establishment of R&D facilities to exploit the new technical developments. Yet between embarking on this research and development and actually producing large quantities of the goods in question, there was a yawning gap, one that became more important each year. By the time the Frankfurt plant was decided upon, the GDR was already years behind its industrialized competitors in the West, in terms of both technology and production capacity.

Although significant, this lag might, at least in theory, have been overcome in the late 1950s and early 1960s. For that reason the years 1958–60 constituted a critical period in the development of semiconductor technology in the GDR. During this time GDR planners and managers pursued three separate strategies simultaneously in their efforts to get semiconductor technology and production up to world standards. The first was internal development, through the establishment of new production facilities and reorganization of semiconductor research and development. The second was technology assistance and transfer from the Soviet Union. And the third was technology transfer from the West, including West Germany, the United Kingdom, and even the United States. To explore this development fully, it is necessary to consider each of these strands separately and in turn, but it is crucial to recognize that these were *simultaneous* developments. Unable to generate this demanding technology entirely on its own, the GDR sought assistance abroad. Through 1960, however, the country was unwilling to commit fully to either West or East. The closing off of options with the West, political pressures for an eastward turn in all areas including technology and production, and the positive attraction of apparently potent Soviet technological capability led to a more complete alignment with the Soviet Union by 1961.

Extensive internal reorganization of semiconductor production and development in the GDR began with the decision to establish a production facility at Frankfurt on the Oder in 1958. Early that year work began on plans for constructing the new plant at a site about 7 kilometers away from the Frankfurt city center, in Marksdorf. At the same time, in order to begin production at a minimal level and to provide training for workers for the new facility, a school building with about 5,000 square meters of space was made available. By mid-year, however, it had already become clear that the likely costs for developing the Marksdorf site would be much higher than originally thought, owing to the need for extensive infrastructural improvements. As a result, the GDR Research Council and those from the industry directly responsible for designing the facility, who were for the most part at Teltow, decided instead on rapid construction of a large, purpose-built manufacturing hall near the school building. Production was to begin there in late 1959. Completion of the project was planned for 1961, when the Frankfurt complex was to provide full coverage of the needs of the GDR for transistors and rectifiers.[55]

The news of the new manufacturing hall did little to impress Erich Apel, the SED's main economic functionary, who wrote to the head of the SPK, Bruno Leuschner, in late April 1959. Apel pointed out that "compared to the international state of semiconductor technology, especially that of American, Japanese, and West German industry, we lie in a state of backwardness that can scarcely be estimated. According to the prognoses which have been worked out, this backwardness will not decrease through 1961 at least, but will instead grow." One way out of this comparative backwardness, Apel suggested, was the establishment of a second production development center for the semiconductor industry at the VEB Works for Telecommunications (VEB Werk für Fernmeldewesen, or WF) at Berlin-Schöneweide, to complement that at WBN in Teltow. The strategy seemed to contradict the general policy of establishing a single scientific-technical center for each industrial sector, but, Apel continued, "in those cases in which the backwardness is so great, it will be necessary to work in parallel."[56]

In making the suggestion "to work in parallel," Apel was clearly following the lead of the head of the Research Council, Professor Peter Adolf Thiessen, who had outlined his comments on the subject in a note to Apel in summer 1958. Centralization of research facilities to make them more efficient and plannable was attractive to GDR planners, but in some areas, Thiessen argued, "parallel work in research and development" was not only desirable but also necessary. This did not preclude planning. In fact, as Thiessen explicitly recognized, it demanded planning. But Thiessen saw the competition between the laboratories and their division of labor as especially fruitful, particularly if their work would be done in conjunction with development laboratories in factories, which would also be responsible for some basic research. He foresaw a complex and dynamic system, in which the virtues of fundamental research were to be translated as rapidly as possible into production, while those closely linked to production would give valuable feedback to colleagues working on more fundamental science.[57] His views—taken seriously by the politically powerful Apel—were symptomatic of the atmosphere engendered by the Second Berlin Crisis, which was conducive to institutional and ideological experimentation.

Apel went on in his letter to describe another major difficulty with the Schöneweide facility: a Soviet military unit responsible for vehicle repair used part of the site, and it contaminated the air and the ground to such a degree as to make diode production impossible. Apel asked Leuschner to try to intervene to correct this problem, preferably by making another site available to the Soviets.[58] As has already been seen with regard to WBN in Teltow, environmental degradation was a major obstacle hindering semiconductor development in the GDR in the late 1950s, and it was to prove significant again and again in the history of the GDR's semiconductor industry. Semiconductor production requires an extremely high degree of cleanliness, which itself demands highly developed air and water filtration technologies. The GDR had difficulties throughout its existence on this score.

Apel's letter pointed less directly to a second problem: the overwhelming domination of the GDR semiconductor industry by the Teltow facility under the direction of Professor Falter. Wresting control of production from Falter—whose WBN was clearly overextended—was probably one of the motivations for building the new works at Frankfurt, and the idea of establishing additional production facilities in Schöneweide would clearly have a similar effect. But the attack on WBN continued and even intensified later in 1959, when Falter was invited to produce a plan for an industrywide Institute for Semiconductor Technology. He presented his plan in December at a meeting of high-ranking state and industry officials chaired by Bernicke, the special deputy responsible for the semiconductor industry; it was "strongly criticized" by all those present. The criticism focused primarily on Falter's old problem, being overly ambitious: "Among other things, it was seen as a shortcoming that tasks of the future industry Institute for Semiconductor Technology foreseen in the plan are so extensive that they could not be accomplished within the next ten years. In this form, the program is utopian."[59]

Utopian thinking was a very serious charge in the Peasants' and Workers' State, and clearly, even though Falter continued to lead the newly created institute, he and his research facility were particularly vulnerable. But it is just as clear that not all problems could be laid at his door. In spite of its move to create a large factory in Frankfurt Oder and the intensive R&D work it had undertaken for nearly a decade, the GDR was not catching up, but was instead falling further and further behind. It was still having considerable difficulty producing first-generation germanium transistors, even as Texas Instruments began commercial production of the integrated circuit in 1961.

In early 1960, on the eve of this breakthrough, Special Deputy Bernicke took stock of the situation. Like Apel, he emphasized the enormous difficulties faced by the industry in terms of research and development and pollution. He also stressed that there were "subjective" factors undermining higher productivity: he implied that workers tended to use rules of thumb in production rather than more formally specified, instrument-based procedures, and noted that cooperation among the various factories engaged in aspects of production of electronic components was poor. The bottom line of his review was a depressing estimate. In this rapidly changing industry, Bernicke detected a "level of backwardness [for the GDR of] . . . five to six years."[60]

Bernicke repeated much of his analysis to a broader audience in the GDR Economics Commission of the Politburo in August 1960, although there was a major and telling change in his estimate of how far behind the GDR was. This time he pointed out that the "backwardness [of the GDR in semiconductor technology and production] . . . is approximately three to four years." As he indicated further, construction of expanded production capacity had begun "in actual fact for the first time at the beginning of this year, more precisely . . . at the end of March,"[61] so not much had really changed in the "objective" circumstances of the industry in the GDR. How had the distance behind world leaders decreased so substantially in the course of just eight months, a period during which little had actually been accomplished that might have improved the situation?

One explanation might be that Bernicke simply cooked the books. Another might be that one set of figures was produced for the state authorities (in the SPK) and another for the broader, more politically charged, party Economics Commission. Both have merit, but it is also important to recognize that we have here a concrete example of the challenge facing GDR policymakers. On the one hand, the GDR was clearly behind the West in this critical technology, and it was necessary to recognize and act upon that fact. On the other hand, it was necessary to avoid painting the situation as hopeless, both for political reasons and for the goal of motivating workers and managers to overcome this deficit rather than discouraging them and preventing them from achieving their task. The estimate of three to four years' lag placed the GDR well within the band of industrialized "follower" nations in this vital technology: it has been estimated that the average lag in the beginning of commercial production of new semiconductor products was between 2.5 and 2.8 years for Japan, West Germany, France, and Italy.[62] An estimate of five to six years' lag placed the GDR in another—and ultimately unacceptable—category altogether.

But whether the lag of the semiconductor industry of the GDR compared to the West was six years or three years, something clearly had to be done to keep it from increasing. This was placed into relief by the growing awareness of the continued and woeful inadequacy of GDR semiconductor technology. Designers of the Frankfurt plant had gleaned their knowledge primarily from foreign literature and lacked the tacit knowledge crucial to getting the plant to work well.[63] Partly for this reason, production of transistors at the plant in Frankfurt was too low, with just 25 percent of the output at all serviceable.[64] Another report sent to Leuschner in October 1959 put the figure even lower, at 20 percent. This in itself was not all that bad on the face of it: in 1956 in the United States, for instance, the overall proportion of transistors that were usable was just 5–15 percent. The October report went on to point out that the technology employed in the GDR was well known internationally to produce yields of 20 percent. But in the case of the GDR, the "serviceable" semiconductors produced were in large part those that would "change their characteristics as they grow older (instability)."[65] In other words, almost the entire production run was virtually useless—one generally dependable economic history of the GDR puts the real "discard quota" at 98 percent—and in any case could not be deployed in demanding applications.[66] The proportion of semiconductors produced that could be used in such applications had grown by 1962, with increased experience in production, but they still lagged considerably behind international norms. The end users of transistors complained of a "miniature ton-ideology" at the Frankfurt works that led to shipment of large quantities of transistors regardless of quality or even suitability for their deployment.[67]

Just as was the case with petrochemicals, it was not possible for the GDR to develop semiconductor technology or industry on its own. Therefore, the choice was between cooperation with the East or with the West. In the context of the Second Berlin Crisis, when all was in flux, both options were pursued, although the latter was clearly preferred by engineers and managers.

In political terms, in the context of the heightening tensions of the Cold War, the obvious choice of a partner for semiconductor development for the GDR would have to be the Soviet Union. Strenuous efforts to establish some sort of cooperation began in the mid-1950s. WBN agitated for assistance in production and research, while Paul Görlich, the head of the Zeiss Works in Jena, campaigned for coordinated research within the eastern bloc.[68] Success was modest at best. After extensive negotiations, two staff members from Teltow went to the Soviet Union in summer 1958 to begin a program of technical exchanges.[69] But Görlich complained in summer 1959 of extremely limited scientific cooperation within the eastern bloc in the area of semiconductor development, which had the effect of forcing the GDR to look westward for assistance. Initial attempts to purchase technical blueprints and documentation from the Soviets to use in design and construction of the new Frankfurt facility were similarly unsuccessful.[70]

Why were the Soviets so reluctant to come to the aid of their German satellite? East German planners considered this question carefully in mid-1959 in a report that reached the highest levels in GDR government and party circles. For one thing, the Soviet Union had "a substantial lead in the development and production of semiconductors even in international terms . . . and thus is interested in strict secrecy." The report pointed out that the Soviet leaning toward secrecy was legitimated to some extent by "the political attitude of some scientists (flight from the Republic and so on)" in the GDR. Moreover, the GDR had to overcome Soviet memories from earlier in the decade when overtures from the Soviets to the GDR (then more advanced than the Soviets) were rebuffed because of "the superior attitude of some of our scientists." The report ended with a plea to the Politburo for intervention to overcome this reluctance. Indeed, it suggested explicitly that Ulbricht write directly to the Presidium of the Soviet Communist Party.[71] Ulbricht obliged in a letter to Nikita Khrushchev of 15 August 1959, asking for provision of a Soviet adviser to be attached to the Frankfurt plant. His role would be to help the plant overcome the problems it was experiencing in production and technology.[72]

Khrushchev in turn assented to the wishes of the East Germans by sending not one, but three advisers to the GDR. During November and December 1959 they spent six weeks investigating and analyzing the GDR semiconductor industry, and they presented a final report on the state of the industry in late December.[73] Nonetheless, no Soviet adviser was directly attached to the Frankfurt plant, and despite a willingness to pay for licenses and documentation from the Soviet Union, "efforts to get these things from the USSR were fruitless."[74]

Bernicke, as a member of the SPK and the GDR's special deputy for semiconductor technology, made these remarks on 9 November 1959, at about the same time as the three Soviet advisers were arriving for their six-week investigative visit to the GDR. While his government prepared to entertain the Soviet visitors, Bernicke himself was about to lead a ten-man delegation to England to explore the possibilities of jumpstarting the GDR's semiconductor industry through an infusion of western technology.

In semiconductors, as in most other technological areas, the West was by far the most important source of ideas and inspiration for the GDR. As we have already seen, managers, engineers, scientists, and planners were all acutely aware of the pace and volume of innovation in the United States and of the impressive achievements of other capitalist industrialized countries, including West Germany and the United Kingdom. Gaining access to the technology, whether through purchase of machinery, licenses, or know-how or through copying and transfer of readily available, nonproprietary scientific and technical information, would be essential, especially in the absence of extensive Soviet assistance. This was true for two main reasons. First of all, borrowing from the West, whatever form it took, would permit the GDR to overcome its technological backwardness most efficiently and quickly. Second, although borrowing from the West by paying capitalist firms for licenses may have been unpalatable, it had the virtue of facilitating subsequent export to capitalist countries of the items built using the licenses.[75]

The question the GDR faced was which western nation it should borrow from. The answer may appear self-evident: always borrow from the leader, in this case the United States. And the GDR did pursue possibilities in the United States through the late 1950s. Professor Falter of WBN, who visited a semiconductor exposition at Earl's Court in London in May 1959, reported that the London representative of Zeiss, a Mr. Joseph of Roditi International Corp., Ltd., would serve as an agent for the GDR in the purchase of specialized machinery when Joseph visited the United States in August and September. He also noted that "the American firms of Semiconductors and Raytheon are prepared to deliver production lines [for semiconductor manufacture] and to install them in the GDR," although it does not appear that anything further arose from Joseph's initiatives.[76]

Because semiconductor technology had obvious and extensive potential military applications, however, it fell under COCOM restrictions. For this reason, the United States, which was most strenuous in enforcing the restrictions on its industrial corporations, was not a particularly viable partner in developing this technology. Furthermore, GDR planners and managers seem to have recognized that their realistic goal should not be to catch up with and surpass the leader, but rather to join the gaggle of industrialized nations close behind.[77] Here there were three potential partners: Japan, West Germany, and the United Kingdom.

Japan impressed many GDR leaders in the late 1950s with its technological prowess, especially in the area of semiconductors and as a potential model for the GDR's subsequent economic development.[78] But extensive cooperation between the GDR and Japan in electronic technology really developed in the 1970s and after.

West Germany was also a potential partner in this area. It had obvious advantages, in common language and technological traditions, and in certain areas it was a major player. The technical leader of the Frankfurt (Oder) works, Dr. Raabe, visited the high-technology firm of Leybold in Cologne (which worked closely with the GDR in the area of electronics well into the 1980s) in August 1959 to negotiate provision of plant and know-how with an estimated value of 1.333 million marks. In the same year, the SPK argued for the purchase from Siemens of patents for producing pure silicon and silicon-carbide for semiconductor production.[79] Since silicon was fast becoming the preferred material for semiconductors, this would be vital.

But the disadvantages of cooperation with West Germany were equally obvious to the East Germans. Political tensions ran high, especially in the late 1950s and early 1960s, and economic competition rather than cooperation was the watchword. Furthermore, the West Germans were not as impressive in semiconductor technology as were the British, who cut a very respectable figure in both basic research and production. They were clearly behind the United States, but they were firmly in second place.[80]

In late November and early December 1959 the GDR therefore placed many of its eggs in the British basket. Bernicke led a ten-man delegation that included most of the key figures in the GDR semiconductor field, among them the plant manager of the semiconductor factory at Frankfurt, high-ranking representatives from Teltow and the VEB Muldenhütte (which produced purified semiconductor raw materials), an architect for the civil engineering authority building the Frankfurt plant, and applied scientists from research institutes in Freiberg and Ilmenau.[81]

The mission had three main objectives. First, the group wanted to visit modern semiconductor factories. Second, they wished to examine the possibility of purchasing specialized equipment and machinery for manufacturing semiconductors and for research and development. And finally, they wanted to negotiate purchase of complete manufacturing facilities for diodes, low-frequency transistors, and possibly also high-frequency transistors. Preparations for the visit were extensive and included prior approval by the SPK for provision of foreign exchange for purchases and negotiation of licensing and know-how agreements in Britain. The negotiating partners were identified and contacts organized through the good offices of Arthur Lewis, M.P., who also represented the GDR's electro-technical foreign trade agency in London.

Lewis's role in arranging this visit was crucial, and Bernicke noted that visits to semiconductor factories by foreigners were seldom approved. Lewis had made "possible what had first seemed improbable," allowing members of the delegation to visit plants of Mullard (British Philips) in Southhampton, British-Thompson-Houston in Lincoln, and Siemens-Edison in Swan. Dr. Raabe also had the chance to see the Standard Telephone Works in London. British factories of U.S. manufacturers, such as Texas Instruments and Semiconductors, were, on the other hand, inaccessible. Oddly enough, Bernicke implied that even thoughts of using subterfuge to get access to these American subsidiaries would be of no use. Security arrangements were so tight that factory employees wore white lab coats with "not only the name and factory identification number, but also [the employee's] own photograph."

Site visits to the British factories were enormously useful and facilitated savings by pointing out what was necessary and what was unnecessary for further development. Questions of purity of materials and climatic conditions for the production of low-frequency transistors, it turned out, were rather less important than GDR researchers believed them to be. But specialized machine-building units that were not committed to any long-term production program but instead were attached directly to the semiconductor factory were "absolutely necessary" since they would "secure the possibility of assembling technological facilities from one day to the next." What was needed was to move new processes as quickly as possible from laboratory experimentation into production, with the production process itself becoming "experimental." The GDR delegation also noted that the works they visited used a silicon-based coating material produced by Imperial Chemical Industries (ICI) in which to dip finished transistors to stabilize them. They noted both the particular factory's address and the details of the product (commenting parenthetically that "no one stopped us from doing that") and sent off for samples, which they planned to turn over to the chemical industry of the GDR for copying. All in all, the savings in time and money likely to accrue from these visits were substantial.

The delegation made significant progress also toward its second goal, securing delivery of specialized equipment and machinery. Deliveries, they noted, would take between three weeks and six months, depending on the item. But the delegation's third goal appeared virtually unattainable: "Purchase of production lines by factories for manufacturing semiconductors is not possible." One London firm, Bader, was willing to produce specialized manufacturing lines for diodes and low-frequency transistors. But this would be only the machines. Bader was not able to deliver what the East Germans most wanted—that is, high-frequency transistor manufacturing facilities and know-how for the diode and low-frequency transistor lines.

Eventually the GDR acquired specialized equipment for the semiconductor industry from Great Britain, to the tune of 1 million marks in foreign exchange—a modest figure perhaps, but a fairly large one in the context of the perennial foreign exchange crises of the GDR and the Second Berlin Crisis.[82] The knock-on effects of these imports would be substantial, too. As Bernicke noted in a report on the backwardness of the industry in January 1960, "obtaining all necessary machines through imports is unthinkable." Although Bernicke did not mention the reason for this, it was undoubtedly owing to COCOM restrictions. In any case, because of the restrictions on imports, it would be necessary to establish shops for producing specialized machinery, in part because this was good practice, as the trip to England demonstrated, and in part because "the individual machines purchased in England would have to be copied in order to secure the equipment of the new semiconductor works."[83]

Bernicke's ruminations make it clear that the dream of catching up with the advanced capitalist countries in the area of semiconductors through imports was fast dissipating by 1960. The combination of COCOM restrictions, limited foreign exchange, continued loss of qualified technical and scientific personnel through emigration to the West, and the ever escalating Berlin crisis led the GDR into a largely unsatisfactory compromise position. Bits and pieces of specialized machinery came from the West, mostly from Britain and West Germany, but turnkey plants were unavailable, which meant that the technological system in general continued to be largely East German, featuring a peculiar mixture of Soviet and western technological style. A policy of using imported machinery as templates for reproducing the machines domestically saved foreign exchange, but at the cost of hindering dynamic technological change, a problem exacerbated by the GDR's limited R&D capacity in semiconductors. In this industry, it was a disastrous combination.

As a result of these and other problems (such as insufficient allocation of raw materials and labor for construction), even in 1963, despite impressive increases in semiconductor production in the GDR from rates in the late 1950s, the new plant in Frankfurt was still under construction. Most manufacturing was still on the site of the old vocational school. Production increases, moreover, were the result of use of imported western specialized machines, intensified scientific and technical effort within the GDR, and direct aid from the Soviet Union. It is not clear what finally changed the Soviet mind about whether to help its East German allies, but the likely cause was the intensification of the Berlin crisis. In any case, specialists in diffusion technology and chemical treatment of crystals arrived in Frankfurt in mid-1960 and began to put the Soviet stamp most heavily and clearly on GDR semiconductor technology.[84] GDR planners and managers were aware of the latest developments in miniaturization and microelectronics, especially in the United States, and tried to develop programs to imitate them.[85] But their inability to master the earlier technology fully meant that this new direction only placed further strain on the GDR system of innovation and research-based production.

Semiconductor technology and petrochemicals technology, as developed in the GDR by the early 1960s, had two major features in common. First, both were falling further and further behind the West. Second, and related to the first point, through the process of direct technological intervention by Soviet engineers, they were taking on increasingly Soviet characteristics.

Petrochemicals and semiconductors represented areas of high-technology development that were crucial instances of the GDR's growing integration into Soviet technological culture. It is important to keep in mind, however, that high-technology industries, though important, often have a limited impact on economy, industry, and technology more generally. One key to generalized technological impact is the prevailing system of technical standards and the generic industrial techniques adopted by the society. These involve the fundamental building blocks of the economy and its technology—from the size, shape, and pitch of screw threads to the steel plates and timber boards that the screws hold together and the tolerances of the machines that manufacture them all. Standards and socialist techniques in the GDR were also Sovietized in the critical period during the late 1950s and early 1960s, with results that reinforced both the artifactual differentiation from the West, which we have seen in this chapter, and the cultural alienation discussed earlier.

Good fences, they say, make good neighbors. If so, the double-ringed barrier surrounding West Berlin, much of it in concrete, stretching more than 100 miles and dotted at regular intervals with heavily guarded watchtowers (260 in all), should have made for excellent relations between the neighboring German successor states. The Berlin Wall, constructed in August 1961, along with the lesser known barrier created much earlier along the border between the two German states, had the effect of stabilizing increasingly tense relations between the two German successor states. This stability in turn allowed the routinization of a remarkable and anomalous situation. Consider that East Berlin was at once the Russian sector of Allied-occupied Berlin and the official capital of the German Democratic Republic. A telephone call from West Berlin to the eastern part of the city was treated as local, whereas one from east to west was international.

The wall has been written about frequently and eloquently.[1] But its potency as an image and a symbol deflects attention from a panoply of developments in the late 1950s and early 1960s, some of which preceded the erection of the wall, and all of which made the wall a much more effective barrier than it would otherwise have been. Many of these developments involved technology, as we have already seen in the case of trade and technology fairs and high-technology industries. They continued and hastened the process of bisection of German identity that had begun well before the construction of the wall, and afterward they buttressed the concrete wall with a virtual one. Obstruction of physical contact between the populations of the two German successor states was accompanied by—and to a certain degree made possible—efforts to break the artifactual and intellectual links between them. These attempts were never completely successful, but they became more and more effective by the early 1960s.

The separation of German technological culture into two very different entities involved not only the hardware, as discussed in the last chapter, but also the "software" of socialism. This can be seen most clearly in two cases, that of Group Technology and that of norms and standards. Examining Group Technology involves an extended foray into the relationship between technology and ideology as East Germans searched for a socialist artifact. Although the search was unsuccessful, studying the search process itself yields insights into East German technology at its crossroads. The second case, that of norms and standards, is generally overlooked in economic and technological history, but is of fundamental importance for understanding technological compatibility between countries.

Group Technology and the Search for the Socialist Artifact

In the early 1950s, as the dust slowly settled from World War II, and state and party officials began serious deliberations about how they should build their new society, they soon encountered two sets of perplexing problems with regard to technology.[2] In order to accomplish their primary task—defining the difference (and superiority) of socialist technology in comparison to its capitalist counterpart—they needed, first, to adapt historical precedents to the situation of the GDR and, second, to address a range of thorny ideological and practical concerns.

Nothing should have been easier than finding and adapting historical precedents for socialist technology, mainly because only one state, the USSR, had any long-term experience with this in the late 1940s and early 1950s. Furthermore, Soviet influence on the GDR was both direct and profound at this time. But unfortunately for GDR planners, and despite considerable effort expended in this cause, they found little to help them in Soviet history. Part of the problem was that Soviet attempts to define socialist technology were at best ambivalent, if not downright contradictory. Throughout Soviet history, prevailing practice vacillated, often wildly, between a traditionalist wing and a nontraditionalist faction. The traditionalists perceived danger (military and technological) from the West, vaunted Soviet technological capability, emphasized military technology, and stressed autarky. The nontraditionalists minimized danger from the West, accepted Soviet technological limitations, stressed civilian technology, and were open to outside influences.[3]

Contradictions within the Soviet leadership were not the only problem with the Soviet model. The USSR was not a particularly useful source of inspiration for East Germans because it was larger than the GDR, enjoyed a vastly superior resource endowment, and was generally far behind the GDR in terms of industrial development. Thus, despite continued attempts to learn from Soviet precedent, in practical terms GDR planners and industrialists were forced to generate their own ideas about socialist technology.

This task posed both ideological and practical difficulties. For one thing, in Marxist ideology capitalism was the necessary precursor to socialism and therefore, even in theory, it was clear that the technology of the two would be closely related. More important still, in actual practice key aspects of capitalist and socialist technology were not just closely related, but identical. Engineers in both systems valued maximizing production and minimizing costs. They thus subscribed to identical, if often somewhat vague, norms of efficiency, which influenced design. They also subscribed to identical, and much better defined, standards for design and performance of artifacts and materials. These standards were established by the DIN (Deutsche Industrie-Normen) and the ISO (International Standards Organization).

Still, it is often possible to establish difference, if one works long and hard enough. One of the earliest and most concrete examples of such resourcefulness was a speech by Heinrich Rau on the occasion of the Sixteenth Conference of the Central Committee of the Socialist Unity Party (SED) in 1953.[4]

Rau, born in 1899, had joined the Communist Party (KPD) in 1919. Although trained as a skilled metalworker, he was for much of the Weimar period a full-time politician, a KPD member of the Prussian provincial parliament between 1928 and 1933. During the Nazi period he spent time in jail, abroad, and then in a concentration camp. After the war he held a series of high offices in the Soviet zone/GDR, serving as chairman of the SPK between 1950 and 1952, and then as GDR minister for machine building between 1953 and 1955. Rau thus had the background and standing to serve as a spokesman for the GDR regime in outlining the future role of industry and technology in the "New Course" adopted throughout the eastern bloc following the death of Stalin in spring 1953. This period was a critical one in the GDR because of the regime's ongoing crisis, which resulted in the uprising of 17 June 1953. Rau's basic message was what one would expect, given his position and task: industry was the most important element of the GDR's economy, the nationalized machine tools/machine-building sector its centerpiece. Improvement of industry would permit general and fundamental betterment of the political and economic situation of the country, which in turn would serve as the basis for significant improvements in the standard of living.

Technology played a pivotal role in Rau's remarks. Indeed, his rhetoric indicated technology's centrality to socialist ideology and practice. Technological development, he claimed, brought forth "violent convulsions": "the production process is continually revolutionized and driven forward."[5] Rau also contrasted capitalist and socialist technology explicitly: "While technology in capitalism, especially in its imperialistic stage, works in service of surplus-value production, in service of the realization of the basic economic law of modern capitalism, and therefore in service of the sharpened exploitation of the working class, technology for us plays an important role in the continuous improvement of the living conditions of the working class and of the whole population."[6]

These remarks seemed to imply that technology itself was neutral, and that what mattered was the socioeconomic system within which it was deployed. But Rau went on to discuss some aspects of specifically socialist technology that would become part of an ideal model:[7] socialist technology would be technology at the highest possible level (although the parameters for measuring height were generally not mentioned explicitly); automation, mechanization, and assembly-line work would be important, in part because they allegedly stood at the forefront of technological progress, in part because they would increase productivity, and in part because they would serve to ease the burden of workers; finally, in socialist technology, workers would participate in design, both of artifacts and of the production process itself.

Socialist technology would thus differ in its essence from capitalist technology. But how was this vision of socialist technology to be realized?

Clearly, one way the GDR leadership felt it might realize the vision of establishing a socialist technology would be to borrow from the Soviet Union, especially given the USSR's major accomplishments in petrochemicals and semiconductor technologies. But there was a continued pull toward the West in the GDR, owing to ingrained traditions and also to a recognition that overall the western capitalist countries seemed to be producing excellent technology in several areas.

The disadvantages of the strategy of promoting technological change by playing the Soviet card, therefore, are—and were—obvious: if western technology led the world, and if the GDR, too, wanted to be at the global technological forefront, there appeared little point in turning to the Soviet Union. For that reason, the most obvious explanation of why the GDR eventually played the Soviet card technologically was that all other options had evaporated and that desperation precluded any other course.

In making this point, it is important to emphasize another, which might otherwise be lost: the GDR throwing in its lot with the Soviets in the late 1950s and early 1960s appeared justified because, for the first time, the Soviet Union did indeed have something to offer the East Germans. Sputnik symbolized the accomplishments and potential of Soviet technology. At a more workaday level, the new Group Technology, introduced by the Soviet inventor Sergei Mitrofanov in the late 1950s, appeared to offer real technological and economic potential and also to justify ideological proclivities. This seemed to be a distinctly socialist technology, although, as we shall see, it was also used to good effect in capitalist countries. Further, it contrasted sharply—and positively—with previous examples of Soviet-influenced techniques, such as Stakhanovite (in the GDR, Hennecke) methods of simply working harder, or methods that favored working faster without regard to wear and tear on equipment. Unlike these methods, which could at best be stopgap measures, Group Technology seemed to have the potential to lead the GDR out of its crisis.

Mitrofanov's Group Technology had its origins in the machine-building industry, but it was not a machine. Rather, it was a technique, a way of organizing production processes.[8] The basic idea behind it was to group together scientifically objects of similar forms or ones that required similar manufacturing processes. The manufacture of the objects—for instance, bolts for use in machine tools, or camera parts—would then proceed by group, which would allow the use of universal machine tools, traditional in the German machine-building industry, and would minimize the amount of retooling that would have been needed had the objects been produced more randomly. Essentially, then, Group Technology allowed many of the benefits of mass production within small-series manufacture (and in some ways prefigured what we now call flexible production). Its potential was enormous for industries such as machine building or fine-instrument manufacture, which used vast numbers of more or less idiosyncratic parts to produce a small number of objects.[9]

For the GDR, of course, since its strengths lay precisely in such industries and since its production runs were often quite small, Group Technology seemed especially promising, just as it did in Czechoslovakia. At the end of the 1950s the Zeiss Works, which pioneered in the application of Group Technology in the GDR, produced about 189,000 separate types of parts, with about 70 percent of them in production runs of between 1 and 200.[10] The promise of obtaining the benefits of economies of scale even in these small and medium-sized production runs led GDR planners to take seriously Mitrofanov's claim: "I am certain that through Group Technology you will save more than 1 billion [East German marks] by 1965."[11] Group Technology's usefulness, moreover, could extend well beyond the technological and economic arenas, for it appeared to conform to—and to confirm—the idea of socialist technology that had been developed during the 1950s in the GDR. It thus spoke to a deeply felt need for inspiration from, and cooperation with, the Soviet Union. For all these reasons, Group Technology was a subject of interest in East Germany just before the wall went up, from the production facilities of Zeiss Works in Jena to the chambers of the Politburo in Berlin.

Several key factories in the GDR began applying and developing Group Technology in late 1959.[12] The highlight of the movement came in early spring of 1961, when Mitrofanov himself paid a two-week visit. He toured the Zeiss and Karl-Marx-Stadt factories that used his methods, met technologists interested in his technique at a central conference on 28 February in Jena, and appeared in Berlin at a meeting with high-ranking SED officials in the House of the Central Committee.[13] As one might expect, the rhetoric flowed freely during the visit, and there is every reason to be skeptical about the depth of the sentiments expressed. Still, given the energy expended at some of the highest levels in GDR politics and industry during the visit, and given the attention lavished on Mitrofanov's methods in industry and the media after it took place, it is worth paying some attention to what was said and by whom, especially in Berlin.[14] The discussions there indicated a genuine sense among policymakers that Mitrofanov's technology represented something new and different.

The 1 March 1961 meeting in the House of the SED Central Committee in East Berlin was chaired by Erich Apel, the party's top officer of economic policymaking, and was concerned primarily with details of planning and party work that would be necessary to implement Mitrofanov's methods across a variety of industries. At the end of his long remarks, however, Apel returned to the theme of Group Technology as both a technological and a political system, as a socialist technology.

Indeed, for Apel, Mitrofanov himself symbolized the fusion of technological knowledge and ability, practical orientation, and political commitment that epitomized the new socialist man: "We have outstanding people in our republic, and our party is also working on solving the problems of technical advancement, but in you we all see very precisely the prototype of the new socialist life. You are familiar with practice, you are a scientist and outstanding inventor, and you are at the same time a party worker."[15]

This archetypal socialist man returned several times to the GDR for similar meetings about his archetypal socialist technology through the mid-1960s, but Group Technology did not deliver on its promises. Its initial economic benefits were much more modest than Mitrofanov's claims had indicated, and savings through application of Group Technology never came close to the boasted billion marks. Although 1961 was proclaimed the "Year of Mitrofanov" in GDR propaganda, and although 200 factories committed themselves to the new technology, not a single factory in that year was able to apply Group Technology to more than 5 percent of its finished parts. One of the biggest hindrances to adopting the method, ironically, was the situation that had led to its embrace. The Second Berlin Crisis, the construction of the Berlin Wall, and the policy of "freeing from disturbance" (*Störfreimachung*) created chaotic conditions that made adoption of new methods virtually impossible.

Just as important, to the extent that Mitrofanov's method was successful—and there is no denying that it did have some impact on production and costs in the GDR and elsewhere, and was a precursor for later flexible production methods—its application was not limited to socialist countries. Companies in capitalist countries, such as the United States, the United Kingdom, and even West Germany, imitated the method without in any way compromising the fundamental orientation of their technology or their political-economic system. Group Technology, it seemed, was not a socialist technology after all—although, interestingly enough, a textbook advocating its adoption, published in England in the mid- 1970s, highlighted its potential for liberation of workers and its particular compatibility with democracy.[16]

Despite the disappointment associated with the adoption of Mitrofanov's methods, the fateful decision to build the wall and to throw in the GDR's lot unreservedly with that of the Soviet Union did have the effect of distancing the GDR from the capitalist West technologically. Cooperation with the Soviet Union in such high-technology areas as petrochemical production, plastics manufacture, and semiconductor production linked the GDR artifactually to the Soviet Union and pulled it away from the West.[17] More important, as part of the break with West Germany through the construction of the wall, the GDR also decided to break with prevailing DIN industrial norms and to embrace instead the Soviet Union's GOST (State Standards of the Union) norms.

The Story of Standards in the GDR

Put simply, standardization involves different producers of raw materials and components of machines and technological systems agreeing to norms for producing those raw materials and components so as to ensure identical quality and performance, thus promoting interchangeability and compatibility among the machines and systems. The push for standardization has deep roots, both in national (and international) systems of measurement and weight, such as the metric system, and in systems of manufacture, such as the nineteenth-century U.S. munitions industry. The story of Eli Whitney's pursuit of interchangeable parts for rifles through standardized, and very precise production techniques is perhaps best known, although John Hall of Harpers Ferry Armory was much more important in this development. It became a vital feature of "the American system of manufactures" and later of "mass production."[18]

Germany's smaller market, entrenched craft traditions, and late and partial unification ensured a different path to industrialization than that pursued by the Americans, and standardization did not figure anywhere near as prominently at first.[19] Short-series, small-scale manufacture by a large number of producers for a large number of different consumers, frequently for regional markets, did not require a great deal of standardization; the continued primacy of the craft tradition probably worked actively against it. But the combined pressures of total war between 1914 and 1918 and of increasing international competition in the period immediately after the war, especially from the Americans, caused the Germans to rethink their strategy. Shortly after the end of World War I, German business embarked on a program to "rationalize" German industry.

Ronald Shearer has pointed out that part of the attraction of the word *rationalization* in interwar Germany was its potential to mean all things to all people.[20] But one of the key aims of the Imperial Board for Economic Efficiency (Reichskuratorium für Wirtschaftlichkeit, or RKW), which was the organization German business counted on to promote rationalization, was to foster standardization of components, products, and processes within German industry. One of the main organs for accomplishing this was the Deutsche Normen-Ausschuss (German Norms Committee, or DNA), which in turn controlled the soon world-renowned Deutsche Industrie-Normen (German Industrial Norms, or DIN). Founded in the final year of the war to promote standardization for the sake of the war effort, the DNA was a typically German institution, which combined the public and private, the large and the small, fairly seamlessly into an institution serving a wide clientele, but with substantial freedom of maneuver. Its financing came partly from its membership, which consisted of companies, industry trade associations, and state institutions, and in part from the sale of materials related to norms that the committee had agreed upon and that were accepted by firms within and outside Germany. This allowed it to retain a considerable degree of independence. The DNA also earned money independently from consulting work done for individual firms and state authorities.[21]

The Germans were not the only ones with a national standards organization in the interwar period, although theirs eventually became one of the best known. The British, the first to industrialize, were also the first to establish a national standards organization, the Standards Development Organisation, in 1901–2.[22] The followers, the Netherlands (1916), France, Switzerland, and the United States (1918), were all prompted by the war to found their own national organizations. International economic turbulence and the desire to mitigate the effects of this through international cooperation during the 1920s led to the founding in 1928 of the International Federation of the National Standardizing Associations (ISA) in Prague. Its work of coordinating the efforts of the national organizations and organizing international norms continued until the outbreak of World War II in Europe in 1939, despite rising international tensions. Even National Socialist Germany took part, with an extensive transition from DIN to ISA norms occurring for the most part between 1936 and 1939; the changeover was made more palatable to extreme nationalists by the fact that, in the development of the ISA system, "the DIN system was very strongly heeded."[23]

With the end of the war and the division of Germany into four separate zones of occupation, the DNA ceased functioning as well. But in late 1946, despite the deepening rifts among the former Allies that would become the Cold War, the DNA was allowed to resume pan-German operations, and with the lapse of the ISA, DIN norms were reestab-

lished.[24] Like the Leopoldina, Allied air-traffic-control regulations in occupied Berlin, and the German Olympic team, the DNA was an all-
German organization that preceded the founding of the two German
successor states and continued to work effectively despite the growing
tension of the 1950s.[25] Unlike those other organizations, however, the
DNA ceased functioning on an all-German basis in 1961 simultaneously
with the construction of the Berlin Wall. And in further contrast, the
DNA's activities affected the fundamental orientation of technology,
which is one of the reasons its history is vital to an understanding of
post-1945 German history.

The resumption of activities of the DNA did not at first lead to all-
German norming and standardization, until the early 1950s. Furthermore, the GDR regime remained committed to it as an all-German institution throughout most of the decade, although its deployment of
standards and norms—which had the force of law behind it—was already
unlike that in West Germany, where standards and norms were vol-
untary. This distinction did not make much difference at first, but it
loomed larger in the course of time.

The first office of the DNA in the Soviet zone of occupation opened in
Dresden on 1 February 1949, but the main GDR office moved to East
Berlin in April 1951. An official publication of the DNA evaluated the
significance of this step in 1957: "With its main office in Berlin and its
branch offices in East and West Germany, the DNA was now in the
position to pursue further the German norm system in the true sense of
its name with the participation—and for the benefit—of the people in all
of Germany."[26]

The DNA had been excluded, along with the Japanese standardization
agency, from the successor organization to the ISA, the International
Standards Organization (ISO), when it was founded in 1946. By late 1951,
however, both countries were invited to join the ISO. But the DNA was
to be the sole representative of Germany, and East and West Germans
had to form a common front in their approaches to the international
organization.[27]

As the GDR began to take some control over its own affairs in the early
1950s, with the winding-down of Soviet occupation and dismantling,
there was some discomfiture at this situation. In 1952, for instance, the
Norms and Quality Control Section of the Central Office for Research
and Technology of the SPK considered fully the question of participation
in the DNA and was extremely critical in its assessment, although the

section believed that there were definite advantages to participation. One was access to "a large archive of foreign, and especially English, American, and French norms, which can be employed in working out [German norms]." In addition, "some norms of the DNA are of such extraordinary and even international significance that they would not be possible for us to develop at present on our own." Still, there were considerable drawbacks, mostly resulting from the dominance of the West and its interests in the DNA. In fact, owing to a shortage of activity on the East German side, the Eastern Branch Office of the DNA was at present functioning "only as a letter carrier for the DNA." This meant in turn that differences in economic structure between the GDR and West Germany were not taken fully into account. Thus, while the advantages of cooperation still outweighed the disadvantages, the latter had to be monitored, and this had to be accompanied by "an improvement in [the GDR's] norming work, especially through strengthened cooperation in this area with the Soviet Union and the peoples' democracies."[28] A confidential memo written just over a year later, in the context of the workers' uprising of June 1953, reinforced many of these same points, underscoring the political importance of the DNA and the need for the GDR to place "politically reliable" personnel on it.[29]

By the mid-1950s, however, in the context of lessened tension with the West and a surer grasp of the political situation at home, official policy had come down fully in favor of cooperation with the DNA. The Office for Standardization (Amt für Standardisierung, or AfS), which was founded in the GDR on 1 November 1954 to take over the previous work of the standardization section of the Central Office for Research and Technology, pointed out in 1955 that "the government of the German Democratic Republic is interested in a pan-German norming system which, by going beyond the temporary division of Germany, possesses as unified a character as possible. For this purpose, the German Norms Committee [DNA] is supported as a pan-German norming organization. Experts from the GDR work together with experts from the Federal Republic in the specialized norming and working committees on common tasks related to norming."[30]

There were, however, voices pressing for change. Early on, and certainly by the mid-1950s, East German authorities recognized that their different economic organization required different technological norms.[31] But what was the alternative to the DIN and participation in the DNA?

One way was for the GDR to establish its own standardization organization. This, though, had three major drawbacks. First, it was a difficult step for a small country, since it would involve a considerable amount of work that would duplicate or attempt to replicate international developments. Second, it would mean sacrificing the prestige and worldwide acceptance of the DIN label, something the East Germans were acutely aware of. Third, it would involve abdicating membership in the ISO, since East German membership was only through the DNA, the sole accredited representative of German industry at the international organization. Essentially, then, creation of an independent East German standardization agency would have a devastating impact both on current exports and on future export potential for GDR industry.

A second alternative was to embrace Soviet norms, the so-called GOST norms. This would have the advantage of broadening East Germany's relatively small market by linking it to one that was much larger. But this, too, would involve foregoing the advantages of the DIN's worldwide reputation and representation on the ISO.

Nonetheless, the political pressure building up in East Germany by the late 1950s for movement eastward led to an investigation of the feasibility of the transition from ISA/DIN to GOST norms for the GDR's most basic industry, machine building, which was undertaken by the polytechnic (Technische Hochschule, or TH) in Dresden, the Ministries for Heavy Machine-building and for Machine-building, and the AfS. The results of the feasibility study were clear. Moving to GOST would not be wise, for several reasons:

1. Most East German scientists and engineers would not approve of such a move, since they valued the work of the DNA highly.
2. The existence of two different systems of norms on German soil might cause difficulties in case of "future reunification" and would, at the same time, make it difficult or impossible to send an all-German delegation to the ISO.
3. The costs to the Treasury, although they would be one-time-only, would also be quite high.

The conclusion of the report in 1957 was quite clear: "For the German Democratic Republic the transition from the ISA [sic] to the [G]OST fitting system is an unwarranted expectation."[32]

Still, conferences on harmonization of standards within the socialist camp, which had begun in the mid-1950s, continued.[33] Furthermore, already in 1957, as the Second Berlin Crisis loomed, there were indications of change. The investigation into the feasibility of changing from the DIN enlarged on its conclusion, stating that although the transition to GOST was not really possible, "a system is to be applied for products of machine building which makes possible a balance between the ISA [*sic*] and the [G]OST fitting systems."[34] East Germany in the late 1950s was a place where options were desperately kept open, as can be seen in the case of the chemical industry, where the changeover to petrochemistry was announced a year later, at the same time as a renewed commitment to acetylene-based coal chemistry.[35]

The real onset of the Second Berlin Crisis in 1958 changed the tenor of the discussion about standardization, which began to emphasize more and more the ideological implications of technological choice. Vigorously and repeatedly, East German officials now stressed the extent to which the DIN norms were "capitalist" norms. Implicitly at least, the officials indicated that the DIN norms served an insidious purpose within East German industry and society, allowing infiltration and perpetuation of capitalist values and influence through seemingly innocuous channels, such as the pitch of screw threads. Those attending one high-level SED meeting in summer 1958, for instance, heard that a review of all the DIN norms was necessary because "DIN norms are worked out under the conditions of the capitalist economy and correspond to it."[36]

The implications of this point of view about the DIN for the DNA were obvious. If the DIN were an insidious means of transfer of capitalist values, the DNA was the sneaky organization promoting that transfer, an "organ of the western monopolies and their NATO policies."[37] There was the danger of unforeseen capitalist intrusion into the East German experiment through western norms; moreover, the DNA, even though East German participation in it had stimulated technological development, would serve as a potential locus for luring away East German scientists and engineers to the West, while at the same time serving as a vantage point from which to spy on the East. (The reverse, of course, was not mentioned.)[38] The preferred solution at that point in mid-1958 was to create two separate standardizing organizations with equal rights in the two German successor states, while a pan-German committee with equal representation from the two German states would represent Germany on the ISO.[39] Why exactly the DIN was allegedly recognizably capitalist, while the ISO was a highly valued organization, was a contradiction, the resolution of which was not addressed in the documents.

At the same time, it is important to recognize that not all the feeling at the time in East Germany was negative or anti-DIN. Rather, some stressed the liberatory potential of "socialist standardization," or, as it later became known, radical standardization.[40] This was a potential that socialist political relationships seemed especially able to unleash, not least because standards and norms in the GDR had the force of law behind them. In retrospect, however, both of these terms are somewhat suspect, neither being adequately defined at the time, and there is every reason to think that many of those who used them did so cynically. But there may have been real enthusiasm among some East German elites about this admittedly vague idea. A draft of the law for standardization prepared by the AfS in October 1958 trumpeted that "standardization . . . is . . . in the position, freed from the traditions of norming in capitalism, cut free from the dependence on the objectively functioning law of the anarchy of production and competition in capitalism, and utilizing all of the possibilities of the socialist societal order, of building the key preconditions for the rapid increase of productive forces."[41] In a speech in 1960 one major figure pointed out that "socialist standardization involves a fundamental break with the traditions of capitalist standardization within the German Democratic Republic. The implementation of radical standardization therefore requires political enlightenment more than anything else. . . . Standardization is therefore not only a technical-organizational problem, but above all a political one."[42]

Again, the increasingly strident tone of the rhetoric of standardization—socialist, radical, and otherwise—was linked closely to the increasing tension of the Second Berlin Crisis. Standardization would be one of the key weapons in the defense of the economy against the "arbitrary measures of disturbance" undertaken by "Ultras from Bonn," a general task set at the eleventh conference of the Central Committee of the SED in December 1960.[43] Through technology, standardization would allow decoupling of the GDR economy and society from those of the West and, simultaneously, a closer affiliation with the eastern bloc. By early 1961 all sectors of GDR industry were beginning to think in terms of establishing procedures whereby future standards would routinely be worked out in conjunction with other socialist countries rather than using the DIN as a baseline.[44]

Even in the spring of 1961, however, there was still some residual resistance to a complete break with the West. A series of answers to "frequently asked questions" on standardization, provided in March 1961 by the SPK to the party publication *Einheit,* stressed that there should be no thought of an either/or situation with regard to norms. "The question is therefore not: DIN or GOST? Rather the task is to achieve radical standardization through the creation of GDR standards. . . . *In this we rely on all sources of knowledge available to us."*[45]

By the summer whatever remained of this ambiguous attitude had dissipated. In June the Politburo considered favorably the suggestion that scientists and engineers in the GDR become more actively involved in standardization, one of the goals being "to free it from the capitalist forms of norming." A single set of compulsory norms for GDR industry and technology was to be developed (the Technische Güte- und Lieferbedingungen [Technical Conditions for Quality and Delivery], or TGL), which "was to be brought into harmony . . . systematically with GOST." Although membership in the ISO would still only be possible through the DNA, and the GDR would still therefore have to remain associated with the DNA, the government should work toward independent membership in the ISO.[46]

The drift of policy was unmistakable, and the final step was just as clearly linked to the construction of the Berlin Wall. Shortly after it was built in August 1961, the GDR decided to end the membership of its factories and other institutions in the DNA, effective 31 December.[47] In fact, even before that deadline, simultaneous with the construction of the wall, communications from the West German branches and committees of the DNA to its East German counterparts were returned to sender with the designation "addressee unknown."[48]

With the ending of East German cooperation in the DNA, the construction of the wall had a virtual counterpart. On a fundamental level, regardless of the experimentation that took place in GDR technology, economy, and society afterward, East German technological culture broke with that of West Germany in August 1961. Adoption of Soviet standards was never fully embraced in the GDR, and the transition toward technical norms of the eastern bloc was in any case a slow process. Gradual adoption of some Soviet norms did not therefore mean immediate and utter incompatibility with West German technology. But the extent to which they were adopted was eventually considerable. This, combined with the fact that standards and norms in East Germany, unlike in West Germany, were backed by the force of law, brought about a fundamental reorientation of principles of design from traditional German principles toward Soviet ones. By 1963 DIN materials were being withdrawn from daily use in major GDR factories and retained in centralized facilities solely for informational purposes. Getting rid of the DIN remained a high priority.[49]

Of Socialist Software and Socialist Technology

The years of the Second Berlin Crisis and the immediate aftermath of the construction of the Berlin Wall were a critical time in the development of East German technological culture. At the beginning of the period, in the late 1950s, decision-making on technology was shaped by the unresolved and fundamental tension in the GDR between political loyalty to the Soviet Union and traditional commercial and technological attachment to the West. This tension was especially evident in crucial high-technology areas, such as petrochemicals and semiconductors, but it was also present in the experiences of GDR engineers and managers as they interacted with their western counterparts, and in the software of socialism. Initially the GDR was unwilling to resolve the tension one way or the other. Instead, recognizing that wholly domestic development of technologies that met or exceeded international standards was an impossible task, GDR scientists, engineers, managers, and planners pursued a strategy of seeking assistance from the Soviet Union while at the same time purchasing equipment and know-how from the West.

Several factors, however, called this strategy into question. One was the Soviet launch of Sputnik, which, along with other technological achievements of the USSR, seemed to herald the realization of the supremacy of socialist technology. Continued hemorrhaging of scientific and technological talent to the West was an additional factor undermining the westward orientation: close technological ties with the West would require frequent contact with and visits to the capitalist countries, putting this talent at added risk. A third was continued problems with foreign exchange and the horrendously high and growing cost of purchase of capitalist technology. As the Berlin crisis progressed, demonstration of mutual political loyalty from both the Soviet and the East German sides became essential, and this had economic and technological implications and dimensions.

Thus, although there were still some areas in which western aid was both sought after and essential, such as chemical process technology for plastics production, the early 1960s saw an increasing Soviet orientation of East German high technology. The reorientation went far beyond lip service, and expressed itself at a fundamental level in the artifacts with which the East Germans designed and produced petrochemicals and semiconductors. Blueprints, people, and machines from the Soviet Union combined to redirect and refocus decades of German technological tradition. Although some of those traditions remained after the construction of the Berlin Wall, and although some of the changes had been set in motion before it was built, East German technology was recognizably different from that in the West after August 1961.

The reorientation of key high technologies toward the Soviet Union would have knock-on effects in a huge number of producer and consumer technologies, since virtually everything required either plastics or semiconductors, or both. The reorientation also proceeded from the other end of the spectrum with the attempt to embrace Group Technology as "socialist technology" and the adoption of a steady stream of Soviet standards for the design and production of all components of all artifacts. Implementation of this decision came in conjunction with the construction of the Berlin Wall, and it was accomplished with the full realization that technological linkage and political attachment to the Soviet Union would reinforce one another and create a more fully integrated Soviet bloc.

The software of socialism—Group Technology and Soviet-based standards and norms—in effect constituted a virtual wall, in two senses. It was abstract and not concrete; it also fell somewhat short of the real thing, disappointing expectations. Group Technology, pioneered by a socialist inventor, seemed to be the answer to a desperate need for technological as well as ideological leadership from the Soviet Union. It also fit in well with the GDR's key technologies, especially in machine building and optics. But it did not lead to quite as large or fast savings in investment and increases in productivity as were promised initially. Group Technology also turned out not to be peculiarly socialist, since capitalist firms adopted its techniques even more successfully than socialist ones.

Adoption of Soviet norms also failed to live up to the expectations of the GDR leadership, although for different reasons. Although legally binding once agreed to by government authorities, the norms were adopted only piecemeal, and never completely supplanted those developed in the West. Furthermore, insofar as they were adopted, they were often mere translations of the corresponding western, generally DIN, norms. Cooperation with the DNA may have been halted, and DIN norms and standards may have been kept in central storerooms in factories so that the rank and file among engineers and managers would not encounter them on an every-day basis. But the DIN norms continued to form the basis for much of the norming system of the GDR, and the country's technology continued to have distinctive traits compared to that of other Soviet bloc countries.

Still, Group Technology and the adoption—however incomplete—of Soviet standards were both symbol and manifestation of the culmination of a fundamental reorientation of technological culture in the GDR. Group Technology may not have been peculiarly socialist, but the rhet-oric surrounding its adoption indicates strongly that the East German industrial leadership wished it were so. "Soviet" standards may have been based ultimately in many cases on DIN norms, but the very fact that many DIN norms were "translated" into GOST norms indicates an orientation eastward rather than westward in terms of ideology, technol-ogy, and export. And the fact that East German norms—whether influ-enced by DIN or GOST—had the force of law marked a fundamental and growing difference between East and West German technology. Indeed, as Joachim Radkau claims in a highly suggestive essay on technology in the GDR, published in 1990 in the immediate aftermath of the fall of the (concrete) Berlin Wall, this orientation toward Soviet bloc markets, and especially toward the Soviet Union itself, may have been crucial in the subsequent technological development of the GDR. He argues that "the most enduring damages [to the GDR] arose not out of the actions the USSR carried out that had the effect of making the GDR's life difficult, i.e. dismantling and unequal trade treaties. Instead, the enduring damage arose from the things that made the life of the GDR all too comfortable: through the USSR's purchase of outmoded machines that had no chance of being sold in western markets."[50]

There was to be no such thing as a "socialist artifact" in the sense longed for by the GDR leadership in the 1950s. Still, through the mutu-ally reinforcing processes of technology transfer in all its forms and of political development in its broadest sense during the critical period of the late 1950s and early 1960s, a recognizably "eastern bloc technologi-cal style" for artifacts produced in the Soviet-dominated area began to emerge. Certainly, substantial differences remained among the various eastern bloc counties, not least between the Soviet Union and the GDR. But there were many similarities, conditioned by shared structural traits and cultural values. Among the most important of these were central planning of the economy, plan fulfillment, limited choices in raw materials and components because of limited and overly specified suppliers, legally binding norms, lack of cost consciousness on the part of designers and managers, "an exaggerated interest in mass production owing both to egalitarian ideological precepts and resource scarcities," and "giganto-mania."[51] By the 1970s and 1980s these determinants—many political and ideological—led to goods and machines that were frequently disappointing in design and/or quality. The goods and machines in turn influenced politics in the eastern bloc: inferior consumer goods made it difficult to motivate managers or workers through material enticements, while inferior producer goods ensured the production of more of the same.

But in the early 1960s the ultimate failure of the GDR system of innovation was by no means a foregone conclusion, and certainly not for leading GDR managers and engineers. After August 1961, surrounded by its concrete and virtual "antifascist protective barriers," the GDR was able to continue its socialist experiment unhampered by the ambiguity of the political, economic, and technological arrangement that had followed the end of the war. Accordingly, the East Germans set out to design their new world. They knew that technology would be essential to the realization of their vision. It would also be a main feature in its failure.

Part III | From Fresh Start to Endgame, 1961–1990

| **The Controlled Experiment in Technological Development**
Technology in the
New Economic System

■n terms of technology, the construction of the Berlin Wall in August 1961 had two major effects. On the one hand, it slowed to a trickle the formerly great wave of emigrants to West Germany who had decided upon *Republikflucht*, most of whom were young and many of whom were scientifically or technologically qualified. On the other hand, it brought about some resolution of the former tension between westward and eastward orientation in terms of technology. The wall both necessitated and permitted a clear eastward turn. Overall, the wall did indeed serve as a sort of protective barrier behind which the GDR could pursue the socialist experiment and the reorientation of East German technological culture under relatively controlled conditions, free from the imminent threat of collapse owing to direct pressure from the West.

Although it changed character over time, the experiment undertaken in the GDR in the 1960s was driven primarily by ideological commitment and by political expediency. Notions of socialist technological excellence, of the power of scientific planning of technological change, and of the capacity of the GDR to reform its system from within underpinned many of the programs developed in the 1960s. Allegiance to the Soviet Union and to the Soviet bloc—always a factor in GDR politics, but given new significance owing to the deliberate decision to cut the country off from the West with the wall—also shaped technological choice and change.

These internal ideological and political forces interacted with external ones as the decade of the 1960s unfolded. Several of these external forces are worthy of mention, but three interrelated ones were critical to the evolution of technology in the GDR. The first was the pace and direction of world technological change, especially in the high-technology industries, such as electronics and chemicals, which contributed to technological change in industry across the board. The GDR made genuine breakthroughs in both these fundamental areas during the 1960s, but continued to lag far behind the capitalist countries. A key characteristic of these new technologies was their synergetic relationship with other technologies, which tended to break down traditional barriers between industrial sectors. This was severely at odds with the corporate autarky that characterized GDR industrial and technological organization. In other words, emerging trends in world technological change and the emerging organization of GDR innovation systems stood in contradiction to one another, and this had an impact on the development of GDR technology in relation to technology elsewhere.

Second, the changing nature of international technological development—which involved an eliding of the traditional demarcation between industrial sectors—was linked to a growing internationalization of technology, which involved sharply increased trafficking in machines, licenses, and know-how. International trade increased notably across the board, and, although it is virtually impossible to measure this precisely, international transfer of technology is likely to have increased to an even greater degree. The GDR's relative isolation for political reasons from international markets in both goods and technology, combined with its chronic shortage of foreign exchange, meant that the country could never take full advantage of the dynamism inherent in the international marketplace. At the same time it was forced to compete, directly or indirectly, with products manufactured by companies that could and did take full advantage of these changes.

Third, and linked to the first two factors, the Soviet Union played a vital role in GDR industrial and technological development as a marketplace, as a provider of key raw materials, and as a partner in technological and scientific development. During the 1960s, however, the Soviets, like the East Germans, were affected by the changing nature of technological innovation and by the evolving international marketplace. They were also anxious for security reasons to keep sensitive technologies out of the hands even of their closest allies. During the mid-1960s, therefore, the Soviets began to display resistance to playing the role the GDR required of them, with a considerable impact on the East Germans' economic and technological prospects.

Clearly, the external factors shaping the development of GDR technology in the 1960s meant that the experiment undertaken in the aftermath of the wall's construction could not be carried out under the kind of fully controlled conditions the GDR leadership would have liked. Taken together, these factors also had a pronounced negative effect on GDR technological development, which by the late 1960s had severe economic and political consequences. But it all started much more optimistically, even though there was, as always, an economic and technological crisis.

Technology in the Immediate Aftermath of the Wall's Construction

One of the dilemmas posed during the Second Berlin Crisis involved the extent to which a formal political and economic break with the West was possible in light of the extensive economic and technological dependence of the GDR on the capitalist world, and especially on West Germany.[1] Even before the construction of the wall, GDR decision-makers had begun to move toward *Störfreimachung*, or the process of making East Germany "free from disturbance." The wall in a sense put an end to the immediate political crisis and, in the short term at least, solved the problem of the "brain drain" to West Germany. But it lent a new sense of urgency to dealing with the profound economic and technological crisis in which the GDR found itself by the early 1960s. Heavy reliance on the West, after all, was no longer a viable option. By late 1961 the GDR needed to do two things: first, to pursue integration into the eastern bloc with renewed vigor; and second, to fine-tune its own domestic scientific and technological capability, especially in high-technology areas.

As described in earlier chapters, the East Germans had been making efforts to integrate themselves technologically into the eastern bloc for some years. These efforts included, for instance, borrowing Soviet technical drawings and expertise in the design, construction, and operation of plants in the semiconductor industry and other industries, and harmonizing GDR technical norms and standards with those of the Soviet Union. Such activities continued and intensified in the aftermath of the construction of the Berlin Wall, but to a greater extent than ever before East German policymakers pursued the promotion of socialist division of labor in terms of technological development, primarily through specialization.

For a small yet technologically advanced country such as the GDR, specialization within an integrated Soviet bloc had attractions. One of the main difficulties the country faced from the beginning of its existence—as a result of relative isolation through the division of Germany, the nature of the Soviet occupation, and the Cold War—was a sort of technological hubris. GDR ambitions to rebuild the country's industrial base and to compete on equal terms, not only with much larger West

Germany, but also with other leading industrialized countries, overextended the country's limited and severely taxed resources. The result was a broad range of activities in every major technological area without the requisite depth in many cases. Specialization would allow concentration of resources on specific technologies. Given East Germany's advanced technological capability within the eastern bloc, the country stood to gain from agreements to specialize, since it was likely to benefit from export of high-value-added machinery and equipment to its socialist neighbors. Connections to the Soviet Union were, of course, central to this course of action. As an advisory report to the Politburo put it in January 1962, "*The establishment of close economic cooperation with the Soviet Union is the key question* [to be resolved] *in making our economy free from disturbances.*"[2]

During 1962, in the context of adjustment to the new dispensation following the construction of the wall, discussions on specialization within COMECON intensified. Negotiations regarding machine building, one of the GDR's strongest technological sectors, showed both the promise and the limits of this strategy. A document prepared in spring 1962 set out the GDR's agenda in this regard, and it was ambitious. Despite much discussion, by the early 1960s specialization in the areas of machine building and electrical goods had not gone beyond "very limited beginnings." The main problem to date had been the fact that "the problems of division of labor and specialization [were] not [based] on long-term national plans (10–15 years), which have been coordinated within COMECON." The suggestion for overcoming these difficulties was to develop coordinated, long-term national plans of at least ten years. Planning for specialization should begin with products that either were not produced at all or were produced only in limited quantities within COMECON countries, and should proceed from research and development through production and marketing. In keeping with the long-range-planning perspective, the country that would eventually manufacture the machine should be designated at the first stage. The products should be of the highest technical standard, and should be produced according to unified GOST and/or ISO norms. Bilateral trade relations within COMECON, which had a negative effect upon specialization, would have to be replaced by a multilateral system.[3]

Such ambitious aims formed the basis for the specialization discussions between the GDR and the USSR that began in Moscow in late April 1962. These talks had an inauspicious start. The Soviet delegation opened the negotiations with a hefty critique of the GDR, questioning the East Germans' willingness and ability to realize agreements from the previous year on specialization within COMECON.[4] By the first week of May things had deteriorated even further. Only in heavy machine building had the two sides reached any agreements. In other key areas, such as machine tools, which was one of the GDR's true strengths, there was no resolution. The head of the GDR delegation for machine tools complained, "We have the impression in the working group that we have not come here for negotiations about specialization, but rather solely to a certain sort of trade advising, in order to fulfill demand which has not yet been covered by the domestic production of the Soviet Union." The matter was brought to the attention of high party functionaries in the GDR "to clarify the difficulties that had come about at a higher level."[5]

Relations did improve slightly as time went on, although other difficulties emerged. The GDR, for instance, attempted to gain agreement for the export of automatic lathes from the Werkszeugmaschinenfabrik "7. Oktober" (Machine Tool Works "7 October") in Marzahn to the Soviet Union, but the Soviets turned down the proposal on the grounds that they had sufficient capacity of their own. The Soviet stance meant that Marzahn would have excess capacity, but the Soviets countered that the factory should switch to more specialized production of grinding and polishing machines for interior surfaces, which the Soviet Union would be keen to purchase. This proposition was attractive to the East Germans, but the difficulty was that a vital component of these machines, cutting shafts, was beyond the technical capabilities of either the GDR or the Soviet Union. The cutting shafts would therefore have to be imported in substantial quantities from Italy.[6] In this case, as in many others, attempts to specialize conflicted with attempts to break free from disturbances, and the technological limits of the Soviet bloc became agonizingly apparent.

At the close of the negotiations in late May 1962, the Soviet delegation continued to proclaim the virtues of specialization and to articulate a vision of the place of the GDR in the COMECON context. They claimed that "the GDR should specialize primarily in labor-intensive machines and equipment, which are characterized by precision and a high technological level." And they suggested further discussions on this basis. But East German delegates did not believe this was the true Soviet objective. Instead, they remained convinced that the GDR was being used to the Soviets' own ends: "Our experts repeatedly got the impression that some mid-level functionaries are guided in their decisions by the idea that the GDR is a reservoir for closing gaps hindering their own increases in production."[7] This view was reiterated in the delegation's final report, which also noted that one of the implications of the Soviet stance was that the GDR would be forced "to alter completely the developmental perspectives foreseen for the factories VEB BWF Marzahn und VEB Fräs- und Schleifmaschinenwerk Leipzig."[8]

The wall, it seemed, had stabilized the political situation, but the Soviets were, if anything, even less inclined than before to take the GDR's needs into account. Although in this case the blame was placed on "mid-level" functionaries, it would become clear in the course of the decade that the machine-building delegates' impressions not only were accurate, but also applied to the highest levels of Soviet leadership. The idea that the Soviets were becoming less and less accommodating to the needs of their German ally applied across the board. As noted earlier, the Soviets became more reluctant to supply crude oil in necessary quantities to the GDR, with the consequence that the East Germans had to consider more intensive exploitation of their lignite resources. The Soviets also dragged their feet with regard to cooperation in the area of computing technology.[9] And the general trade agreement signed in 1965 between the Soviets and the GDR was extremely disadvantageous to the smaller country. All these factors, and especially the last, appear to have contributed to the decision by East Germany's leading party economic functionary, Erich Apel, to commit suicide in December 1965. Thus, although the GDR continued energetically to pursue the aim of specialization and technology transfer within the eastern bloc, the East Germans were most active in the immediate aftermath of the construction of the wall in the one place where they believed they might exercise full control over technological development, at home. But domestically, too, 1962 was a year of frustration and casting about for new ideas and solutions.

Like the construction of the wall, the reorganization of the GDR system of innovation after August 1961 had long-term causes, and its full impact took many years to become apparent. One of the major developments of the early 1960s in this area was the elimination of the East German aeronautical industry and the related restructuring of research into automation.

Germany's aviation industry had been one of the most advanced in the world through 1945, but the Allies naturally wished to restrict its activities, especially in research and development. Both sides in the developing Cold War recruited aeronautical engineers from Germany to work on their missile and airplane design and production programs, but the Soviets were particularly effective in this regard. In October 1946 they forcibly deported virtually all aeronautical engineers, scientists, and technicians to the Soviet Union, where they remained for several years, the last of them returning to the GDR in 1954. The returning engineers were put to work primarily on projects to develop and produce middle-range jets and commercial air carriers. Focused on Dresden and Karl-Marx-Stadt, the burgeoning aviation industry employed about 25,000 workers and "became the most important and most expensive industrial innovation project of the late 1950s."[10]

The success of the GDR's aviation industry depended upon selling at least some aircraft to the Soviet Union. But the Soviet decision, beginning in 1957, to focus its military spending primarily on missiles rather than on long-range bombers meant that its own aviation industry had to retool, and it moved into precisely the same markets in which the GDR had hoped to compete. Diminishing Soviet interest in the products of the GDR aviation industry became overwhelmingly apparent by 1959, and in early 1961 a high-ranking Soviet official informed Heinrich Rau, by then the GDR foreign trade minister, that "it is the opinion of the Presidium [of the Supreme Soviet] that the airplane industry in the GDR must be converted." By March the decision had been announced to dismantle the industry entirely.[11]

Compared to many decisions made in the GDR, this one was surprisingly definitive and radical. And it made a great deal of sense. After all, the projected markets for aviation that had been the basis for the industry's existence were simply not there. And the resources, especially in terms of highly trained personnel, devoted to the aviation industry could be redeployed elsewhere. Some of the scientists, engineers, and technicians, of course, took the opportunity to head to the West, where they could continue their professions either in West Germany or elsewhere. But most of them remained in the GDR, moving into R&D sections in industry, to the Institute for Light Construction (Institut für Leichtbau, or IfL), or into the Central Institute for Automation (Zentralinstitut für Automatisierung, or ZIA).[12] The reshuffling continued as the wall went up, and formed part of the ongoing reorganization of the GDR system of innovation after August 1961.

The ZIA was central to this reorganization, for automation was both a central ideological aim of socialism in the GDR and a likely strong suit for GDR industrial development. The GDR had inherited—most prominently through Carl Zeiss in Jena, but also through other companies—a significant proportion of Germany's office-machinery, electro-technical, and optics industries, all of which were important to the development of computing, which in turn formed the basis of automation. Work on a digital computer had begun in 1950 at the technical university in Dresden under the direction of Nikolaus Joachim Lehmann. In 1953–54, in the VEB Carl Zeiss, Herbert Kortum and Wilhelm Kämmerer began work on an optical calculating machine (Optische Rechenmaschine, or OPREMA), a working model of which was available in December 1954. OPREMA was the GDR's first functioning computer. The two versions of it produced at Zeiss in the mid-1950s were used until 1963 and laid the basis for information technology in the GDR.[13]

As a result of this early and, even in international terms, extremely successful work, automation became one of the major tasks set by the SED as a prerequisite for "catching up with and surpassing capitalism in terms of technology." It held a central position alongside mechanization and nuclear power for the "industrial transformation" envisaged in the second Five-Year Plan, approved at the SED's Third Party Conference in 1956.[14] Work continued at several different venues, although Kortum at Zeiss gained in power and influence as the decade proceeded. By 1959 he was able to gain permission to establish a Central Institute for Automation that would be located in Jena and would employ personnel who had worked at Zeiss's automation laboratory, but would also be institutionally independent of the Zeiss firm and directly responsible to the SPK. Kortum would leave Zeiss and assume the directorship of the ZIA officially on 1 January 1960.[15]

The ZIA had four main tasks. First, it did its own research and development on automation processes that were not being developed elsewhere in the GDR. Second, it coordinated and supervised the work of all East German development centers working in the area of automation technology. Third, it offered advice to industry in application of automation systems. And finally, it was to be active in standardization work in the area of automation. By 5 May 1960, when the ZIA was up and running, it employed 250 persons, of whom 212 came from Zeiss. These numbers were supposed to grow rapidly, to 500 by the end of 1961, and to 1,000 by the end of 1964. Organized into various sections, the scientists, engineers, and technicians were to focus on such tasks as "automation in production, control, and measurement technology"; "theoretical problems of automation and computing systems"; "technical development of computing systems"; and "complex automation."[16]

Setting in motion such a large organization dedicated to complex technological research and development was an arduous task, but two things made it still more difficult. The first was the relationship between Zeiss and other industrial firms and the institute. The second, related problem was the personality of the ZIA's director, Dr. Kortum.

Even in the negotiations to establish the ZIA, Kortum pressed for a large staff, and he was able to get many of them from Zeiss. His request to hive off even more parts of Zeiss's R&D sections, however, was turned down by the SPK in 1959, in the final negotiations to form the institute, and was something Zeiss's directors were both aware of and opposed to. But during 1960 Kortum continued to try to recruit additional personnel from Zeiss and from other factories, such as the VEB Funkwerk Erfurt and the VEB Keramische Werke Hermsdorf. In the context of the alarming and increasing shortage of scientific and engineering talent in the GDR as the Second Berlin Crisis came to a head, disputes over recruitment of personnel were particularly bitter. Disagreements of this sort with Zeiss took on additional significance because the ZIA was also beholden to the company for laboratory facilities and space. Zeiss's leadership had had misgivings about appointing Kortum to his position in the first place and now showed considerable reluctance in allowing use of the company's apparatus and laboratories, as well as in providing accommodations for the growing numbers of ZIA personnel.[17]

Undoubtedly, one of the reasons why these inevitable territorial disputes grew so heated had to do with the personality of the director, Dr. Kortum. Kortum did not get on well with the first deputy director of the Zeiss Works, Herbert Weiz, who, from 1958, was also a member of the SED's central committee. Normally neutral and sober documents from the period indicate "personal tension" between the two, "which exists . . . because of the personal qualities of Dr. Kortum." Erich Apel, the SED's main functionary for the economy, himself reported on the case to Ulbricht, speaking to him of "the well-known difficulties" in the formation of the ZIA, "which are connected in no small way with the character of Dr. Kortum."[18]

A clash of this sort in the GDR could only be resolved through intervention at the highest level. The area over which Kortum presided was considered so important to the country's prestige and competitive prospects as to overcome any reservations about his personality, at least initially. In summer 1960 Ulbricht directed Apel to inform the SPK and local party functionaries in Jena "that—in spite of all the subjective diffi- culties that arise in the beginning stages of the establishment of the institute—[they are] to force forward the establishment of the institute with all available resources . . . [and] to make available the necessary personnel." Kortum was to be brought into regular meetings with the SPK to specify the measures needed to enable the plans for the expansion of his institute to be realized.[19]

But the persistence of this problem in a crucial area of technology, in the midst of the general political-economic crisis of the late 1950s and early 1960s in East Germany, eventually led to more drastic measures, which in turn were linked to the crisis of the aviation industry. In early 1961 the ZIA was simply closed down in Jena and moved to Dresden. The move offered several advantages. First, Dresden had a surplus of scien- tific and engineering personnel from the now defunct aviation industry, and many of these people went to work in the ZIA. Second, the move promised some cost savings, important in view of the GDR's financial crisis. Third, Dresden was far away from Jena, which made the problem of establishing the division of responsibility between Zeiss and the ZIA a far less visible source of friction, and also helped slow down the outflow of qualified personnel from East to West Germany even before the con- struction of the wall. The locational advantage offered by Dresden was reinforced by a key personnel change: ZIA's problematic director, Dr. Kortum, was replaced by Professor Jancke.[20]

By the time the wall went up, the ZIA was established in Dresden, and East German authorities could hope that their drastic measures to re- form a key institution in the development of automation technology would have a positive effect. But although the centralized decision- making structure of the GDR offered rapid response to crisis in this and other instances, it also had tremendous drawbacks. The previous (and, despite the problematic relationship between the directors, often fruit- ful) connection between the ZIA and Zeiss was broken, and the research directions developed through that connection were disrupted. Establish- ing the new ZIA required redefinition of tasks, integration of new project teams, and design and construction of new premises. All in all, a "pause in the process of innovation" occurred, which lasted until at least 1963.[21] In the area of automation, in which the GDR was already lagging behind the West, this self-imposed obstacle was devastating to the GDR's pros- pects in high-technology development.

As East German scientists and policymakers struggled to reorient and rejuvenate the ZIA in the aftermath of the construction of the wall, they also became aware of other problems facing the GDR system of innovation, some of long standing and some relatively recent. In the electronics industry, producers were still plagued with shortages, high prices, and poor-quality transistors—the worst of all possible worlds—from GDR suppliers. The problems began with the manufacture of basic materials and continued into production and distribution. The price of germanium in East Germany was about nine times what it was in West Germany. Yields of high-quality transistors of all sorts continued to lag far behind typical international levels. And instead of addressing the problem, manufacturers simply adopted "a 'miniature tonnage ideology'" that in one case saw the delivery of 6,000 transistors, of which only 1,000 were useable. Attempts nonetheless to keep up with growing demand for finished electronic goods from consumers and industry led to an increasing rather than a decreasing level of dependence on imports, mostly from the capitalist West.[22]

License policy was also proving to be a difficult aspect of the GDR system of innovation. In this case, there was a general critique that focused primarily on the chemical industry. In 1960 the Buna Works in Schkopau had paid 1.3 million DM in hard currency to Karl Ziegler for a license for his low-pressure, high-density polyethylene (HDPE) process. Two years later, however, "no conception existed as to when or even how the low-pressure polyethylene facility would be built." In February 1960 the Leuna Works in Merseburg had agreed to pay £298,000 by spring 1963 to Humphreys & Glasgow in London for licenses for an ethylene production facility that was not supposed to begin production until 1968.[23] In the meantime, the GDR remained unable to produce polyethylene, a vital modern plastic, on an industrial scale.[24]

Attitudes of engineers and managers also continued to be problematic. Discussions were carried out in all industrial sectors on how best to improve general technological levels and how to involve workers and engineers in making incremental innovations in products and processes. Some of these discussions focused on industrial areas, such as semiconductors and some parts of the chemical industry, that had clearly begun to lag seriously behind the West. But in other areas, such as machine building and machine tools, the danger was not so much lag as complacency. In September 1962, for instance, the chief engineer at the VEB Großdrehmaschinenbau "7. Oktober" in Berlin was quoted as saying:

"In our factory, there is nothing else to improve. We already have the best technology."[25] Further discussion centered on the perennial need to transfer research results into production.[26]

All in all, the number and scale of the difficulties facing the GDR in terms of scientific and technical development in the early 1960s continued to be depressingly large. Yet the wall gave policymakers a sense of finally having the space and time to confront these challenges and to demonstrate once and for all the technological, economic, and political superiority of socialism to capitalism. They grasped the opportunity to do so in a series of dramatic reforms beginning in 1963.

Technology under the New Economic System, 1963–1966

Aging Stalinist though he was, Walter Ulbricht presided over a daring and extensive attempt at systemic reform during the 1960s. The centerpiece of the reform movement was the New Economic System of Planning and Management of the Economy (NES), approved in principle by the GDR Council of Ministers in July 1963. From the outset, the NES has been a focal point of discussion by policymakers and scholars, many of whom regarded (and in some cases still regard) it as a litmus test of the very possibility of reform of Soviet-style economic and political systems. For many, the NES provides vital clues to answering a variety of questions about the nature of centrally planned economies: Were such systems doomed by their very nature? Or was the NES an opportunity to fine-tune one such system, rendering it viable in the long term? It failed, but what caused the failure? And could it have succeeded?[27]

The gravity of the questions indicates that the NES was also a turning point in the history of the GDR. Technology was an essential component, in terms of both NES objectives and targets of planning, and NES implementation. But it was more than that. During the NES, more than in any other period, technology served as the linchpin linking the theory and practice of communism in the GDR; it also revealed the fundamental tensions inherent in the communist experiment and seemed to indicate some of communism's natural limits.

The NES represented a reformist vision for the socialist world. Based on the ideas of Evsei Liberman, a Soviet professor of economics whose ideas were legitimized through their publication in *Pravda* in September 1962, the NES sought to introduce elements of decentralization and the market economy to Soviet-style socialism. Rather than an economy based almost exclusively on a centrally developed and administered plan, the NES proposed that much of the responsibility for carrying out the centrally devised objectives for production was to be devolved to the various industrial associations (Vereine Volkseigene Betriebe, or VVB), which were organized by industrial sector. The VVBs became legal personalities and were eventually subject to new laws for making contracts. The carrot and the stick for making sure that the VVBs carried out their essential tasks under the new system were a series of "economic levers," which included such variables as prices, costs, turnover, profit, and bonuses, and which therefore looked suspiciously like capitalist "levers." However, prices were never completely freed up, centralized planning was never fully discarded, and strict limits were set on profit and bonuses. Still, given the previous Stalinist centralized planning that had characterized the GDR's economy and those of its eastern European neighbors, the NES constituted a major change.[28]

In its first years, it also appeared to be a resounding success, measured in terms of growth of physical output. Despite a stagnant labor market, the GDR was able to turn in rates of growth in net material product of about 5 percent per year between 1964 and 1968. The extent to which this was attributable solely to the NES is debatable, however. One commentator has pointed out that most of the NES reforms were not even implemented until 1968, which meant that the reform program alone cannot have accounted for this growth. Instead, growth appears to have been based primarily on two NES-related measures that were implemented early on: the Bonus Fund Decree of 1963, and the general slack allowed to the economy through the NES's initially realistic plan targets and its dedication to decentralization.[29]

In any case, technology was both a means and an end within the context of NES. The system of "levers" utilized by NES had been legitimized by the Soviet willingness to entertain the ideas of Liberman in 1962. Similarly, in 1961, the willingness of the Communist Party of the Soviet Union to define science as a "force of production" had moved it ideologically from the superstructure to the base. This allowed the GDR to do the same thing officially in 1963. The GDR also took this opportunity to define applied social sciences—as used, for instance, in economic planning—as a force of production as well.[30] For East Germany, this ideological redefinition must have been a godsend, for it legitimated a practical necessity. Short of labor and skilled in science and technology, the GDR economy could only achieve satisfactory growth through the fostering of science-based industry.

But what did this ideological redefinition mean for technological development in the GDR in practical terms? First of all, it meant that science and technology policy gained a new measure of legitimacy and priority in planning and allocation of resources. One important indicator of this change was a series of alterations in the bureaucratic status of research policy within the GDR government apparatus. The Central Office for Research and Technology (Zentrales Amt für Forschung und Technik, or ZAFT) was established within the SPK in 1950, where it remained until 1957. ZAFT was responsible for the planning of research and development, but had in real terms only advisory and investigatory functions. Actual decisions on research directions and allocation of funding were in the hands of individual factories or industrial groups. With the creation of the Research Council in 1957, ZAFT was placed under the control of this new elite group, but again retained primarily advisory functions. It was really only in the 1960s, after the construction of the Berlin Wall, that science and technology policy took on a key role in the central administration of the GDR. In October 1961 ZAFT was moved up to the status of a State Secretariat for Research and Technology. In July 1967 the State Secretariat became a full-fledged Ministry for Science and Technology. Each organizational change entailed an increase in the importance of research and development in the planning apparatus that was central to power in the GDR.[31] Expenditures for research and development grew in tandem with this enhanced bureaucratic status. Between 1959 and 1963 spending on research and development increased by more than one-third.[32] During the 1960s growth rates for R&D spending were substantial.

But the enhanced bureaucratic status of research and technology, and increased spending on it, were not the only indicators of major changes in the aftermath of the construction of the Berlin Wall and in the context of the New Economic System. The ideological redefinition of science and technology in the GDR in the early 1960s also involved, as a key component of general measures to decentralize planning and production, the introduction of the principle of "contract research," which was something completely new to the eastern European communist economies. Research for specific projects was contracted out by industry and the state to various laboratories, either in other industries or in the universities and polytechnics.[33]

Changes in the ideological place of science and technology in the GDR had major ramifications for the GDR system of innovation, both in institutional terms and in terms of allocation and deployment of resources.

But what impact did this have on the output of the system of innovation—in other words, upon the machines and processes that fed the GDR's economy and its consumers? The mid-1960s were, after all, years of tremendous growth rates in material production, made possible by technological improvement.

At least some of this increase in output was due to the realization, after many years of effort, of several high-technology projects. The output of plastics in the GDR, for instance, began increasing substantially in the early 1960s, and especially after 1963, with the mastering of polyethylene production technology, among others. Between 1955 and 1966 the total output of plastics increased by a factor of 3.5, an annual rate of increase of about 12 percent. Most of this growth occurred between 1960 and 1966, when output more than doubled. During this period, plastics production in the GDR continued to differ from world norms, being dominated—although to a lessening degree—by polyvinyl chloride (PVC), which accounted for nearly 60 percent of output in 1955 and about 44 percent in 1966. Polyethylene production, which in other major industrial countries had overtaken PVC by 1966, was still quite limited in the GDR in 1965, at just 2 percent of total plastics production. But output of polyethylene increased by a factor of four between 1965 and 1966, when large-scale production of low-density polyethylene came on-line at Leuna. To be sure, polyethylene production still lagged far behind world norms, but at just over 8 percent of total plastics manufacture in 1966, the GDR appeared to be catching up. This increase in the output of various sorts of plastics had a knock-on effect on other industries and on the design of consumer and producer goods as plastics and synthetic fibers were increasingly substituted for more traditional materials, such as wood, metal, and cloth. The relatively slow adoption of polyethylene production appears to have had a substantial impact on design, and was part of the reason for the old-fashioned look of many GDR consumer articles beginning in the 1960s.[34]

During the mid-1960s, too, the Frankfurt semiconductor works dramatically expanded production of semiconductor components for the electrical industry. By 1965, 82.3 million East German marks' worth of semiconductors counted toward total electronic component production of 223.3 million marks. This total nearly tripled again by 1969, while the value of semiconductor output increased well over four times. By 1971 the total value of electronic components produced in the GDR was 1.1 billion marks, while the value of semiconductor manufactures was 535 million marks.[35] Again, the knock-on effects were considerable, as industries from chemicals to machine tools and from the producer sector to the consumer sector altered the design of their products and the processes for producing them to take advantage of electronics technology.

The accomplishments of the GDR in technology-intensive areas became more and more apparent to the everyday East German as the 1960s went on. In 1965 the first experimental color television broadcasts were made, while the following year saw the GDR's first atomic power plant come on line in Rheinsberg. By 1968 more than 60 percent of all households in the GDR had a television, a figure that rose to nearly 70 percent in 1970. And by the beginning of the 1970s, 15.5 percent of GDR households had a car, while well over 50 percent had electric refrigerators and washing machines.[36] Certainly, the GDR was still lagging behind the Federal Republic, where as early as 1962–63 more than half of households possessed a refrigerator and one-third of all "employee households" had some sort of automobile.[37] But the communist country was demonstrably able to provide key consumer durables to a large and growing proportion of its population.

It is important to keep in mind that all these developments in large-scale production of plastics and semiconductors, as well as the breakthroughs in other industrial sectors that were passed on to consumers by the mid- to late 1960s, were the result of long-term trends that were not necessarily caused by the NES. Changes in the institutional and funding basis of the GDR system of innovation could be undertaken relatively quickly, but despite the hopes of Ulbricht and the other supporters of the NES, they would take a considerable amount of time to result in new and dramatically better products and processes. Quite simply, time for realizing the full benefits of the changes to the GDR system of innovation through the NES ran out, overcome by the irresistible forces of political intrigue and international events.

Before discussing the failure of the NES, however, it will be useful to consider its initial years from another angle. For the NES was not simply a case of economic policy and ideology determining (or attempting to determine) technological development. The very ideological and economic changes envisaged by leaders in the GDR during the NES period presupposed and relied upon extensive technological change, which revealed tensions in technology policy and suggested the natural limits of the communist project itself. As usual, everything came together in the planning process, although to an extent unknown before or afterward in the history of the GDR.

The first atomic power station in the GDR, the Rheinsberg facility, which came on-line in 1966. It symbolized the GDR's close relations with the Soviet Union and its apparent technological capability during the hopeful years of the New Economic System. *Bundesarchiv, Koblenz, Bildsammlung Bild 183/E0506/04/5*

Planning an economy depends in large part upon two things: First, information on the resources available to the economy and on the demand for goods within the economy must be both timely and reliable. Second, the information must be processed in a sophisticated and rapid manner, allowing quick and agile decision-making. Perfect information perfectly processed in real time constituted a dream for socialist (and even capitalist) planners throughout the twentieth century.[38] That dream, of course, was never realized, and there is considerable doubt as to whether or not it is even theoretically possible.[39] Even approaching this dream, however, as the GDR and other eastern bloc countries were driven out of ideological necessity to do in the 1960s, required extensive technological development, especially in areas such as semiconductors, computing, and systems theory. This is one reason for the high priority assigned to electronics in official party pronouncements and economic planning in the 1960s and for the high profile accorded to cybernetics during the same period, once the ideological battle surrounding it had been won with Ulbricht's support by 1965.[40]

Trying to achieve the goal of technologically sophisticated planning, however, appears to have brought to the fore fundamental tensions within the East German system of innovation. Whatever its virtues, the East German system of planning had not been particularly good at fostering product and process innovation in high-technology industries during the 1950s, as previous chapters have shown. Capitalist countries were, by and large, better able to deliver new products and processes. Arguably, one of the main reasons for this discrepancy could be found in the more decentralized nature of planning and innovation under capitalism. Funding for research and development and procurement was a tool used by more or less centralized state authorities in capitalist countries to direct the innovation enterprise. But the tools here were rather more blunt and rather less coercive than under the socialist system. The bulk of R&D work was carried out in a more decentralized—and often quite competitive—way, often within the confines of more or less autonomous companies, universities, and research institutes.

In other words, it appears that in order to achieve its goal of more effective centralized control of the economy through the deployment of sophisticated data processing, the GDR would have had to decentralize R&D efforts far more radically. The NES was characterized by strong attempts at decentralization, but it seems that achieving the aim of effective innovation in the area of electronics would have required still greater efforts, which would have been unacceptable to a Soviet-style state. This was one important contradiction within the East German system brought out by the attempts to improve planning during the 1960s.

The primacy of considerations of planning in the development of this key technology may also have had unforeseen, and largely deleterious, consequences for it. Nikolaus Lehmann, a pioneer in GDR information technology, in a book coauthored after the fall of the wall, claims that the emphasis on using computers primarily for planning purposes, rather than, for instance, for designing machines or solving scientific problems, lent a heavy "administrative technological" slant to computing development in the GDR, with disadvantageous consequences.[41] The political objectives of the regime are thus likely to have had important effects on the development of computing technology.

The reverse, moreover, was also true: political tensions arose directly from the development of computing technology. As became clear in the discussions that ended the NES (or the Economic System of Socialism, or ESS, as it had come to be known by the late 1960s) in the early 1970s, the adoption of more "scientific" planning techniques and technologies implied a greater reliance on applied scientists and mathematicians. The logic of the situation was that this would involve a concomitant decrease in the power and control of politicians and policymakers, something the politicians were by and large not willing to contemplate. Thus, although high technological standards for planning remained something East German policymakers embraced in principle, they were unwilling to bring them about for political and ideological reasons. The unwillingness to take the necessary steps in this direction amplified the already very noticeable inadequacies of the system of innovation in the GDR, continuing the unfortunate patterns of technological change that had emerged as early as the 1950s.

Renewed Crisis and the End of the Ulbricht Era, 1966–1970

By 1966 the West German economic miracle was clearly coming to an end as the economy dipped into a severe recession. In contrast, the East German economy still seemed buoyant, especially in high-technology areas and in the production of technical consumer goods. But even here, growth slowed to an average annual rate of about 5 percent between 1966 and 1975. Although this far exceeded rates of growth in the West during this period, it was well below the double-digit increases of much of the

1950s, and lagged behind most of the other eastern bloc countries.[42] Furthermore, the East German growth rates occurred on a far smaller base than those of West Germany, so that the distance between them in terms of standard of living continued. Even more important, some shortages cropped up in several areas, not all of them technically sophisticated.

The government's response was to embrace still more strongly programs to promote high-technology development, since Ulbricht and his supporters continued to believe that this would serve as the basis for improvements in the supply of consumer goods. In the ESS Principles for 1969 and 1970, which were approved in 1968, priority in planning and allocation of resources was given to "structure-determining" industries, which included chemicals and electrical goods. Characteristic of this "planning according to structure-determining tasks" was an emphasis on technologically advanced products and centralized (and fairly long-term) production and R&D planning. The latter characteristic has often been cited as evidence that the ESS constituted a move away from the decentralization characteristic of the NES and back toward a more centralized, Soviet-style model of economic planning and practice. More effective promotion of research and development was to be accomplished through the concentration of production into very large units, as enterprises were organizationally integrated with their suppliers of parts and materials into combines. A similar linkage was to occur between industry and academic science, which were to be "institutionally tied together in large-scale science centers [*Großforschungszentren*] and large-scale research associations and in this way to implement the intention to subordinate research to the production interests of industry."[43]

Ulbricht's efforts to promote technologically sophisticated industries as a basis for further industrial development and consumer provision ultimately met with failure. To a large degree, that failure was a direct result of those efforts, which created imbalances in the economy and thus substantial shortages of key goods. Investment in high-technology industry had been high under the NES, but that was possible only because investment in less technologically advanced areas was kept relatively low. Furthermore, despite attempts at price reform under the NES, the costs of production bore little relation to the price at which goods were sold. Combines that manufactured new, improved products could and did charge prices that bore no relation to the cost of materials, and to which the state added a hefty surcharge, while more traditional goods remained heavily subsidized.[44]

There were, of course, other factors at work in the failure of the NES. The initial ham-handed efforts at planning the economy during the 1950s had already created a culture of innovation within which interdisciplinary contacts and contacts between enterprises were infrequent and of poor quality. The NES had tried in vain to alter that structure. Add to that the increasing reluctance of the Soviet Union to support its German ally in various crucial ways. By the second half of the 1960s, for example, the USSR refused to cooperate fully with the GDR in the development of computing, partly for trade reasons, but also on account of security concerns related to this militarily vital technology.[45] Additionally, the Soviet Union reneged on deliveries of key raw materials, including petroleum, which halted the transition of the East German chemical industry from coal-based to petroleum-based chemistry. Across the board, difficulties in obtaining key raw materials from the Soviet Union forced East German industry to become more rather than less autarkic in its outlook, which in turn promoted technologies (such as acetylene-based chemistry) that were out of synch with international trends. And this had a knock-on effect on the competitiveness of East German products on foreign markets. It was an unfortunate cycle, which the NES did little to counteract.

The combination of all these factors had an impact on the domestic scene: although goods such as televisions were available in greater and greater numbers for purchase by East German families, shortages of items such as toothbrushes and toilet paper were becoming more acute. There were only two possible ways out of the situation. The first would have been to push the reform effort to more radical extremes still. But this had been rendered impossible by the combination of the frustration engendered by the aging and still unsuccessful NES, on the one hand, and the Prague spring of 1968, on the other. The alternative was to abandon the reform effort in favor of a more conservative path, which promised a return to the old certainties of planning while at the same time providing more consumer goods. Under the slogan of "the unity of social and economic policy," Erich Honecker was able to oust Walter Ulbricht from his position as leader of the SED in 1971, thus becoming the GDR's second leader.

Ulbricht's New Economic System was undertaken as a radical project to revamp the GDR's economic system and system of innovation. Initiated in the aftermath of the radical political stabilization that followed the construction of the Berlin Wall, the NES involved some important changes to the GDR system of innovation through such measures as contract research and decentralized responsibility for R&D. But, on balance, it still did not change the system radically. It did not grapple with fundamental problems of the sharing of information among various institutions, the effective linking of fundamental with applied research, and the motivation of researchers.

Still, despite these admissions, it is unlikely that the NES or any other set of reforms could have overcome the fundamental problem of the GDR economy and its technology: the country was simply too small to be viable on its own, either in terms of traditional raw materials or ideas. Forced to throw in its lot with the Soviets, it soon found that it could not rely on them for what it desperately needed because the USSR was suspicious of the GDR technologically, commercially, and in terms of military security. No amount of internal reform in East Germany could counteract that. Eventually, the GDR's solution to this technological conundrum mirrored the solution of the political-economic problem: it abandoned essential and far-reaching reforms in favor of half-measures, seeking substitutes for success.

|

The palace coup that pushed the aging Walter Ulbricht out of power in the early 1970s involved a series of complicated political maneuvers, which were in the end won by the faction surrounding the GDR's new leader, Erich Honecker. The old leader had managed to alienate powerful constituencies, not least the Soviets, through his reluctance to engage in détente with the West and his apparent mishandling of economic policy. Honecker's takeover of power was therefore a profoundly political affair, but it was one prompted in large part by economic and technological conditions, which although generally improving, continued to disappoint everyone, not least GDR consumers.

The ascendancy of Honecker, who stressed the "unity of economic and social policy," meant that consumers would be moved from the periphery to the center of the planning process. Housing and consumer goods would be the primary focus of state spending. Export-oriented industries, including such traditional sectors as the chemical and machine-tool industries, continued to be the darlings of the state planning apparatus and received considerable investment. Still, many expensive industrial investment programs, especially in high-technology areas, were in effect abandoned during the 1970s through persistent underinvestment and generalized neglect at the highest levels of policymaking. In particular, for instance, computerized numerical control (CNC) technology for machine tools was simply ignored in the GDR when it came into prominence beginning in the early 1970s. Jörg Roesler goes so far as to claim that "the SED leadership which had just come to power under Honecker had for the moment closed the book on Ulbricht's efforts to keep pace in GDR industry with the scientific-technical revolution."[1]

One does not have to be an economist to recognize some fundamental problems with this system. When the state is, for all practical purposes, the primary investor in the economy as a whole, shifting priorities to consumer goods production and construction of housing requires that there be correspondingly lower levels of industrial investment. If industrial investment is insufficient, productivity will at best be static. In crude terms, this means—in the medium term, at least—no increases in the amount of goods available for export (which were often producer goods). Increases in the amount of goods available for distribution to consumers could be obtained only at the expense of producer-good production and/or of imports necessary to increase such production, which in the longer term would have a deleterious effect on the amount of consumer goods available.

How, then, was steadily growing availability of consumer goods to be obtained over the longer term? Higher levels of foreign debt were one way, and this was a strategy the Honecker regime (along with others in eastern Europe) employed with gusto. Another was to seek better relations with the Federal Republic, which would have the effect of making more credit and more hard currency (through gifts and visits from relatives and friends) available to the GDR economy. The Honecker regime excelled in making *Ostpolitik* a paying proposition.

Politically, then, Honecker and his government were highly effective in getting others—and generally their capitalist rivals—to pay for policies that had the effect of stabilizing the GDR regime. These lucrative foreign policy successes (at least in the short to medium term) go far toward explaining the—admittedly frequently fragile—viability of the GDR regime under Honecker from 1971 to 1989. But these explanations do not suffice, for they ignore key elements of GDR domestic policy during the same period, which enhanced the GDR's ability to survive and even (at least in comparison to other eastern bloc countries) to flourish in the short and medium term, but which also helped ensure the country's long-term downfall. Honecker, after all, not only maintained the GDR's traditional focus on scientific and technological development, but also oversaw the expansion of efforts in two important areas related to technology. The first was the development of a sophisticated system of recycling of secondary materials and development of substitute raw materials; the second was the expansion and redirection of the Ministry for State Security (Ministerium für Staatssicherheit, MfS, or Stasi).

At first glance, the two make an odd pair, and to my knowledge the links between them have not yet been noted by scholars. Recycling and ersatz materials development tended to involve a relatively low level of technological sophistication. Partly because of this, the secondary raw materials system (Sekundärrohstoff, or Sero) was a highly visible area of technological and organizational development, which featured high levels of participation among the general public. The Stasi, in contrast, was an elite, highly secretive group that, in the area of science and technology, concentrated primarily on high-technology sectors. The aim was to promote leading-edge technologies believed to have a pronounced economic impact.[2] In fact, as we shall see, the Stasi's efforts did not have the desired effect of pushing the GDR toward overcoming its deficits in the area of innovation, which distinguishes it further from the effort regarding secondary and substitute raw materials: the lower profile, less sophisticated program quite possibly had a far greater positive economic impact than did the high-profile, highly sophisticated one.

But despite these contrasts, the two can be usefully regarded as two strands of the same impulse. They represented a reinvigorated and expanded—and for those reasons qualitatively new—attempt to develop techniques for overcoming domestic shortages (of raw materials, foreign currency, machines and know-how) through substitution. They also both grew in prominence as a direct result of Honecker's ascension to power, which lends added weight to an interpretation emphasizing commonalities rather than differences.

Secondary and Substitute Materials

From the beginning of its existence, Germany had been a relatively advanced industrial state, but it possessed few of the raw materials necessary for industrialization. The main—and very significant—exception, of course, was the high-grade coal of the Ruhr district. But iron ore reserves were of poor quality, nonferrous metals were practically nonexistent, and oil was available only in minuscule amounts. This last item became critical as petroleum products slowly grew in importance during the late nineteenth and early twentieth centuries, first for lighting and then as a fuel.

This situation had two major implications. First of all, Germany was forced to rely upon export of finished goods in order to be able to import necessary raw materials, and therefore depended on world trade to a far greater degree than other major industrialized nations, such as Britain, France, or the United States. Second, dependence on foreign countries for raw materials and markets was an uncomfortable position in the minds of most world leaders—and certainly those in Germany—in the late nineteenth and early twentieth centuries; it was, moreover, untenable in the case of war. Germany therefore frequently favored development of substitute materials for achieving autarky, or domestic self-sufficiency. From the start, this tendency was supported heavily by the highly developed organic chemical industry. Through 1945 the industry supplied substitutes for a wide variety of economically and strategically important goods that Germany would normally have had to import, including dyestuffs, nitrates, rubber, and petroleum. Generally, the substitutes were produced from the country's abundant coal resources.

The division of Germany after 1945 left the Soviet zone (later the GDR) with even less coal, and of poorer quality, than was available in the West, while most other raw materials remained in short supply. One exception—uranium—was vital in the dawning nuclear age, although the Soviets rather than the East Germans retained strict control over this resource throughout the GDR's existence.[3] Shortages of raw materials, in turn, encouraged even closer attention to the two traditional ways out of this dilemma, foreign trade and autarky.

Both these courses were fraught with danger. Although the risks associated with autarky—the tendency for quality to be lower and/or prices to be higher than for goods obtained on international markets—were practically identical to those that existed before 1945, the dangers associated with foreign trade were slightly different from those of the earlier period. Foreign trade, especially with the capitalist West, was difficult to develop after 1945, partly for political reasons and partly because much of the experience and organization for foreign sales and purchasing lay in West Germany. The GDR's relatively poorer performance in most technological areas compared to West Germany and many other capitalist producers was also a disincentive for other countries to buy its goods. This relatively poor showing in technology, of course, did not apply across the board, and it grew in importance after the 1950s. But in any case fewer sales abroad meant less foreign currency for purchasing raw materials. Moreover, as the 1950s progressed and the Cold War intensified in the context of the Second Berlin Crisis, the GDR, with Soviet encouragement, undertook the policy of "breaking free from disturbances" (*Störfreimachung*), which applied to all imports from the capitalist world, from raw materials to finished products.

By the early 1960s the GDR's traditional range of options for overcoming limited natural resources had narrowed, for political, economic, and technological reasons. Basically, the country could either work to build up foreign trade with the eastern bloc, and primarily with the Soviet

Union, in order to obtain crucial starting goods and raw materials, or it could intensify programs pushing for increased levels of autarky. In practice, both paths were taken, although in the atmosphere of heightened optimism following the drastic solution of the Berlin Crisis through the construction of the wall, the former was emphasized. As East German interest in Soviet technology and standards grew in the late 1950s and early 1960s, so did the hope that scientific and technological cooperation and increasing levels of trade between the two countries would flourish. An analogous situation existed with regard to supplies of raw materials from the Soviet Union to the GDR. The Soviets appeared to be willing and able to supply critical resources for GDR industry, not least oil.[4] As noted earlier, however, the optimism in both cases was misplaced. Promised deliveries of petroleum and other crucial resources did not materialize during the 1960s, and the GDR had no reason to believe that the situation would improve in the immediate future.

By the late 1960s, therefore, the GDR could add uncertainty over supplies of raw materials to its long list of economic woes. Walter Ulbricht's fall from power and the takeover by a new team headed by Erich Honecker were accompanied by a renewed emphasis on domestic development of substitutes for imported raw materials and on extremely efficient use of both imported and domestic ones. In fact, the change in policy took effect almost immediately after Honecker replaced Ulbricht as first secretary of the Central Committee in early May 1971. The Eighth Party Congress, which took place in mid-June, considered various documents related to "the second-hand materials economy and trade [*Altstoffwirtschaft*]," which were then translated into political action through a secretarial decision of 1 September. The areas took on renewed significance for economic planning and performance for the rest of the GDR's existence.

Government responsibility for secondary raw materials was under the control of the Ministry for the Materials Economy and Trade. This ministry had been formed at the end of 1965, but its responsibilities were considerably expanded between 1971, when the secretarial decision was passed, and 1976, when the Ministerial Council of the GDR enacted a statute detailing the extended competences of the ministry. Economic realization of the ministry's directives was left largely to the VVB Altstoffwirtschaft, within which the VEB Sekundärrohstoff operated, although the ministry also controlled other organizations, such as the VEB Minol, which was primarily responsible for operating the GDR's filling-station network. It also oversaw the actions of scientific and technical laboratories devoted to research and development in the area of rational use of materials, recycling, and so on.[5]

Organizationally, the ministry, and especially the VEB Sekundärrohstoff, or Sero, managed to extend its influence over virtually all areas of the East German economy during the 1970s and 1980s. The operation of Sero's collection and recycling centers was materially aided by the GDR state apparatus through the appointment of "state-sanctioned deputies for the secondary raw materials economy," who worked to support its aims within state agencies and combines, either full-time or part-time, depending on the size of the organization.[6]

Sero itself, supported by its "deputies" within state and industry, steadily expanded its operations during the 1970s and 1980s as the GDR economy was stretched to its limits. Commenting in 1982 on a report to the Ministerial Council on Sero's extended remit during the previous decade, one SED official noted with satisfaction that "the GDR is in the most advanced international state in the identification, registration, and utilization of secondary raw materials." Its activities, he reported, were primarily in the areas of metals, plastics, textiles, and glass recycling, which remained the most significant areas throughout the GDR's existence. In each of them, though, there was room for improvement.[7]

Despite the party's official insistence on achieving a usage rate for secondary raw materials on the order of 80–85 percent by 1985, there were many deficiencies.[8] Problems with sorting, for instance in the case of "scrap alloys," meant that only 60 percent could be utilized in the production of "ferrous alloys." Some areas performed even worse. Only 3 percent of the rare metals in discarded electrotechnical and electronic goods were sorted in such a way as to make them readily reusable, while only 4–5 percent of the thermoplastics that might have been recycled actually were. Even areas in which the GDR performed better left something to be desired. Glass production was one particularly telling example. Glass was very important for the distribution of vital and widely used consumer goods. Yet less than 40 percent of each ton of glass produced in the GDR used broken (that is, recycled) glass, which was far below the international average. The Federal Republic of Germany had attained a proportion of broken glass of up to 90 percent, particularly in the production of green glass. Partly because of this, in the GDR only 4 percent of containers were made from green glass, while the western European average was 25 percent. Furthermore, up to 20 percent of all bottles deployed in the economy were not returned, while nearly 30 percent of used paper was not recycled.[9]

These deficiencies were important, and not only because the GDR was short of a wide variety of raw materials. It was also argued that better performance in recycling could stimulate high-value-added GDR exports as well. The growing world demand for environmentally friendly machines and for recycling technologies was recognized early on.[10] The GDR was proud of, and wished to publicize, its achievements and its commitment to these technologies.[11]

But the challenge to GDR industry and society was clear as well. The GDR was not producing recycling-related machines and apparatus for export, and it was lagging considerably behind its goal of using 80–85 percent of its waste gainfully by the mid-1980s. The organizational limits to attaining this target had apparently already been reached. The only way of attaining the goal was to improve scientific and technical performance.

In true bureaucratic fashion, the Ministry of the Material Economy and Trade termed its programs to promote recycling and to use "industrial waste products" the "further deepening of the intensification of the process of social reproduction."[12] An additional aspect of this process was the application of science and technology to support these other activities. Working together with the Ministry of Science and Technology, the Material Economy Ministry developed plans and operated laboratories devoted to finding additional applications of generally available materials. The ministry also examined ways of promoting more lightweight construction in order to save materials, methods of improving corrosion resistance, and better means of packaging to avoid waste. Finally, it was responsible for "research in areas for deployment and of technologies for preparation and processing for the intensified use of secondary raw materials and the waste products of industry."[13]

These activities improved the efficiency and methods of Sero and other organizations associated with expanded use and reuse of materials, and prompted fears of foreign governments stealing the GDR's secrets. As the Ministry for State Security noted in a report on the activities of foreign intelligence networks in the GDR in 1979, "in particular research on the better usage of domestic raw materials awakened the interest of the other side and was the cause of specifically targeted enemy activities (e.g., offers of scientific-technical 'cooperation' or else corresponding 'exchange of information')." In the report, such foreign incursions into research and development and processes for utilizing secondary materials ranked alongside similar ones in the electronics, metallurgy, and machine-building sectors.[14]

The extensive activities of western spies and the pride of the GDR in its accomplishments in this area of secondary materials appear, however, to have been misplaced. Most of Sero's activities remained rather low-technology, and the machines and apparatus used in the various recycling programs and programs for more efficient use of materials never made much of an impact on the GDR's sales abroad. Although the dream of making a virtue of—and gaining a substantial payoff from—the GDR's need to develop an extensive recycling program and related technologies was a good one, given developments throughout the industrial world in the late 1970s and 1980s, it remained very much a dream.

In the waning days of the GDR, during late 1989 and early 1990, Günter Schabowski, the member of the Politburo who had announced the opening of the Berlin Wall on 9 November 1989, talked frequently to foreign reporters. On one occasion he tried to explain that, although he was a high-ranking party official, he was also just an ordinary guy. Like many GDR citizens, Schabowski told the reporters, he went home in the evening, sat down in his easy chair, turned on the television, and popped open a can of beer. His remarks may or may not have had the intended impact on foreign audiences. But they certainly had the effect domestically of further undermining the credibility of the GDR regime. For every citizen of the GDR knew that beer was not generally available in cans in the GDR, but only on draft or in bottles. The ability to purchase beer in cans meant privileged access to foreign currency and to the special shops in which to spend it.

This anecdote is telling, not just as an insight into cultural assumptions, but as an indication of the centrality of "used materials economy and trade" to the everyday lives and consciousness of ordinary East Germans. Metals were in short supply and were used primarily for the production of producer goods, consumer durables, and export items. Consumer goods were packaged in more readily available materials, which could be readily reused. For drinks, this was most notably glass, and bottles were generally used several times before being channeled into the recycling stream when they were worn out or broken. By the end of its existence, the GDR was achieving excellent results in gathering, processing, and reusing glass and other materials. Sero eventually constructed a "collection network with no gaps." It organized the reutilization of vast quantities of goods, and played a modest role in facilitating the continued existence of the GDR in the crisis-ridden 1970s and 1980s.[15]

But Sero's successes did not translate into generalized economic or technological well-being for the country. This was primarily because the actions that led to some success were the product of necessity rather than of deliberate planning as part of a general economic strategy. As such, Sero generally acted at a fairly low technological level, performing well in an extended emergency, but rarely reaching to medium- and high-technology areas such as advanced machines and apparatus for recycling, which might have had export potential and a broader positive economic impact. In contrast, its counterpart organization, the Stasi, operated at the high-technology end. It, too, counted many successes, but also had similar problems in translating them into generalized economic or technological well-being for the country.

The Stasi's Role in GDR Technological Development

Since the fall of the Berlin Wall and the implosion of the GDR, nothing has been more prominent in news reports and analysis than the Stasi (or MfS). Historians and others immediately saw an enormous and unprecedented opportunity to gain a glimpse into the workings of the security apparatus of a modern state and immediately pressed for access to the organization's documents. By and large, they have been successful, if the growing raft of books and articles about the East German secret service is any indication.[16]

The results of this documentary windfall, however, have been somewhat disappointing so far. Much of the most interesting material was located in the files of the Main Espionage Administration (Hauptverwaltung Aufklärung, or HVA), which was responsible for the activities of agents abroad. The files were virtually all destroyed in the days following the opening of the wall. The documents that remain indicate a workaday and generally very dull world of spying, far removed from the fantasies of Ian Fleming or John LeCarré. For instance, one of the files of a GDR agent sent undercover abroad, which I investigated, consisted mainly of West German intercity railway timetables and widely available prospectuses from various firms.[17] Furthermore, the agency set up to process and oversee access to the documents, known colloquially as the Gauck Authority after its head, Joachim Gauck, has had to work within a thicket of laws and regulations that make it extremely difficult to find out what documents are available, let alone get the opportunity to see them. Nonetheless, enough materials are now accessible from the Gauck Authority and in the form of secondary sources to indicate clearly, if incompletely, the significant impact of the Stasi's work on the GDR economy and technology, especially during the 1970s and 1980s.

The Ministry for State Security was initially established not for economic or technological reasons, but rather for political ones. It emerged in the late 1940s and early 1950s as a product of typical practice under a Stalinist regime, on the one hand, and of Cold War tensions, on the other. Throughout its history (and even since 1989), the Stasi has been notorious primarily for its careful scrutiny of and control over its own citizens and its frequently successful and devastating infiltration of West German government and bureaucracy.

As early as the 1950s, the Stasi also began to engage in scientific and technological espionage. For the most part, the task was primarily one of internal scientific and engineering security, especially in the area of atomic research. In February 1956 it installed "operatives for 'cadre and security questions' in the Office for Technology and in the Office for Atomic Research and Technology." Just four months later it expanded its activities by establishing an internal section for the assessment of scientific and technical information.[18]

Through the late 1960s, most of the MfS's activities in this area were concerned with internal security and with collection and assessment of scientific and technical intelligence, and the science and technology units remained relatively small, with well under 100 personnel in total. (There were approximately thirty-five people operating in this area during the 1950s.) But in 1969 and 1970 the units were reorganized and their activities expanded, involving thirty-four new staff. Particular emphasis was placed on the acquisition of militarily important technologies. Then, after 1970, and especially after Honecker came to power in 1971, the area came into its own. The Scientific and Technical Sector (Sektor Wissenschaft und Technik, or SWT) of the HVA grew rapidly in the ensuing years, reaching a total of around 400 personnel by the end of the GDR's existence.[19] This total includes secretaries, drivers, and other auxiliary staff as well as officially appointed agents, but it does not include the "informal agents" (informelle Mitarbeiter, or IM) who performed much of the work of the SWT and whose activities the official agents oversaw.

Nor was the SWT the sole Stasi group responsible for science and technology. Broadly speaking, the SWT of the HVA was assigned the task of collecting, evaluating, and disseminating information and goods collected from "highly developed 'capitalist states.'" By 1989 the more internally directed Main Section XVIII (Hauptabteilung, or HA XVIII) of the MfS, broadly responsible for the domestic economy as a whole, featured a further 647 personnel. Many of them were engaged in providing internal security in high-technology industries and research establishments. Some were also responsible for aspects of foreign trade and international economic cooperation. And once again, a sizeable number of the official agents in the HA XVIII oversaw an even more substantial group of IMs.[20]

The leap in the number of Stasi agents involved with science and technology is an indicator of subtle but important changes in the organization's strategy and remit in response to the new regime under Honecker. Throughout its existence, the Stasi had essentially four major areas of activity with regard to science and technology. It was responsible first and foremost for the security of the GDR's own technological information and personnel. Second, it was charged with the acquisition and evaluation of publicly available information, primarily through perusal and evaluation of international scientific and engineering periodicals and other readily available published sources, such as patent publications and firm prospectuses. A third aspect of its remit was the acquisition, assessment, and dissemination of private information on patents, processes, and know-how, generally culled from agents working in government and industry abroad. Finally, the Stasi was responsible for the acquisition of high-technology machines and apparatus from capitalist countries for GDR industry and government, generally in contravention of western Allied restrictions as imposed by COCOM.

In undertaking all these activities, the Stasi was engaged in answering the age-old political-operational question of all agencies related to espionage and intelligence: "Who is who?" It also specialized in getting those identified as crucial informants or suppliers to cough up the goods. Once that was done, the Stasi had to supervise the turnover of the information and/or machines to the GDR government and industry without revealing the source so as not to endanger its agents.

All this was common practice, not just for the Stasi, but for all secret services. And all of it continued from the Stasi's founding until its demise in 1989–90. Throughout, the largest number of personnel was undoubtedly devoted to the first two tasks, internal security and evaluation of publicly available information. But after Honecker came to power, two marked changes occurred. For one thing, the Stasi shifted its emphasis from the acquisition of information related to *basic* scientific and engineering research to a focus on information about *applied* research and know-how. This required a substantial increase in the number of agents, assessors, and evaluators employed by the MfS and a growing concentration on the third general area of its remit, acquisition of privately held information on production processes and know-how from foreign firms.[21] Furthermore, the fourth area of traditional activity for the Stasi with regard to science and technology, the acquisition of machines and apparatus, became relatively more important than before, for two reasons: the increasing bankruptcy of the GDR system of innovation, and the ever stricter imposition of COCOM restrictions, particularly after 1980.

But what did all this mean in practice, and how did the Stasi's activities affect the GDR system of innovation? Unfortunately, because of the factors already noted, it is unlikely that these questions can ever be answered satisfactorily, in spite of substantial and valuable efforts by scholars in the aftermath of the country's collapse. One of the earliest pieces of research based on newly available Stasi records was produced by Jörg Roesler. Investigating the Stasi's role in promoting innovation in the GDR, Roesler makes crucial contributions to our knowledge by emphasizing the role of HA XVIII in the GDR system of innovation and by showing the limits on the Stasi's influence on that system. But his work focuses primarily on two case studies in the areas of machine tools and textile machinery, cases that may or may not be representative.[22] Another scholar, Kristie Macrakis, is engaged in a project that aims to provide a detailed picture of the Stasi's activities in the area of science and technology through more intensive research in the Gauck Authority records and through interviews with agents.[23] Although the research she has published so far is more thoroughly documented than Roesler's, it is necessarily far from complete, focuses very heavily on the SWT and on computing technology, and is frequently anecdotal. Macrakis's published work thus far also highlights a problem inherent to this type of research: the sources, often interviewees, are frequently unwilling to be identified, which makes it virtually impossible for other scholars to assess the reliability and representativeness of their statements and information.

Although I have pointed out the limits of others' work in this area, I myself can offer no more than a few additional pieces of the jigsaw puzzle. Furthermore, the story I am telling is based on documentary rather than oral evidence, and is also highly impressionistic and anecdotal. Nevertheless, I think it is useful in that it helps complete a picture, however rough, of the GDR system of innovation as it developed during the last two decades of the country's existence. One key implication of the picture that emerges is that historians must look well beyond the Stasi in trying to understand the failures of the GDR system of innovation.

If we look at the *modus operandi* of the Stasi, there were generally four steps involved in a mission to transfer science or technology from capitalist countries to the GDR. The steps generally occurred in sequence, although some of them took place practically simultaneously. The first was to identify the target, whether a particular company or laboratory, and within it an individual machine or technological system, or specific information or software. It appears that Stasi officers in Berlin identified particular companies or laboratories for further investigation, and they then worked to win over or to place as an IM an employee of the company or laboratory abroad, generally in West Germany. The second step was to mobilize an agent, generally an IM, to collect the hardware or information. The IM, of course, often played a key role in this stage, by identifying promising technological and scientific developments to the Stasi officer in charge.

The next step was the transfer of the information or machine to the GDR. The precise way in which this took place depended crucially on the size, complexity, and sensitivity of the information or machine. If the item to be transferred was easily transportable and relatively straightforward, border officials were simply instructed to allow the IM to pass uninterrupted into the GDR, generally from West Berlin. In the 1980s, for instance, HA XVIII issued advice to border officials regarding the assistant general director of the Erfurt-based Kombinat Mikroelektronik, who was to be allowed to pass unencumbered and undisturbed through border controls at Berlin's Schönefeld airport "daily, without any time limitations." The grounds were that the man "is deputized by the state security service to import embargo goods." Similar advice was given regarding a technical worker from the VEB Applications Center, who would be traveling by S-Bahn (the local railway within Berlin, which also connected the city's eastern and western halves), and for a director of a West German firm who would be entering by automobile from West Berlin.[24]

If the item—generally a machine, but sometimes even a whole plant— was bulky or under embargo restrictions, it would take a more circuitous path. Vienna was a favored starting point for arranging the finance and transport of the item, which then wended its way through other, more or less friendly, generally eastern bloc countries.

Finally, the information or machine had to be transferred to relevant people or organizations within the GDR. This was often the easiest part of the process, although, as we shall soon see, there were frequent problems here as well.

Each step in this process had to be carried out under maximum secrecy, not just because it was necessary to protect sources to maintain access to desperately needed science and technology, but also because of the potential danger to the safety and even the lives of the agents involved. Each step was also fraught with additional, less life-threatening problems. For instance, the apparently simple task of identifying the target should not be underestimated. In a time of rapid technological change and increasing specialization, the volume of information coming to the Stasi officers in Berlin was enormous, and it kept increasing. Although by the 1970s and 1980s there were large numbers of officers compared to the 1950s, they were still relatively few considering the variety of fields that needed to be covered. Thus, the number of potential targets always far exceeded the capacity of the MfS to process them. The mobilization of IMs was made more difficult by occasional defections, most famously in the case of Werner Stiller. Stiller was a physicist who held high rank in the HVA and defected to the West in January 1979. Shortly afterward, about thirty agents active on behalf of the Stasi in the West had to be recalled from the foreign secret service in considerable haste and with much disorder in order to prevent further damage. Additional agents and informers were also "closed down." Information provided by Stiller wrought havoc within the Stasi, and it also enabled the West German secret service, the Bundesnachrichtendienst, or BND, to publish detailed descriptions of Stasi efforts and methods in scientific and technical espionage.[25]

Transfer of information and hardware to the GDR from the capitalist West was the single most dangerous step. If the goods in question were under embargo, they had to be purchased illicitly, using various front organizations. They then would make their way to the GDR indirectly, over a circuitous route that often included many different countries. One example from 1988 illustrates this point well. At the end of 1987 the state secretary of the Ministry for Electrotechnics and Electronics contracted the Stasi to purchase a VAX computer 8800, produced by the Digital Equipment Corporation (DEC), on behalf of the Robotron electronics combine. In this particular case it is not clear, but exceedingly likely, that the purpose was the usual one of obtaining a single machine of this particular type in order to copy and to produce it in larger quantities for the GDR and eastern bloc market.[26] The Stasi commissioned an "embargo transport line which had proven itself repeatedly," Sentrade Import-Export GmbH in Vienna, to carry out the task. Sentrade managed to obtain one of the machines, but in February and March 1988 it had problems gaining transport papers for the truck carrying it to travel from Yugoslavia to the GDR via Hungary and Czechoslovakia. The truck, which was registered in Bulgaria, was consequently sent back to that country, where the driver was interrogated for four days under suspicion of "having brought damage upon the People's Republic of Bulgaria through the manipulation of wares and papers."

Attempts by Sentrade to get the computer released remained unsuccessful well into May, although in the meantime East German import officials had arranged for it to be shipped by plane from Sophia. At the beginning of June, presented with an offer of DM 4.9 million from an unknown Bulgarian, Sentrade then informed the Stasi's front organization that it had given up trying to get the machine back. And finally, a month later, the GDR import authorities received an unprompted telephone call from the Bulgarian export company, Inco, offering to sell the GDR a VAX 8800 computer, complete with transport by truck to East Germany, all for the price of $1 million in cash and an additional $1.15 million in the form of a check. As it turns out, it appears that the Bulgarians were not getting an especially good deal here, since at then current exchange rates, $2.15 million was only DM 3.7 million.[27]

Naturally, the GDR complied, and the computer arrived safely in East Germany on 26 July. It is likely, of course, that this was the very same machine seized earlier by the Bulgarians, but the usual practice of relying on oral contracts and reputation rather than written contracts for the purchase of embargo goods made it impossible to verify this.[28] Its path, like that of many other such "semi-legal" imports, was complicated, insecure, and ultimately quite expensive. Embargo restrictions were not the only thing that hindered the import of such wares. Various pirates, men on the make, and "friendly" governments contributed too.

The final step in the process, the dissemination of information and hardware imported by the Stasi within the GDR, was a difficult one as well. Protecting sources was a crucial consideration, but even more important was the attempt to deflect the obvious conclusion that many would have reached if the Stasi's activities had been widely publicized: the need for such imports from the West was an indication of the ultimate nonviability of the socialist system of the GDR. Keeping the Stasi "label" off imported goods and information did not completely avert this, of course, but it hindered the rapid stampede of rumor into certainty.[29]

These general problems and dangers of the Stasi's activities in science and technology during the last two decades of the GDR's existence must be placed into historical context. It was surely unfortunate for the GDR that its interest in electronics in general and computers in particular, which had languished during the 1970s, flowered anew at about the same time that Ronald Reagan became president of the United States and once again heightened the Cold War tension that was already increasing in the last years of President Jimmy Carter's administration. Reagan oversaw growth in arms spending in the United States as well as the development of the so-called Strategic Defense Initiative (SDI), or Star Wars. The Star Wars program seems to have been as provocative and seductively attractive to those nations—most prominently from the eastern bloc—that were excluded from it as it was misleading in its promises.[30]

Renewal of the arms race, together with SDI, entailed an increased level of surveillance on the part of COCOM. Since the demarcation between civilian and defense technologies—at best always fuzzy—had been practically erased in the area of high technology, heightened COCOM restrictions bit hard on the aspirations of the GDR, especially with regard to semiconductors and computing. To begin with, it became more difficult to get goods, although it was usually possible to secure them in the end, at a price. An internal Stasi report from the mid-1980s, for example, indicated that the mark-up on list price for goods produced by the Digital Equipment Corportion was 3–8 percent if the goods required an export license. And if the goods stood under embargo through COCOM, the mark-up was 30 percent. If they were under the strictest embargo, the mark-up could be as much as 100 percent of list price. The size of the mark-up differed by company, but the tighter the restriction on export of the good, the more it cost.[31]

The Stasi's activities in the area of science and technology were at least as far-reaching as they were expensive. But obtaining funding for its operations was rarely a problem for the Stasi, in part because the GDR's leader, Erich Honecker, had been associated with the ministry before becoming first secretary, and he remained committed to its activities. The Stasi was also extremely adept politically in the GDR, managing to convince those in positions of power of the dire need for and utmost importance of its activities for both security and economic and technological progress. Reports on the Stasi's activities in science and technology, the contents of which were made known to high-ranking party and state officials, always stressed the massive savings to the economy that those activities entailed. One report from 1971 claimed that information and goods obtained by the Stasi and transferred to the economy had led to savings and/or "general economic utility" of tens of millions of marks. The report also argued that the Stasi delivered value for money, indicating that "the semi-legal acquisition of samples and documents using only 1.6 million [marks] had led to a proven utility of 17 million in the first half of 1971."[32]

What the report obscures is that the "investment" of 1.6 million marks had been in the form of hard currency, while the measurement of "utility" was undoubtedly expressed in East German marks: the official exchange rate may have been one to one, but the East German mark was in real terms worth only one-fourth of a West German mark, and perhaps much less. But if the Stasi could document a "return on investment" of more than ten times (at least in terms of official exchange rates), the hard-currency funds, which were hotly pursued by a wide variety of ministries and combines within the GDR, would clearly be made available to support espionage activities. The foreign exchange for paying agents, buying information, and purchasing goods came from a variety of sources, including funds from compulsory exchange payments by foreign visitors to the GDR and East Berlin, and transit fees for using the air, road, and rail corridors to West Berlin.

The issue of whether or not the Stasi's activities in the area of science and technology were worth it is a difficult one to assess. In a certain sense, in the context of Cold War tensions, they undoubtedly were worthwhile, since they kept the GDR government and military informed of the technological state of play of the enemy. Strategically, there was a role for the Stasi, which the GDR government, like those everywhere else in the two opposing blocs, felt compelled to support, financially and otherwise. But what of the Stasi's activities to support economic development through acquisition of foreign science, technology, and know-how for primarily civilian use? These, after all, constituted a significant part, and possibly even the lion's share, of its activities, whether measured in terms of personnel committed or funds deployed. Here, it is worth highlighting once again that the Stasi's role in the promotion of GDR science and technology throughout the 1970s and 1980s focused almost exclusively on high-technology areas, most notably semiconductor production, electronic data processing, and sophisticated sectors of the chemical and machine-tool industries.[33] The decision as to whether the Stasi's promotion of these areas was worthwhile depends crucially on whether one believes that they were essential to the economic success of the GDR regime.

For the sake of argument, let us assume, together with the Stasi and the top levels of the GDR regime, that high-technology production was critical to the country's well-being. Did goods and information collected through the Stasi's frequently illicit and "semi-legal" channels in fact contribute to the GDR's capability in high-technology industries? Or, alternatively, did they actually diminish the country's capability in these industries? Or did they make little difference in the end? It is difficult to assess such issues satisfactorily at a very general level; instead, it must be recognized that the quality of the Stasi's contribution depended upon the kind of activity it undertook and the particular area it covered. Some examples will help clarify this point.

A report giving a comprehensive overview of the activities of the SWT during the first half of 1971, the beginning of the period under consideration here, provides clear instances of positive Stasi contributions. The ministry's intelligence on international prices for high-technology goods, which were collected through its domestic and overseas espionage organizations, allowed the GDR to negotiate more effectively with partners abroad. Armed with information and documents provided by the Stasi, East Germany was able to purchase atomic power plant, and gas and petroleum pipelines, at prices far below what the sellers had in mind—savings that were estimated at more than 100 million marks over the next ten years.[34] Given that the goods acquired were vital to other industries, both high- and low-technology, as well as to the GDR's energy policy, these results are concrete evidence of the positive and important impact of the Stasi on GDR economy and technology. Just as clearly, moreover, these are instances of relatively straightforward and comparatively inexpensive practices: essentially, it was sound business thinking to try to gain information that would enhance the GDR's negotiating position in dealings with other countries. The Stasi's activities in this area did nothing to undermine the economy or the development of technology in the GDR; rather, they facilitated provision of critical goods and provided an example of sensible practice in purchasing foreign technology. Consequently, the Stasi's efforts to collect and disseminate information, not only on prices, but also on R&D directions and other matters, grew over time, until by the mid-1980s its list of "priorities" in its information-collection effort amounted to sixteen closely printed pages.[35]

Other cases are more ambiguous—those in which the role of the Stasi combined positive with negative influences on the GDR economy and innovative capability. One instance of this was the procurement of foreign-made computers, technical data, and software for the Robotron combine, mentioned above. This case is a good example of the ambiguity of Stasi influence, and therefore worthy of more extensive consideration.

By the early 1980s Robotron had managed to develop a 16-bit computer. But its accomplishment was spoiled by the fact that it came years behind similar technology in the West. Worse still, it was insufficient for computer-aided design and manufacturing (CAD/CAM) applications and those related to automation of factory processes, for which a considerably more powerful machine, along the lines of the DEC computer, was needed. The decision to produce a 32-bit machine proceeded quickly, but several plans to develop it were tried and discarded for a variety of reasons during the first half of the 1980s. Some of the plans proved impracticable because of shortages of capacity for producing various components, while others were abandoned apparently because the research team no longer deemed them worth pursuing for other, unspecified reasons. Attempts to persuade the USSR to supply the machines failed because the Soviets produced only enough machines to keep up with demand from their own domestic market.

At the end of 1985 the Ministry for Electrotechnics and Electronics became fed up with the delays, and it ordered Robotron to abandon all of its internally developed plans and to focus instead on copying "1:1" the DEC VAX 11/780. Robotron's engineers objected that the machine would already be ten years old by the time it came into production, and argued in favor of copying newer machines. But the ministry insisted on its decision, which was based primarily on the relatively easy and secure supply of electronic components, 75 percent of which could be produced domestically. Half of those, moreover, could be supplied on short notice, and the variety of suppliers available in the "nonsocialist world" meant that it would always be possible to find the components in case of emergency. Given clear and realistic direction, Robotron engineers came up with the new machine, although it required nearly two additional years. On 14 May 1987 Günter Mittag, the secretary of the SED's Economics Commission and a member of the Politburo, exhibited the computer, the K 1840, with some fanfare at a press conference, although the camera operators from the East German television documentary program *Aktuelle Kamera* were expressly forbidden to film the DEC machines Robotron had copied, which were still in use in its "prohibited area." The fact that a large number of other machines of this class were already in use in GDR industry was to be explained as the result of imports from the Soviet Union, although "in actual fact these are computers that were acquired from DEC through the evasion of embargo restrictions."[36]

The development of the K 1840 would clearly have been extremely significant for the GDR economy and technology had the country lasted past 1990. That it was copied was less important than the fact that it existed—that Robotron engineers were capable of reproducing it at all. It testified to the GDR's ability to produce goods, not at the forefront of world technological capability, but not far behind it either. Even more important, this was a machine with broad economic and technological impact. Given embargo restrictions, domestic production would allow its application across a much wider spectrum of GDR industries than would be possible by simply importing machines from abroad. Consequently, it would permit a large number of industrial areas to design better and more quickly and to automate key processes, especially those demanding real-time automation. And it would therefore be required in large numbers for the domestic economy. The Stasi itself, moreover, also professed to believe that the K 1840 might contribute to "building up the computing technology export line."[37]

This last point leads us finally to the downside of the Stasi's impact on GDR technology. It was simply unrealistic at best, and misleading at worst, to assert that East German copies of DEC computers had export potential. At most, the East Germans might be able to sell them within the eastern bloc, but trying to sell them elsewhere would mean that the GDR would be subject to retaliation from powerful western industrialized countries, led by the United States, whose intellectual-property interests had been violated. Moreover, while enabling the copying might help broad sections of GDR industry, it could do nothing to enhance the prospects for sales abroad of electronics—a desirable, prestigious, and high-value-added export sector for all industrialized countries. At the same time, enabling the copying had another, more subtle deleterious effect on the electronics industry. The history of Robotron's efforts to build a 32-bit computer is a telling case study of the problems with innovation in the GDR economy. Researchers recognized the needed lines of inquiry for research and development in high-technology industries. To be sure, they were stymied by various factors, including most prominently their own poor organization, the inability to decide among competing priorities, and insufficient support from complementary industrial sectors. But the fact that the Stasi could be counted upon to supply at least one version of a desired artifact to the researchers to make up for these deficiencies must be added to this list. That capability of the MfS fostered a culture of dependence, almost of laziness, in science and technology, which grew into a larger and self-reinforcing system: industry could become more and more lax in its development efforts and its attempts to overcome supply problems because the Stasi would provide necessary information and artifacts; the Stasi's role in the GDR system of innovation grew as it was called upon to supply more and more information and artifacts. This self-reinforcing system in turn consigned the GDR, more than ever, to eternally trumpeting its achievements in essentially outmoded technologies.

Similar points could be made about the Stasi's activities with regard to the chemical industry, which, despite its prominence and worldwide reputation from the beginning of the GDR's existence, was frequently disappointing in its ability to innovate. Here, though, I will sketch out another area, one in which the role of the Stasi, while again ambiguous, appears to have been on balance more detrimental than helpful to the development of GDR technology.

In the early 1970s the entire electronics industry—not just in the GDR, but also in the capitalist world—was abuzz with talk about a new technology for producing semiconductors, so-called ion implantation. Essentially, this technology would permit faster production of more accurate and dependable electronic connections between various components on a single integrated circuit. In the summer of 1971 the Stasi indicated its full awareness of the revolutionary potential of the new technology: "If it is possible to take this technological path [ion implantation], it will bring about increases in productivity on the order of 1:10, which means that the existing world production systems for electronic components would have to be abandoned."[38]

The Stasi then seized the moment as part of its own dawning revolutionary potential in the Honecker era, which had just begun. Rather than turn the development work over to any of the combines, the Stasi "acquired" a prototype of an ion-implantation plant from abroad and set a team of its own agents (IMs) to work on it. They were scheduled to build "a small-scale pilot plant, which was supposed to produce directly" by the beginning of 1972.[39]

With this project, the MfS had seemingly picked a winner, for ion-implantation technology was indeed revolutionary in its impact on the semiconductor industry throughout the world. But the problem with the Stasi's involvement in ion-implantation research and development was not that it was misdirected in technical terms—it clearly was not. Rather, the work was misdirected in terms of *technology policy*, crucial aspects of which the Stasi was certainly arrogating to itself. The Stasi did not have the staff, even with the support of IMs, to undertake massive R&D work. To take it up regardless deprived the teams working in the combines of the experience of participating in key projects at the cutting edge of technology. It also served to exacerbate one of the key problems in the GDR system of innovation—weak linkages between suppliers and their customers. For the Stasi did not have to operate in the real world of "real existing socialism"; it could instead draw upon the products and experience of real existing capitalism in its R&D efforts.

Sero and the Stasi were not the only two organizations operating within the GDR system of innovation during the last two decades of the country's existence, nor were they necessarily the most important ones. As Roesler has pointed out, the GDR was capable of producing world-class technology without the Stasi and outside the area of recycling, and it was even more capable of producing shoddy merchandise and a poor record of innovation in many areas of technology and the economy.[40] Sero and the Stasi, however, were two important institutions whose responsibilities grew considerably in the desperate attempt to overcome this latter tendency. And the remit of both expanded as the new Honecker regime tried to square the circle between limited industrial investment and poor innovation performance, on the one hand, and the desire to substantially improve the lot of the GDR consumer, on the other. The two organizations were crucial elements of economic and technology policy that involved substitution in a desperate attempt to foster economic success and well-being. Domestic goods, used more intensively, substituted for imports of materials from abroad. Imports of ideas and artifacts substituted for domestic production. But neither, as we have seen, could overcome the general tendency of the GDR system of innovation toward discouragement and poor performance.

Was the GDR system of innovation so fundamentally flawed as to defy any attempt to improve it? Or could Sero and the Stasi have functioned differently, to more positive economic and technological effect? The thrust of the argument in this book has been to contend that the GDR

The one-millionth Trabant, produced in 1973, pictured in front of the factory at Zwickau. Compare the design with the photograph of the Trabant on page 2. The car had not changed much from the original model designed and produced in 1958—an indication of the ineffectiveness of the GDR's system of innovation from the 1960s on. *Bundesarchiv, Koblenz, Bildsammlung Bild 183/M1122/22N*

was condemned, for systemic and contingent reasons, to underperform compared with West Germany in terms of science, technology, and the economy. But that does not mean that it had to perform quite as badly as it did, or that that performance necessarily had to deteriorate so substantially after the 1960s.

Part of the reason for this steadily deteriorating performance record was that the two institutions designed to overcome the poor capacity of innovation and to foster dynamic technological change were not conceived broadly or boldly enough to make a difference. Their activities remained limited, when this need not have been the case. Sero, and the organizations of the Ministry for the Material Economy and Trade in general, could have been more attentive to the medium- and high-technology potential of recycling and related industries, which might have stimulated the GDR machine-building industry to innovation and lucrative export performance. And the Stasi might have been more attentive to the low- and medium-technology potential of its programs for collecting intelligence. Rather than an almost exclusive focus on high-technology industries, some attention to other, more workaday industries might have had a positive impact on their ability to innovate, in turn allowing them to produce more goods of better quality for both domestic and foreign markets. But instead, Sero remained active primarily in the low-technology area, while the Stasi confined itself primarily to prestigious high-technology sectors. Consequently, neither was able to promote diffusion of its impact across a more varied profile of industries, which would have had greater and more positive effects for the broader economy.

As a result, the GDR economy under Honecker dedicated itself to pursuing a mission-oriented technology strategy of the type undertaken by the United States, which emphasized single-minded pursuit of the technological cutting edge. The GDR, however, possessed the resources and traditions of a diffusion-oriented economy—one that specializes not in developing, but rather in diffusing best practice and technology. West Germany, meanwhile, capitalized on those diffusion-oriented traditions.[41] So the distance between the two German successor states, already pronounced during the 1960s, grew to a yawning and unmistakable gap, readily evident to any observer from East or West. This gap grew wider still during the 1980s, as the regime dedicated itself still further to the mission-oriented strategy, throwing all its weight behind a single and very expensive high-technology industry, microelectronics.

|

The technological optimism of the GDR in the late 1950s and especially the early 1960s, under the New Economic System, gave way to despair in the late 1960s and the 1970s. In response, the GDR resorted to substitutes for success in the form of the Stasi and the secondary raw materials system (Sero). But even those substitutes, combined with renewed efforts to reform and revive the GDR's own domestic capability for innovation under Erich Honecker, could not turn the tide. On the eve of its final decade of existence, the GDR was not closing the technological gap with the capitalist world, and especially with West Germany. Instead, the gap was widening.

Clearly, this state of affairs called for some action, but of what sort? Renewed efforts to bolster the effectiveness of the Stasi and Sero would be one way forward. But the GDR's leadership also considered it necessary to make more dramatic adjustments to their system of innovation. By the mid-1970s they had decided on a radical course of action: they would invest heavily in microelectronics and data processing in order to make up lost ground with the West. In this, they were in step with the other major members of the eastern bloc.

Scholars disagree about the exact meaning of this growing commitment to microelectronics, but all agree on its importance. According to Raymond Bentley and others, this move by the GDR into microelectronics was a fateful decision. Bentley implies that its consequences for the GDR economy may even have been devastating: "the GDR's investment . . . in microelectronics [in the last two decades of its existence] was too high. Despite the . . . investment, the country was unable to keep up with developments in Japan and the USA, and the technological level of GDR's products in the electrical, electronic and instrument building sector was low. The opportunity cost of the ambitious investment in microelectronics for other branches of East German industry was too great."[1]

Other commentators, writing earlier (in the 1980s) and more generally

The Planeta offset machine (above) and the Zeiss microscope (left). Both were examples of the GDR's continuing ability to produce high-quality goods even into the late 1970s and early 1980s. Such successes, however, were not transferred effectively into other technologies. *Sammlung industrielle Formgestaltung, Berlin*

(about the Soviet bloc as a whole), claimed it was the nature of the new technology itself, rather than any misinvestment, that posed the greatest challenge to the communist system of innovation. Having relied for years, especially in the Soviet Union, on reverse engineering and assimilating western goods in order to maintain only a short lag with the West, the eastern bloc was faced with new technologies, including microelectronics, composite materials, and biotechnology, which did not lend themselves to earlier practices.[2] As Joseph Berliner noted as early as 1976, "the physical form of an integrated circuit gives no clue to the closely controlled manufacturing technology required to produce it." This meant that there would be diminishing returns for transfer of technology from West to East.[3]

W. R. Lee and Nigel Swain, in a comparative study of the GDR and Hungarian computer industries, also view developments in microelectronics in eastern Europe in the 1970s and 1980s as significant. But they, unlike Bentley, see such developments not as a cause, but rather as a symptom of Soviet bloc shortcomings in the area of technology: "The CMEA computer industry . . . was not so much a source of decay as the material embodiment of the socialist economy's failure to innovate and respond [to] the challenges of the late twentieth century's shift of techno-economic paradigm."[4]

Unlike other countries in the eastern bloc, the GDR was able to draw upon a rich tradition of activity in microelectronics and computing. But it was a tradition that had lain moribund for some time before being resurrected in the late 1970s under Honecker. Besides resuscitating that tradition, the GDR also had to copy and improve upon western developments. Copying posed less of a problem in East Germany than elsewhere because of the country's relatively high level of technological development. Improvement was more problematic, not least because it challenged the GDR to perform well in interdisciplinary, cross-institutional interchange of information for both the development of the technology and its diffusion.

Resuscitating the Tradition

Although the United States was the country in which the modern electronics and computing industries assumed much of their shape, Germany, until the postwar period, was one of the most advanced in this sector. Working in Berlin in the 1930s and 1940s, Konrad Zuse produced a series of calculating machines, of which the Z3, completed on 5 December 1941, was the first programmable electronic calculator in the world. An improved version of this machine, the Z4, was produced later in the war and hidden from the Allies until it could be recovered in the late 1940s.

Zuse's work is remarkable for several reasons. First of all, it demonstrates some of the strengths of Germany in this regard. Second, it was done independently; Zuse developed his machine without knowledge of developments in the United States or elsewhere. Third, both the Z3 and Z4, unlike computing machines in the United States, were electromechanical devices that used relays rather than vacuum tubes as their main construction components. Although Zuse contemplated using vacuum tubes, the number that he would have needed (around 2,000) provoked "disbelieving shaking of heads" in wartime Berlin, not just because the tubes were unavailable in such numbers, but also because many experts believed that a device using tubes in such numbers would never work. Zuse continued his work after the war, although in West rather than East Germany.[5]

The area that would later become East Germany was the home of a substantial part of the German electrical and office-machinery industries, which would serve as the basis for computing development in the postwar period. Nikolaus Joachim Lehmann, working at the TH-Dresden, began in 1950 to develop a digital calculating machine, which eventually resulted in a primitive computer. Beginning in 1953, Herbert Kortum worked independently toward this end at the Zeiss company. Both developments, especially that of Lehmann, faced a fundamental difficulty that was similar to Zuse's: limited availability of electronic components.[6] It was a problem that dogged the GDR electronics, computing, and office-machinery industry throughout its existence. Foreign exchange was not available in sufficient quantities to allow imports to cover the needs of the electronics industry, and domestic capacity was late in coming on-line and always lagged behind international best practice. Later, trade restrictions and embargoes exacerbated these problems.

But the practical difficulties of developing this industrial sector did not prevent the GDR's leadership from identifying it as a priority early and repeatedly. The Third Party Conference in 1956 identified automation as one of the centerpieces of its program for high-technology development, along with mechanization and nuclear power.[7] This presupposed a commitment to developing the electronics and computing industries in the GDR. Later in the 1950s the GDR invested heavily to produce semiconductors on a large scale at Frankfurt on the Oder (see chapter 4). Research and development work was done at a Central Institute for Automation in Jena under Kortum's direction (the institute moved to Dresden in 1961) and at several industrial laboratories. The country's leaders generally tried to work toward creating a large electronics industry and diffusing its products into most other industrial sectors.

This initial effort to build up these industrial sectors flagged somewhat in the 1960s. True, in 1964 the GDR's Ministerial Council undertook a program to promote machine-based data processing in the country, emphasizing basic research.[8] But approval for a COMECON-wide computing program came only in the late 1960s. The Unified System for Electronic Computing Technology (Einheitliches System der elektronischen Rechentechnik, or ESER) started officially in 1969. Based in Moscow, an ESER oversight committee supervised the development of large-scale computers and related software that were "IBM analogues." Tasks were divided among the member states, and the first computer was produced in 1974. Later in the 1970s the eastern bloc began another program, the System of Mini-computers (System der Kleinrechner, or SKR). Machines produced under SKR were to be "DEC analogues (now known as VAX computers)." Finally, and later still, the eastern bloc began a program for producing personal computers based on the IBM system.[9]

Put another way, despite ESER and other programs from the late 1960s, the GDR and the rest of the eastern bloc did not make much progress in computing and electronics during this decade of rapid technological change. It was not until the late 1970s that the GDR leadership began to single out electronics and microelectronics as a priority for development. Not even the directive for the Five-Year Plan commencing in 1976 accorded electrotechnics or electronics particular emphasis among the eleven major industrial groups dealt with in the plan, although it did insist that the industrial sector take measures to prepare "decisive preconditions for the significant increase of exports, especially in products . . . in data compilation and copying technology."[10] By autumn 1977, however, the party's Central Committee had taken important steps to raise the industry's profile in planning and investment decisions, and at the beginning of 1978 the Mikroelektronik combine was founded in Erfurt. But it was not until the 1980s that robotics, automated production processes, and electronics received a major commitment. By that time, of course, the GDR was very far behind the rest of the world. The effort to overcome this lag would require massive expenditure of resources, whether material, financial, or human.

Electronics in the 1980s

Besides party pronouncements of various sorts, concrete measures indicate that the Honecker era was one in which the GDR electronics and computing industries grew substantially, in terms of both research and development, and production. R&D personnel in the electrical and electronic-engineering industries grew by more than one-fourth between 1971 and 1988, with much of the growth occurring in the late 1970s, and electrical/electronics featured the largest number of R&D personnel of

Figure 1. Gross Industrial Production and the Electrical/Electronics Industry in the GDR, 1971–88 (1970 = 100)

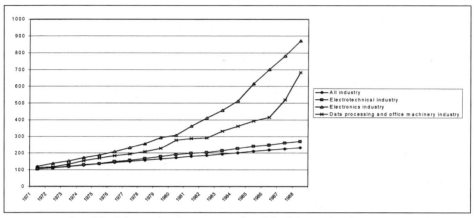

Source: Statistisches Jahrbuch der DDR (1984): 140; *Statistisches Jahrbuch der DDR* (1989): 142.

the major technology-intensive industries in the GDR. In all, the Ministry of Electrical and Electronic Engineering and its associated factories employed almost one-quarter of all R&D manpower in 1963, a figure that rose to one-third by the early 1970s, where it remained for the rest of the GDR's existence. The nearest competitor to the sector in these terms was the Chemicals Ministry, with less than one-fifth of all R&D personnel. Throughout the Honecker period, moreover, Robotron and Carl Zeiss were the largest employers of R&D personnel within the sector, together utilizing more than 12,000 scientists, engineers, and technicians in the early 1970s. By the early 1980s that number had grown to well over 16,000, with about half in each of the combines. R&D personnel in the two combines subsequently declined to about 15,000, where it remained till the end of the GDR's existence. But in the meantime, the Mikroelektronik combine in Erfurt was increasing its R&D effort dramatically, from well under 4,000 personnel in 1971 to nearly 6,000 in 1988. Again, most of the growth occurred in the late 1970s and early 1980s.[11] Additional financial resources accompanied this growth in the number of R&D personnel employed in the sector. Again, it was the electrical and electronics industry that received the lion's share of R&D funding among the GDR's main high-technology industries. In 1971 the industry expended about 1.1 billion East German marks, a figure that increased gradually to about 1.6 billion in 1978. By the early 1980s new

Figure 2. Percentage of Semiconductors among Production of all Electronic Components in GDR

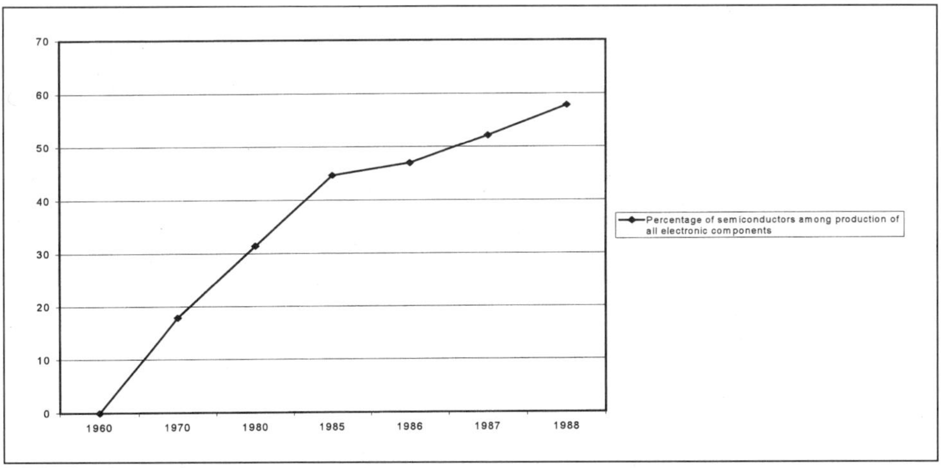

Source: Statistisches Jahrbuch der DDR (1989): 148.

commitments to the industry resulted in an increase of approximately 50 percent in R&D expenditure, although it stagnated at about 2.3 billion marks through 1985. There was also a significant increase in funding between 1985 and 1987, when expenditure on research and development in the industry rose to about 3.7 billion marks. In the meantime the other major research-intensive industries in the GDR increased their expenditures on research and development as well, although much more gradually. In all, from 1981 to 1988, the GDR spent about 20 billion marks on microelectronics research and development.[12]

The payoff for such increased R&D efforts was dramatic increases in production, as seen in figure 1. Between 1970 and 1988 industry as a whole more than doubled its level of production. Increases were steady, but they were also gradual. In the same period, the data-processing and office-machinery industry increased its production nearly sevenfold, while the electronics industry's level of production increased almost ninefold. The most dramatic increases for the electronics industry occurred during the 1980s, when the trend line became dramatically steeper. For data processing and office machinery, there were two spurts in the 1980s, the first fairly gradual (1981–86), the last very steep indeed (1986–88).[13]

But what exactly were the East Germans making during these years? Figure 2 shows that the composition of production of electronic components in the GDR changed substantially, and that much of this change occurred during the Honecker era. At about 19 percent of total value of production of all electronic components in 1970, semiconductors were a relatively insubstantial part of the industrial sector's production program. The proportion of semiconductors within the sector's output is a stark indication of the severe technological backwardness of the GDR at the end of the Ulbricht era: as early as 1965 semiconductors, including transistors and integrated circuits, accounted for nearly one-third of total output of electronics component production in the United States and the United Kingdom.[14] Under Honecker, concerted attempts were made to redress the balance in this area. By 1980 semiconductors accounted for about one-third of the value of all electronics components manufactured in the GDR, and by 1987 that figure had risen to more than half of total production value of electronic components.

Figure 3 gives an indication of the trends in production of specific semiconductor components and computers in the GDR between 1960 and 1988, although this figure, unlike figures 1 and 2, portrays physical output of components and computers rather than their value. This figure permits several observations. First of all, the trend lines for production of transistors and of integrated circuits were very similar throughout the period, although the quantities involved were numbered in the millions for transistors and in the thousands for integrated circuits.[15] Second, it is worth noting that all the indicators bar one ("electronic data processing stations," or computers) rose substantially through time, with especially rapid growth during the 1980s. Finally, the trend for computers bears some investigation. Production of computers rose rapidly between 1980 and 1985, reaching a plateau through 1987 before falling substantially in 1988. The raw numbers in this case require further clarification. On the one hand, the decline in numbers conceals important improvements in design and performance of computers in the GDR. On the other, the decline in absolute numbers is a very clear indicator of the failure of the GDR's strategy in microelectronics.

Besides devoting considerable domestic resources of manpower, knowledge, and finance to the development of electronic and computing potential, the GDR also mobilized resources to obtain equipment, information, and know-how from abroad. One obvious way of doing this was for the GDR to look eastward towards its COMECON neighbors. Purchasing materials from and fostering cooperation with the Soviet Union remained important policy objectives for the GDR leadership. But the level of cooperation in this militarily sensitive area, together with diffi-

Figure 3. Production of Semiconductor Components and Computers in GDR, 1960–88

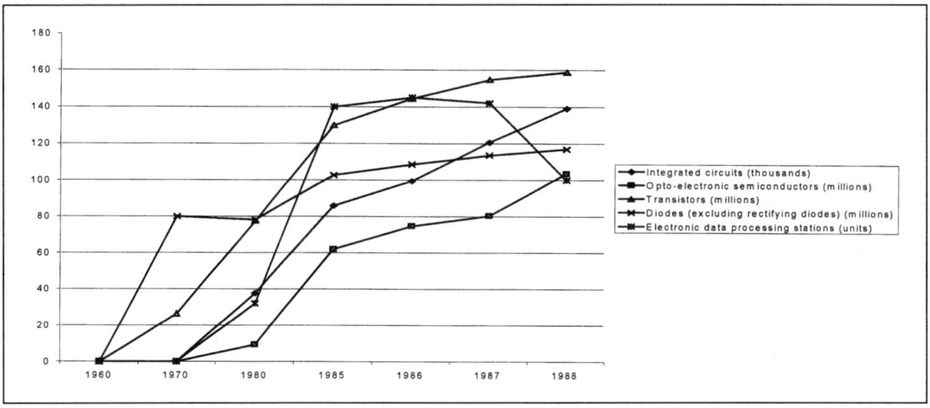

Source: Statistisches Jahrbuch der DDR (1984): 140; Statistisches Jahrbuch der DDR (1989): 142.

culties in guaranteeing supply of vital goods, continued to disappoint the East Germans.[16]

Consequently, the West remained the focal point of technology procurement and transfer efforts. Decisions on specific electronic components for use in apparatus and machines manufactured in the GDR, for example, were made not just on the basis of domestic availability, but also in part on the basis of the breadth of suppliers of the components in foreign, and mainly capitalist, markets. Chapter 7 outlined the process for the copying of machines capable of being used for computer-aided design and manufacturing on the basis of the DEC VAX 11/780 in the mid-1980s. Part of the reason for focusing on older style technology was the wide availability of components, both at home and in the West. Chapter 7 also indicated some of the ways that the Stasi was deployed to gain information and equipment from the West, and it is worth emphasizing again that this effort was heavily oriented toward electronics and computing technology. In 1979, for instance, the Ministry for Electrotechnics/Electronics received appropriations of 48 million hard-currency marks for "specific imports" from the capitalist West. A further 60 million hard-currency marks—always highly sought after and in short supply—were made available for the coming year to purchase "apparatus and equipment that are difficult to procure (embargo) . . . [which] cannot be obtained in the framework of compensation trading." This sum was made available to Gerhard Beil, a state secretary and first deputy minister in the Ministry of Foreign Trade, and Alexander Schalck-Golodowski, a shadowy figure who was also a deputy minister, but who was far more important in his role as head of the highly secretive "Commercial Coordination" Agency (Koko), which had the task of evading COCOM embargo restrictions.[17] Undoubtedly a large proportion of these funds found its way into Stasi coffers.

One other way of promoting such transfers from the "West" was to exploit contacts with major Japanese firms, especially in the 1970s and 1980s. As early as the 1950s GDR officials had identified Japan as a country worthy of admiration and emulation: it featured a high level of state intervention in the economy; it had significant technological capabilities, although it lagged behind the world leaders in key areas; and, as a country poor in most raw materials, it was highly dependent on export of high-value-added manufactures. That admiration only grew through time, and justifiably so, as the Japanese surged forward in high-technology industries, most notably electronics. By the 1970s Japan was even challenging the world leader, the United States, in this booming area.

The GDR's most important contacts in Japan were with the Toshiba Corporation, although there were also key links with Mitsui and Mitsubishi.[18] There were three main areas of cooperation. First, the Japanese firms supplied the GDR with technical expertise and equipment. Second, they facilitated sales from and to the GDR through their trading companies and their extensive commercial networks. Toshiba, for example, included machine tools produced in the GDR within large projects it undertook and/or managed in Algeria, Northern Ireland, Canada, Thailand, and Malaysia. And, finally, the Japanese firms provided additional technical intelligence based on their contacts with foreign, and especially U.S., firms. In 1977, for instance, Toshiba gave GDR officials technical documents on an American system for control of machine tools with microprocessors. Toshiba was in possession of the files because it supplied the American firm with the electronics used in the end product.[19]

By and large, relations between the GDR and the Japanese appear to have been cordial. But occasionally they grew somewhat tense. When the general director of the VEB Mikroelektronik visited President Saba of Toshiba in March 1981, for instance, he came with a long wish list. It included a study visit by three GDR technical specialists to Toshiba's semiconductor manufacturing operation to gain knowledge of "the tech-

nology of a CMOS SGT on the level of a 16K memory." The same specialists, he requested, should also be able to interview Japanese colleagues
extensively regarding "questions about yields [in production] of 16-K
DRAM-chips in the GDR." To help overcome this problem of yield in
16K DRAM chips, he asked that Toshiba sell Mikroelektronik "a new or
used projection, justification, and exposure facility (either Perkin Elmer
or Cobilt, both manufactured in the USA)." He asked in addition for
provision of other equipment and for a visit of an expert in measurement
technology. "After a long discussion, which went from the side of the
general director of the VEB Mikroelektronik combine to the point of
breaking off business relationships with Toshiba (the discussion was carried out politely), the president declared himself willing" to fulfill most
of the East German wishes. He was more reluctant, however, to sell the
East German firm the specialized equipment and asked for four weeks'
time to consider that request.[20]

The incident raises two important issues. First, it underscores the
heavy reliance of the GDR on Japan for supply of key goods and information for its high-technology industries, and especially electronics and
computing. Second, it brings up a crucial question: what were the Japanese getting out of this difficult cooperation with the GDR? Was it so
much that they could suffer through negotiations of the sort outlined
above?

The GDR could offer the Japanese three things. First, it was capable
of producing reliable and reasonably sophisticated investment goods,
mostly machines, and was willing to sell those machines at very low
prices in order to earn foreign exchange. The Japanese were able to use
the GDR contacts and production capabilities in organizing deals with
other countries. Second, the GDR could provide the Japanese with an
inroad into the eastern European market in general. Third, and most
important, the GDR offered the Japanese hard cash for the goods they
produced, and since those goods often fell afoul of COCOM regulations,
they could command premium prices, which the GDR was willing to
pay, especially for electronic goods.

But unfortunately for the GDR, the cooperation with Toshiba did not
last. Under the administration of President Ronald Reagan, Toshiba was
put under pressure by diplomats from the United States to limit or stop
trading with socialist countries in high-technology areas. The U.S. Central Intelligence Agency was mobilized to make sure the company complied with the U.S. wishes. Consequently, by early 1982 an informant

of the Stasi (IM) reported that a conversation with a representative of Toshiba at the Leipzig Spring Trade Fair had warned of changes in their previous relationship. Although on Toshiba's side "there existed, it is true, a readiness to cooperate with the GDR, nevertheless the previously mentioned circumstances currently . . . offer no preconditions for implementing an agreement in the ways it was done before between the VEB Mikroelektronik combine and the Toshiba firm."[21]

Enormous effort was devoted in the GDR, in the late 1970s and 1980s, to developing capability in the production of semiconductors, electronic products, computing hardware, and software. Nevertheless the country continued to lag behind the West. In the mid-1980s, for instance, the GDR had less than 10 percent of the absolute number of office and personal computers of the Federal Republic, although if the figures are normed to reflect differences between the two countries in number of employees, the GDR proportion was actually 18 percent. In the crucial area of computer-aided design and manufacturing, however, the GDR looked much worse. In 1987 the GDR had just eight CAD/CAM systems per 1,000 employees, while the Federal Republic had 111 per 1,000 employees in 1985, and the United States had 215 in the same year.[22]

These numbers, however, do not even begin to convey the seriousness of the situation for the GDR, for the problem of a relatively small number of microelectronic devices compared to the capitalist world was exacerbated by other factors. One report published in the late 1970s noted that the level of integration of GDR microelectronic devices was only 10–20 percent of the level of international best practice, while the costs were five to ten times international levels.[23] It appears that the problems endemic to the GDR's system of innovation practically from the beginning, and increasingly in the 1970s and beyond—inflexibility, lack of interchange between suppliers and customers, focus on production rather than quality or novelty—were especially pronounced in this area, which depended heavily upon exactly the opposite traits.

The problems faced by the GDR in developing internationally competitive capability in electronics and computing were not all generated internally. The 1970s and 1980s saw a worldwide explosion in demand for electronic devices, which also vastly increased demand for semiconductors and other components. The GDR needed to supplement its limited domestic production of semiconductors with imports from the capitalist West, but such developments affected both availability and price, something that caused considerable concern in East Germany.[24] At the same time, moreover, the Carter and Reagan administrations in the United States tightened existing COCOM restrictions considerably. Again, the effect caused grave concern within the GDR. For even though it was possible for the East Germans to evade embargo restrictions by using the Stasi and its contacts, suppliers grew more reluctant to fulfill the GDR's wishes, the danger of confiscation increased, and prices rose substantially.[25] Instead of improving, the crisis of GDR technology seemed to be worsening. The key question was whether to move forward or to retreat. Since the latter would be an admission of defeat, the former seemed the only real option, and it led in the mid-1980s to a redoubling of efforts to catch up with the West in terms of electronics and computing.

The One-Megabit Chip and Beyond

Semiconductor technology has shown several consistent characteristics since the development of the transistor at Bell Laboratories in the late 1940s. Production has tended to increase exponentially, and costs of components have fallen very quickly. Size of individual components has also decreased dramatically over time. Simultaneously the performance of the components has risen substantially, while power consumption has declined sharply. The integrated circuit was patented in 1959; by the late 1960s large-scale integration (LSI), involving chips with between 100 and 1,000 gateways, was commercially viable. The next step was very large-scale integration (VLSI), involving chips with many thousands of components. This has characterized the electronics industry's development since the late 1960s. VLSI required simultaneous advance on several technological fronts, including the chemistry and physics of the chips themselves, development of etching techniques, and more sophisticated chip design.[26]

The GDR in the first half of the 1980s faced a continued lag in semiconductor and computing technology compared to international best practice. Consequently, in 1986 the GDR decided on its own ambitious VLSI program. *Höchstintegration* (highest integration) was ratified by the GDR leadership, although not without controversy at the highest levels (for example, between the two leading economic functionaries in the GDR, Günter Mittag and Gerhard Schürer in 1987).[27] A large-scale, coordinated program was necessary to bring East Germany back into the international mainstream. Although the development of the one-megabit chip at Carl Zeiss was probably the most prominent objective of the highest integration program, other initiatives were undertaken, both at Zeiss and at other institutions. Key universities and polytechnics in East Germany received tasks ranging from research and development of materials for semiconductor production to design and testing of semiconductors and development of software. The institutes of the GDR Academy of Sciences were also heavily involved in the program. They carried out basic and applied research into areas including diagnostics technologies; lithography, etching, and masking techniques; coatings and adhesives; and microprocessor design and development.[28]

The three major combines included in the highest integration program were Mikroelektronik (KME), Carl Zeiss (CZ), and Robotron. Again, the goals set were ambitious and would require an unprecedented degree of cooperation, not just among the large combines, but also between them and research institutes and institutions of higher learning. KME's Erfurt Works had two main tasks. First, it was to modify and adapt processes and technologies developed at CZ Jena "for the development and mass production of programmable memory, logic circuits, microprocessors, and chips in the expansion of the production palette which has been decided upon." Second, KME Erfurt was to engage in mass production of VLSI dynamic and static memory devices. The latter activity included development work on 32-bit microprocessors, which was to be completed in 1990–91 in conjunction with Robotron Dresden, CZ Jena, and the Academy of Sciences. Carl Zeiss itself had several tasks, including clean-room development, development of 256K DRAM devices (which was to be completed by May 1989), and development of a one-megabit DRAM chip. Robotron in Dresden was to contribute its research capacity primarily to the development of chips for 16-bit, and eventually 32-bit, microprocessors.[29]

By the end of the 1980s the commitment to this program was enormous. A series of Politburo decrees led to a budget of 2.2 billion East German marks for research and development to achieve "highest integration" between 1987 and 1990. A further 6.4 billion marks were made available for investment in physical plant. Nonetheless, serious problems continued to dog the area. When Honecker visited KME in Erfurt in May 1986, for instance, he saw some impressive achievements. And the general director, Wedler, thanked him, Erich Mielke (the head of the Stasi), and Alexander Schalck-Golodowski (the head of Koko) profusely for their support in reaching this level of technological excellence. Wedler also noted, however, that in order to develop a 32-bit microprocessor by 1990 (note the lag compared to Intel, which had reached this level in 1981), he would require approximately 400 additional personnel for circuit design.[30]

A report on progress made through the beginning of 1988 indicated that these substantial problems remained, not only for the 32-bit microprocessor, but for other key programs in the microelectronics sector. A prototype of the 256K DRAM device, it stated, was available on 7 October 1987, a year earlier than planned. But there were likely to be severe problems with moving into pilot production. For one thing, specialized equipment, especially from the Soviet Union, was either not available at all or of insufficient quality and reliability. Attempts were being made at present to change the technology from 100 mm to 125 mm chips, but experience had shown this to be a hazardous enterprise: the report warned that in changing the technology, "they must avoid the errors in the transfer to the new regime that had led in the case of 64K DRAM to a situation in which until the end of 1987 no stable series production with justifiable yields could be reached."[31]

To be sure, the one-megabit chip had been designed, and a prototype was in preparation. But this project, too, was endangered by a shortfall of about 50 percent in availability of apparatus for pilot production. Furthermore, the project leader estimated that the project was 30 percent understaffed. The next-generation chip, the 4-megabit DRAM, was still in its earliest stages of development. Nonetheless, only 20 of 100 planned researchers were active in this effort, and there were shortages of apparatus desperately needed for carrying out R&D work. Coprocessor production capacity, crucial for the realization of the 16-bit microprocessor was insufficient. At the same time, the 32-bit microprocessor project was in serious danger because of "the absence of complex testers and measurement technology (strictest embargo), in order to secure the knowledge which must be transferred from [investigation of] samples [of processors] from abroad into the production process."[32]

Nevertheless, and despite all these handicaps, Zeiss was indeed able to exhibit the proud results of its work on the one-megabit chip later in 1988, although it appears that the prototype—which Honecker took with him to show Gorbachev on his trip to Moscow in autumn 1988—may well not have been made by Zeiss, but rather purchased in the West. If not, it was certainly a labor-intensive copy of western technology. It was unveiled with much fanfare, and the promise associated with its mass production widely trumpeted.[33] At the same time, however, those doing the trumpeting recognized, along with experts in the West, that this development, impressive as it was given the resources of the GDR, would be insufficient to guarantee the GDR's competitiveness in this industry. Series production was still far off, and in the meantime the capitalist West, which was already producing the one-megabit chip in series, was moving on to the next generation.

Obviously, electronics and prestige projects such as the one-megabit chip had enormous value for the GDR. They provided an impressive technological display that was meant to convince both domestic and foreign audiences that East German technology was on the cutting edge. But it was a very expensive show, both financially and also because it did not lead to generalized application of the new chips in the electronics industry as a whole. East Germany still remained very weak in the diffusion of the latest technologies. Furthermore, the channeling of financial and personnel resources into microelectronics, within the context of general scarcity of money and qualified people, inevitably weakened other sectors of the economy through unbalanced development.

Consequently, despite the massive efforts to create a world-class microelectronics and computing industry in the GDR through 1988, and despite the many successes those efforts had achieved, it appeared that the uphill struggle would have to continue, and would have to be forced forward still further, in the coming few years. One trusted party member, reporting on a visit to the CeBit trade fair in Hannover in 1988, saw a need on the eve of the fall of the GDR for "increasing productivity, in order to secure at least a doubling of capacity in the GDR in the next three to four years with available capacity. This is necessary in order to increase export from the Robotron combine to the nonsocialist world."[34]

But even as he wrote, things were getting worse still, because the western embargo, ever a problem, had begun to bite harder. As the Stasi reported in January 1989, the production of the one-megabit chip in series was endangered by the unavailability of a high-voltage implantation device, which heightened embargo restrictions had prevented from arriving in the GDR. One such device had been acquired in the United States by agents of the GDR ("professionals in weapons export") and sent to a military enclave in Argentina, from where it was to be sent to Morocco and then the GDR. But the transport aircraft was not given permission to take off.[35]

A month later, the Stasi reported that Siemens was putting pressure on the companies in West Germany with which it had business contacts not to deliver its technology to the GDR. In particular, the firm Leybold AG, which had been taken over by Degussa and was a long-time supplier to the GDR of leading-edge technology, was affected by this.[36] As reported in a Stasi memorandum:

> The members of the Leybold AG managing board intimate an increasing level of pressure from their concern leadership—Degussa AG in Frankfurt am Main—which has been noticeable for several months and which they indicate is related to corresponding attempts at influence from the concern leadership of Siemens AG.
>
> Thus, for example, all members of the managing board of this firm [Leybold] had to confirm again in writing that they were undertaking no exports to the socialist countries that would contravene COCOM embargo restrictions. The increasing pressure leads one to expect that those forces within the managing board of Leybold AG which view further cooperation with the GDR with caution will gain in influence.[37]

One of the key problems in microelectronics and computing is that each new generation requires an enormous leap in terms of technology and also in terms of resources deployed in its development. Intel, for example, announced the world's first microprocessor, the 4004, in mid-November 1971. It took nine man-months to develop. The company introduced its 32-bit microprocessor, the APX432, in early 1981. It took 100 man-*years* to develop.[38] For the GDR, the problem was mustering such increased human resources in the face of a declining population. After all, each impressive success for the GDR in microelectronics and computing—even though it was tempered by the knowledge that East German technology still lagged far behind the West—entailed a higher commitment of humans, materials, and money to reach the next step. Growing shortages of people and money, problems only exacerbated by trade restrictions, meant that the GDR was eventually condemned to a steadily increasing technological lag with the West.

But does this mean that the GDR was condemned *from the outset* to relatively poor competitive performance, technological lag, and eventual collapse? This question demands speculation upon what did not, rather than what did, occur. Such speculation might range widely, but in the context of this historical study, it must focus on the availability of realistic alternatives to the path actually taken by the GDR leadership. It is clear that there was only one such alternative: to focus investment and R&D expenditure not on leading-edge technologies, but rather on run-of-the-mill ones, and on diffusing them more effectively throughout industry and the economy. In other words, the GDR might have focused instead on less sophisticated electronic components and apparatus, abandoning the most sophisticated sectors of the industry to countries better endowed with trained people and investment capital—countries such as the United States, Great Britain, and Japan. By embarking instead on an R&D trajectory that closely shadowed those countries and was utterly inappropriate for its own demographic, economic, and technological conditions, East Germany guaranteed not only that it would be unsuccessful in microelectronics, but also that it would starve other sectors of ideas and funding. The decision to embark on this path, made in the early 1980s, was not irreversible. But it was never reversed, and so contributed to the country's eventual collapse.

Conclusion

The story of the German Democratic Republic's forty-year existence can be told in many ways, and the rich array of scholarship and popular writing on the subject since 1990 is testimony to that. But to an extent unparalleled in the histories of many other countries, technology and its deployment shaped the unfolding of that story. Decisions about machines and how they should be used, as well as the implications of those decisions, dominated and helped determine the political, economic, and social development of the country from its beginnings in the aftermath of World War II until its collapse in 1989–90.

Part of the reason for the centrality of technology to East German history was ideological. For the party members who monopolized decision-making in this highly centralized country, high-technology development was at the core of the communist project. Ambitious plans for mechanizing, automating, and rationalizing GDR industry emerged in the early 1950s, just as the country was getting on its feet. And speeding up the development of electronics technology, automobiles and airplanes, sophisticated chemicals, nuclear power, and eventually rocketry and computing figured prominently in most party plans from the 1950s onward. Undoubtedly there was a large measure of rhetoric, and eventually even cynicism, in discourse about "socialist technology," "radical standardization," and so on. But there was also a large measure of conviction behind these and other slogans—a belief that the socialist system, with its dedication to planning and shared ownership, was peculiarly suited to modern technology, unlike chaotic, cutthroat capitalism.

Closely connected to this ideological proclivity to embrace modern technology was the practical necessity of employing high technology in order to attain one of the major goals of state socialism: detailed, precise, and timely planning of economic and social development. Such planning, the planners knew, would ultimately depend upon a variety of factors, including sophisticated techniques for gathering data; rapid and dependable communications technology for transferring the data to central planning authorities; equally rapid and theoretically sound analysis of data and development of plans; and flawless communication of the plans to, and monitoring of their performance in, industry, the economy, and society at large. Small wonder, then, that cybernetics enjoyed a period of high fashion in the GDR and that microelectronics and computing ultimately emerged as the country's primary foci for high-tech development and investment.

More important than the ideological and practical centrality of technology to the GDR leadership, however, was technology's position as a linchpin both in the undeniable achievements of the country and in the persistent crises that dogged the regime from the outset. Effective resuscitation of German technological traditions in research-intensive industries in the GDR in the aftermath of German defeat and Soviet occupation after 1945 helped the country to eventually become the richest country per capita in the Soviet bloc, the most technologically advanced, and a respected power in international terms as well. At the same time, unbalanced technological development, especially compared to the three German zones to the west, combined with relatively low population and poor resource endowments ensured relative backwardness compared to fledgling West Germany. Poor policy decisions about technological development exacerbated these inherent weaknesses of the GDR. By the mid-1950s, as a result of all these factors, the country was losing its scientific and technological intelligentsia at an alarming rate to the more vibrant West, a loss that threatened the regime's very existence and precipitated the Second Berlin Crisis (1958–61).

To be sure, the construction of the Berlin Wall in August 1961 stabilized the regime by stanching the outflow of scientists and engineers. But it also brought into sharper focus the fundamental problem facing the GDR both before and after the wall's erection: how was it possible to achieve high levels of economic growth and a correspondingly high standard of living with limited natural resources and a small and stable or declining population? The only solution to this fundamental dilemma was to foster innovation in order to achieve growth and well-being through labor-saving technology at home and high-value-added, high-technology exports to other countries. Ultimately, this attempt failed. But the prospect of ultimate failure did not deter GDR policymakers from embracing the strategy. In fact, microelectronics development from the late 1970s onward was probably spurred as much by the prospect of imminent failure of the strategy in so many other areas of industry and the economy as by any other factor.

Clearly, machines, their design, and their deployment—in other words, technology—played a crucial role in shaping the history of the German Democratic Republic. Saying this, of course, does not at all imply that machines, artifacts, and technological systems *determined* the country's history. In fact, the approach throughout this book has been just the reverse: the underlying assumption has been that machines, artifacts, and systems only exist and gain meaning by virtue of human agency. Technological systems can only be considered "actors" insofar as they embody the inherent assumptions and deliberate desires of those who commission, design, manufacture, and/or deploy them. In that sense, though, they are vital components of the political and social constellation of a given moment in time, and deserve to be recognized as such. Consideration of the role of technology in history does not have to exclude, but can rather enrich, the primacy of human agency and of contingency in historical interpretation.

This gets to one of the major issues at the heart of GDR historiography and consequently deserves attention here. The GDR's existence ended abruptly, and for most people unexpectedly, in 1990. But although the country's existence may have been "short" in absolute terms, it was not so in modern German terms. Forty-plus years old at the end of its existence, the GDR had existed longer than either the Weimar Republic or the Third Reich. It even rivaled Imperial Germany, whose constitutional order lasted just forty-five (or, using more flexible criteria, forty-seven) years. Crisis was constantly looming during that time, and many informed observers believed that the combination of constant crisis and internal contradiction must inevitably spell disaster for the GDR. Nonetheless, even as the country approached its end in late 1989 and early 1990, few predicted anything other than that the GDR would somehow muddle through once again.

Obviously, many—indeed most—informed observers were wrong in this respect at least. Still, the more interesting question is not so much why academics and journalists were wrong about a particular prediction. They frequently are, and this simply underscores the fact that human events very often are so complex as to defy prediction. No, the crucial question is to explain why a country founded in a state of extreme crisis and characterized by crisis throughout its existence was able to survive more than forty years, and even to appear healthy to the outside world for much of that time. The combination of permanent crisis and relative longevity is what sets East German history apart.

Some of the most obvious answers to this riddle lie in the purely political sphere. Soviet support for the GDR in periods of crisis, for instance, was no doubt crucial. Certainly this was true in June 1953 at the workers' uprising and during the Second Berlin Crisis. But perhaps the most telling indication of the importance of Soviet support came at the end of the country's existence, when it was withdrawn. When we recall the famous picture of Mikhail Gorbachev embracing Erich Honecker on the occasion of the fortieth anniversary of the founding of the GDR in early October 1989, we cannot help thinking that the Soviet leader was probably using the opportunity to inform the aging East German leader of the withdrawal of crucial Soviet support. This withdrawal in any case became patently obvious in the next few weeks. And it was undoubtedly a major factor—perhaps even *the* major factor—in determining the timing of the final collapse of the GDR regime.

In terms of domestic policy, the regime was propped up throughout its existence in part by a dense network of intelligence-gathering operations under the Stasi, which controlled and manipulated the GDR citizenry. This machinery was rudimentary as the GDR began, but it became more sophisticated and extensive as time went on. Persistent crisis encouraged the development of more and more effective tools for containing it.

But these factors in and of themselves cannot adequately explain the longevity of the GDR despite constant crisis, for they sometimes conceal as much as they reveal about the historical development of the regime. "Soviet support," for example, took different guises through time. And even though its withdrawal was an essential factor in determining the timing of the GDR's collapse, to focus on it as the key factor in the GDR's longevity would distort historical reality by implicitly downplaying the role of East German politicians in ensuring their country's continued existence. Similarly, a focus on spying tends to obscure the fact that the evidence for its effectiveness is far from clear. Even more important, it ignores that there was extensive passive and active support for the regime, especially at certain times in the country's history. This was, of course, less true at the end than at the beginning or during specific periods such as the mid-1960s, but it is nonetheless important to bear in mind.

Searching for a more satisfactory explanation for the stability and longevity of the GDR regime during perennial crisis requires more complex interpretations. Many have been advanced, of which I will focus on just two key ones. In 1992 the sociologist Sigrid Meuschel, in her book *Legitimation und Parteiherrschaft*, provided one of the first sophisticated "postwall" treatments of this problem.[1] Essentially, she argues that the GDR, for most of its existence, was extremely stable due to a lack of tradition of oppositional practice and the country's lack of institutions that would have allowed gradual reform. But, ironically, this inability to reform gradually, which guaranteed stability in the medium term, guaranteed revolution in the longer term. Drastic institutional upheaval was the only option left in the mid-1980s, when the accumulated results of frequent and unresolved crises were matched with high levels of migration from the GDR and broader systemic crisis in the eastern bloc.

Jeffrey Kopstein's 1997 book *The Politics of Economic Decline in East Germany, 1945–1989* is the first full-length, archivally based treatment of this problematic in English. Unlike Meuschel, who contends that political equilibrium was possible in the GDR owing to the nonexistence of traditions and institutions of opposition, Kopstein argues that political equilibrium was attained owing to the constant threat, from 1953 onward, of effective and fatal opposition. The fact that labor, from that point forward, had a "paradoxical sort of veto power" meant that the opportunities for the party to reform the system from within were severely limited. Indeed, for practically the whole of the country's existence, party officials were managing inevitable long-term economic decline.[2]

Although very different, both these interpretations have much to recommend them. Both authors provide a clear and consistent explanation for the GDR's longevity despite constant crisis and, in advancing their interpretations, consider the role of technology, although it does not occupy a central place in their arguments. Both authors, however, from opposite vantage points, also share at least one characteristic that is difficult to reconcile with the notion of historical contingency. Meuschel implies that there was little historical development in the GDR until the mid-1980s (except slow accretion of unresolved crises, which ultimately made the regime untenable and eventually led to revolution), while Kopstein suggests that there was little historical development after 1953 (except slow accretion of measures and half-measures staving off inevitable economic decline).

In contrast, a more thoroughgoing analysis of the role of technology in the history of the GDR, such as that offered here, provides a more nuanced picture of the country's decline and eventual collapse, neither of which was preordained from the outset. The technologies and the technological systems inherited by the GDR from unified Germany were after all viable and thriving into the early 1960s at the very least. In some cases, moreover, German traditions, together with GDR "tweaking" of those traditions, ensured that they performed well even beyond that. These traditions included such crucial industries as office machinery, machine tools, and optics. The strength of these areas, even in the 1970s and 1980s, is undeniable and goes far to explain the GDR's maintenance of some degree of economic and political stability, reasonable standards of living, and even instances of international competitiveness over the longer term. It was, therefore, not just traditions of political culture and institutions that guaranteed the regime's stability despite constant crisis. The vestiges of traditions of technological excellence underpinned these political and institutional traditions, promoting stability in the country over a surprisingly long period of time.

Traditions of technological excellence and the inheritance of an effective system of innovation guaranteed a measure of stability and affluence as the GDR emerged from the ravages of World War II. But the inability to alter that system to adapt effectively to the demands of new technologies and to promote not just scientific research, but the transfer of that research to industry to attain constant gains in productivity, eventually proved damaging to the GDR.

The causes of this inability to participate fully in international terms in the development of modern technologies lay to some degree in the socialist system as it developed in East Germany during the 1950s. Development of the most modern technologies, such as numerically controlled machine tools, computers, and so on, required more than theoretical competence. To an unprecedented degree, it required interactions among different industries, R&D organizations, and customers. But the GDR's centralized organizational structure hindered such interactions. The system of planning and the lack of effective measures for disciplining suppliers discouraged cooperation among different firms in different industries. Planning necessarily depended on analysis of past performance and therefore tended to favor existing products, as did plan fulfillment, which in turn encouraged avoidance of the unpredictable and sometimes arduous learning curve that the introduction of new technologies would have entailed. And the productivist mentality of the planners tended to disregard the wishes of—and vital feedback from—consumers.

By the late 1950s these problems resulted in relative economic decline in comparison with West Germany, insufficient increases in the standard of living of the GDR population, and growing numbers of GDR citizens voting with their feet by leaving the country. The Second Berlin Crisis was a critical juncture in the GDR's history. The political nature of the crisis is obvious, but I have also emphasized its underlying technological causes and consequences. Until that point, the GDR had altered its system of innovation to conform to the Soviet model, but practicing engineers and managers were by and large still heavily influenced by ideas and training about technology imbibed before 1945. For the most part, they looked to the West rather than the East for technological inspiration, and purchase of know-how, machines, and technological systems from the West continued apace despite continuing foreign exchange difficulties and some attempts to foster technology transfer within the eastern bloc.

The Berlin crisis, however, rendered the continuation of this practice untenable, forcing a recognition that the intimate technological connection with the West was at odds with the GDR's growing political estrangement from the West. Such close technological connections, moreover, made the GDR dangerously dependent on the West. These insights undoubtedly forced a fundamental reorientation of East German technology between 1958 and 1961. But consideration of them alone would lead one to expect a grudging and reluctant resignation to the need for closer connections to the Soviets and other eastern European countries, rather than the active and excited embrace that in many cases actually occurred. This, I argue, can only be explained by the perception of Soviet technological accomplishment, symbolized most spectacularly by the launch of the first Sputnik, but also evident in Soviet achievements in petrochemicals, semiconductor development, and Group Technology. By 1961 the die was cast politically with the construction of the Berlin Wall. At the same time, a technological wall began to be erected by means of more systematic adoption of Soviet standards for the production of goods in the GDR.

The year 1961, then, was a crucial breaking point in the history of the GDR for technological as well as for political reasons. Still, even that breaking point did not mean that the GDR was thereafter condemned to its ultimate fate in 1989. Indeed, in 1961 most of the country's existence remained ahead of it.

At this juncture, two key points need to be made. First, the inability of the GDR's leadership to adapt their system of innovation to promote development of the most modern technologies and to diffuse best practice throughout industry and society was not inherent in GDR politics or society from the outset in 1949, but was instead the product of historical development. In other words, although the GDR's Soviet-style system of government constrained the country's ability to develop a more efficient and effective system of innovation, there were other, ultimately possibly more important factors at work as well. These included the size of the country, the state in which it was left after Soviet occupation, the political tension of the 1950s, limited raw materials, and so on.

The second point follows to some degree from the first. To the extent to which the GDR's system of innovation was responsible for the inability to perform effectively in more modern technologies and to diffuse innovation throughout the economy, it was in principle possible to change that system to make it function more satisfactorily. To be sure, the attempts to do this during the 1960s through the New Economic System and its successor did not by any means solve the problems of the GDR in the area of technology and innovation. Still, they represented real innovations in communist planning and practice, and may potentially have improved the system of innovation. But here, as was frequently the case, the GDR's attempts at reform foundered on developments outside its control. In terms of technological development, the most important of these were Soviet unwillingness to fulfill promises to supply key raw materials, especially petroleum, as well as reluctance to provide technological assistance in key high-technology industries out of considerations of national security.

Even after the collapse of the reform movement in the waning years of the 1960s and the end of the Ulbricht era in 1971, the GDR still had options, but they were dissipating fast. The Honecker regime's decisions in many areas constrained opportunities to improve the GDR's situation. Armed with the slogan, "The Unity of Social and Economic Policy," Honecker oversaw the provision of an unprecedented array of consumer goods to East German citizens. But these were never available in such abundance or at the same level of quality as in West Germany. They were also purchased at a very high price in national economic terms, which involved not only horrendous levels of national debt, but also general neglect of investment in industry and innovation. To compensate for these deficiencies, the Honecker regime attempted to develop substitutes for success through the establishment and expansion of a secondary raw materials organization (Sero) and an organization for collecting and disseminating technological intelligence from abroad (within the Stasi).

The emphasis on substitution is a persistent theme in modern German economic and technological history, and was not restricted to the latter years of the GDR. Still, self-sufficiency in the GDR had different motivations and differing effects compared to other regimes in German history. Unlike the Nazi era, in which autarkic policies were largely embraced deliberately as part of a general preparation for war, policies promoting self-sufficiency in the GDR were adopted mainly because of the lack of viable alternatives. The GDR's efforts to develop self-sufficiency in key areas through technological development or substitutions were also unprecedented in terms of their endurance: unlike the ersatz policies of World War I, these emergency measures became permanent fixtures of GDR economy and society, lasting for decades in many cases.

These unique aspects of the GDR's self-sufficiency policies had unusual effects. They led, for instance, to a situation in which the country "unwittingly preserved fossils of [consumer] articles" long since outdated in the West, becoming a sort of "Galapagos Islands of the Design World."[3] They led to the further development of exotic, often outdated technologies, such as acetylene-based chemistry, which lost out completely to petroleum-based chemistry elsewhere. They also led to one of the most efficient recycling programs in the world and an intelligence apparatus capable of evading most of the West's security restrictions on export of technology to the eastern bloc.

Sero and the Stasi were especially important and interesting institutions within the evolving system of innovation in East Germany. They were designed primarily to overcome severe deficiencies within that system, of course, but neither actually did so. However, as I argue in chapter 7, they had the potential to function better than they actually did. If Sero had worked more effectively with the machine-building industry in developing recycling processing machinery for export, it might have served a much more positive and dynamic economic function beyond making the paltry raw materials available in East Germany stretch a little further. Had the Stasi not been so fixated on high technology to the exclusion of all else, the intelligence-gathering and smuggling operations might have been more effective in promoting the prospects of middle-tech industry in the GDR.But it was not to be. It is worth emphasizing, though, that it also did not *necessarily* have to turn out the way it did.

Even as the limits to the strategies of substituting for success were being reached in the late 1970s and early 1980s, the GDR embarked on a final, grand attempt to overcome its technological and economic deficiencies compared to the West through the intensive and very expensive development of microelectronics technology. Relying heavily on machines and information provided by the Stasi, the microelectronics program starved other R&D areas of financial and personnel resources. And even with the vast effort and expenditure, the program did not allow the GDR to do more than produce poor replicas of already outdated western components. It did virtually nothing to improve the everyday operations of industry in the country. The gamble, in other words, did not pay off. Largely on account of this, there is no question that, whatever possibilities for reform may have existed through that point, the GDR's ultimate demise was inevitable by the early 1980s: the question was no longer whether the wheels would come off, but when.

The answer was not long in coming. Although the reasons that the GDR would ultimately collapse were largely technological, the precise timing of that collapse was political. In particular, the withdrawal of Soviet support in the late 1980s left the GDR leadership no option but to accede to popular demands by opening up the wall.

The aftermath of the fall of the Berlin Wall on 9 November 1989 fully exposed the depths of the problems with the GDR economy and system of innovation.[4] For the first time, visitors from the West began to arrive in large numbers at GDR industrial plants. With the support of the privatization agency, the Treuhandanstalt (THA), which was trying to sell off all state-owned industry in the former GDR, they could poke and prod the physical plant and carefully inspect the books of the erstwhile combines. Most of them did not like what they found, and partly for that reason, the THA's work is still being carried out by a successor organization, the Federal Agency for Special Tasks Brought About by Unification (Bundesanstalt für vereinigungsbedingte Sonderaufgaben, or BVS). But, to the extent that it was successful in its efforts at privatization during the first half of the 1990s, the THA benefited from enormous financial subventions from the German federal government for environmental improvements, infrastructural repair and expansion, investment, and tax incentives.

Many of the problems with selling off the industrial plant of the former GDR stemmed from the state of its technology, which was woeful, especially in the industries that had been neglected by the Honecker regime during much of its existence (in other words, almost all branches except microelectronics). This was brought home to me in 1991 when I visited an industrial plant in the former GDR for the first time to do archival research.

At that time, the archives of the Leuna Works were located in the old part of the plant, which had its origins before World War I as a subsidiary of BASF. By the 1920s Leuna, eventually part of I. G. Farben, had become the largest chemical factory in Germany, and was one of the most technologically advanced in the world. After World War II, despite destruction and dismantling, it remained a mainstay of the GDR economy, providing desperately needed plastics, among other things. Its official name, the VEB Leuna-Werke "Walter Ulbricht," gave some indication of the esteem in which it was held by the central government, at least through the 1960s. It featured prominently in the chemicalization program of the late 1950s, and its relatively new Leuna II plant was the site of the GDR's first large-scale foray into petrochemicals technology in the 1960s and beyond.

I had all this in mind as I walked to the archive through the still impressive plant, where I was nearly overcome by the smell of organic chemicals dripping from the vast network of overhead pipes, pipes that in some cases appeared to be held together with the East German equivalent of chewing gum and baling wire. The atmosphere around the factory was extremely gloomy, not just because of its physical state, but even more because of the specter of massive job losses that appeared to be in the offing despite—and possibly because of—the efforts of the THA to sell the plant. Interest from potential buyers in the property as a whole was practically nonexistent. Carving it up into smaller pieces seemed the only way forward, but even that was attracting few purchasers. Unfortunately, the fears of job loss were soon realized.

As I surveyed the scene before me, I had cause to reflect on just how far Leuna had fallen from its heyday as the region's most important single employer and the technological envy of the whole world. Its sorry state seemed to be the physical embodiment of the explanation for the failure of the GDR.

But two considerations substantially modified that first impression. One occurred to me right then, as I continued on my walk toward the archive: Leuna may have been in a dismal state, but it was still manufacturing organic chemical products in large quantities for the GDR and eastern European markets when the country collapsed, and even well into the early 1990s. Despite years of underinvestment and general neglect by the central government, the factory was still limping along. The remarkable thing, then, was not that the factory had fallen into disrepair, but rather that it was still there, held together by chewing gum and baling wire applied by resourceful employees. It was the physical embodiment of an important element of the explanation for the longevity of the GDR.

The second consideration occurred more gradually, as I stepped back from my more detailed researches into the GDR's chemical industry to think more broadly about the economy and technology as a whole: clearly, upon reflection, the state of GDR technology was not the sole explanation for the country's collapse or for what was happening in the former GDR after unification. The old plant at Leuna, in its state of disrepair, underinvestment, and outmoded technology, was perhaps unfortunately fairly representative of much of GDR industry. But there were major exceptions to this pattern, as for instance the Leuna II plant, or the "Fritz Heckert" machine-tool works in Chemnitz (formerly Karl-Marx City).

Commenting on the Chemnitz machine-tool works in mid-1990, British business journalist Alan Purkiss intimated that its modern and generously outfitted main plant "would not disgrace any western manufacturer," and predicted a bright future for it. Yet that advanced modern technology did not prevent the Heckert works from going into receivership in late 1996. Purkiss chose the Buna Chemical Works in Schkopau to contrast with the Heckert works. Because of its dire technological condition (which was, if anything, worse that that of Leuna), Purkiss predicted that dealing with the plant's state was "a daunting prospect for any partner." Yet the Buna Works, linked with other chemical plants in the area (including a part of the old Leuna plant), has been taken over as a subsidiary of Dow Chemical Corporation and renamed the BSL Olefinverbund GmbH. It is now enjoying heavy investment and technological renewal, which will make it one of the most modern chemical production facilities in the world.[5]

As this example demonstrates, although the general technological state of the GDR may have contributed substantially to the country's final collapse, especially from the late 1970s onward, the technological state of individual factories did not determine their fate in the aftermath of 1989. Instead, several other factors must be mentioned. The major blow was undoubtedly that factories from the former GDR were forced to adopt the deutsche mark without adequate preparation or period of transition in mid-1990, thus eliminating unceremoniously the vital eastern European markets for the plants. By the time programs were devised to try to ease this transition through loans and subventions, it was too late for many companies in the new federal states. Problems with unclear ownership and environmental degradation also helped determine the fate of individual plants, as did the more general state of the world economy, which, on the whole, featured sufficient modern capacity to supply the market of the former GDR effortlessly and without reliance on suppliers from the new states. The result has been crippling job losses, pervasive social problems, and a fear that the area of the former GDR will remain permanently behind that of the old federal republic in economic terms.

On a brighter note, however, technological renewal is proceeding apace in the states of the former GDR, with the federal government underwriting new, extremely modern communications and transportation infrastructure. Attracted by this and even more by the emerging and potentially lucrative markets of eastern Europe, companies such as Dow are deploying managerial, technological, and commercial resources to modernize industry. The success of these efforts in the long term depends on many factors outside the control of the companies involved, of the new federal states, or of the federal government. But it will depend ultimately upon harnessing the abilities of the human beings who received their training in science and engineering in what was, despite all its drawbacks, a modern technological state, and who were able, despite extremely adverse conditions, to keep Leuna and other neglected factories in operation. Despite the enormous changes to the East German system of innovation undertaken during the GDR's existence, some important vestiges of traditions of German technological excellence survived, and still remain.

Abbreviations Used in the
Text and Notes

AdW	German Academy of Sciences (Deutsche Akademie der Wissenschaften)
AfS	Office for Standardization (Amt für Standardisierung)
BAP	Bundesarchiv Berlin, formerly Potsdam
BRABAG	Braunkohlenbenzin AG
BStU	Federal Deputy for the Documents of the State Security Service of the Former German Democratic Republic (Bundesbeauftragte für die Unterlagen des Staatssicherheitsdienstes der ehemaligen Deutschen Demokratischen Republik)
BVS	Federal Agency for Special Tasks Brought About by Unification (Bundesanstalt für vereinigungsbedingte Sonderaufgaben)
CEFIC	European Center of Federations of Industrial Chemistry
COCOM	Coordinating Committee (for East-West trade)
COMECON	Council for Mutual Economic Cooperation
CZ	Carl Zeiss
DAW	German Academy of Sciences (Deutsche Akademie der Wissenschaften zu Berlin)
DFG	German Research Society (Deutsche Forschungsgemeinschaft)
DIN	German Industrial Norms (Deutsche Industrie-Normen)
DIW	German Institute for Economic Research
DNA	German Norms Committee (Deutsche Normen-Ausschuss)
DWK	German Economic Commission (Deutsche Wirtschaftskommission)
ESER	Unified System for Electronic Computing Technology (Einheitliches System der elektronischen Rechentechnik)
ESS	Economic System of Socialism
GOST	State Standards of the [Soviet] Union
HVA	Main Espionage Administration (Hauptverwaltung Aufklärung) of MfS

IM	"informal agents" (*informelle Mitarbeiter*)
ISA	International Federation of the National Standardizing Associations
ISO	International Standards Organization
KME	Microelectronics Combine (Mikroelektronik Kombinat)
KPD	Communist Party of Germany
MfS	Ministry for State Security (Ministerium für Staatssicherheit, or Stasi)
NES	New Economic System of Planning and Management of the Economy
OPREMA	Optical Calculator (Optische Rechenmaschine)
PTR	Imperial Institute for Physics and Technology (Physikalisch-Technische Reichsanstalt)
RKW	Imperial Board for Economic Efficiency (Reichskuratorium für Wirtschaftlichkeit)
SAGs	Soviet Joint-Stock Companies (Sowjetische Aktiengesellschaften)
SAPMO	Federal Archives Foundation for the Parties and mass Organizations of the GDR (Stiftung Bundesarchiv der Parteien und Massenorganisationen der DDR)
SBZ	Soviet Zone of Occupation in Germany (Sowjetische Besatzungszone)
SED	Socialist Unity Party (Sozialistische Einheitspartei Deutschland)
Sero	Secondary Raw Materials Company (VEB Sekundärrohstoff)
SKR	System of Mini-computers (System der Kleinrechner)
SMAD	Soviet Military Administration in Germany
SPK	State Planning Commission (Staatliche Plankommission)
SWT	Scientific and Technical Sector (Sektor Wissenschaft und Technik) of the HVA
TAN	"technically determined work norms"
TGL	Technical Conditions for Quality and Delivery (Technische Güte- und Lieferbedingungen)
TH	Polytechnic (Technische Hochschule)
THA	Treuhandanstalt
USSBS	U.S. Strategic Bombing Survey
VCI	Chemical Industry Trade Association (Verband der chemischen Industrie)
VEB	People's Own Enterprises (Volkseigene Betriebe)
VEB WBN	Works for Electrical Components for Communications Technology (VEB Werk für Bauelemente der Nachrichtentechnik "Carl von Ossietzky")

VEB WF	VEB Works for Telecommunications (VEB Werk für Fernmeldewesen)
VLSI	very large-scale integration
VVB	Union of VEBs (Verein Volkseigene Betriebe)
ZAFT	Central Office for Research and Technology (Zentrales Amt für Forschung und Technik)
ZIA	Central Institute for Automation (Zentralinstitut für Automatisierung)

Notes

Introduction

1. On "failed" innovations, see the special issue of *Social Studies of Science* 22 (1992). Related to this notion is that of "competing technologies." See, for instance, W. Brian Arthur, "Positive Feedbacks in the Economy," *Scientific American* (February 1990): 92–99; and Raymond G. Stokes, *Opting for Oil: The Political Economy of Technological Change in the West German Chemical Industry, 1945–1961* (Cambridge: Cambridge University Press, 1994).

2. David Childs, *The GDR: Moscow's German Ally* (London: George Allen and Unwin, 1983), 162; Eberhard Schneider, *The GDR: The History, Politics, Economy and Society of East Germany*, translated by Hannes Adomeit and Roger Clarke (London: C. Hurst, 1978), 102.

3. German Institute for Economic Research (DIW), *Handbook of the Economy of the German Democratic Republic* (Westmead: Saxon House, 1979), 35, 37 (quotation).

4. Vincent Edwards and Peter Lawrence, *Management Change in East Germany: Unification and Transformation* (London: Routledge, 1994), 52–54.

5. Raymond Bentley, *Research and Technology in the Former German Democratic Republic* (Boulder, Colo.: Westview Press, 1992), 143.

6. Johannes Bähr and Dietmar Petzina, "Innovationsverhalten und Entscheidungsstrukturen in der Wirtschaft der Bundesrepublik und der DDR—Fragestellung und Bilanz," in *Innovationsverhalten und Entscheidungsstrukturen. Vergleichende Studien zur wirtschaftlichen Entwicklung im geteilten Deutschland 1945–1990*, edited by Johannes Bähr and Dietmar Petzina (Berlin: Duncker & Humblot, 1996), 11–20.

7. See, for instance, Susanne Franke and Rainer Klumpe, "Offsetdruck als Herausforderung für innovatives Handeln: Die Innovationsaktivitäten der Druckmaschinenhersteller Koenig & Bauer AG (Würzburg) und VEB Planea (Radebeul) in den sechziger Jahren," in Bähr and Petzina, eds., *Innovationsverhalten und Entscheidungsstrukturen*, 215–50; Katharina Hein, "Space Research in the GDR: Development of the Unified Telemetry System (Einheitliches Telemetriesystem, ETMS) within the Interkosmos Cooperation," in *Science, Technology, and Political Change*, edited by Benoit Severyns, Dieter Hoffmann, and Raymond Stokes (Turnhout: Brepols, 1999).

8. The Deutsche Forschungsgemeinschaft (DFG) funded a very large-scale, multiyear investigation into innovation in the two Germanies between 1945 and 1990,

and some of its results are now being published. One collection of essays resulting from the DFG project is Bähr and Petzina, eds., *Innovationsverhalten und Entscheidungsstrukturen.*

9. See, for instance, the contributions by Rainer Karlsch on innovation in synthetic rubber at two former I. G. Farben factories, and by Roland Kowalski on innovation in construction of scientific apparatus in the West and East German Zeiss successors, both in Bähr and Petzina, *Innovationsverhalten und Entscheidungsstrukturen.*

10. The amount of literature here is enormous. One of the most impressive pieces is Anthony Sutton's three-volume work, *Western Technology and Soviet Economic Development, 1917–1965* (Stanford, Calif.: Hoover Institution Press, 1968–73). Vol. 1 deals with the period 1917–30, vol. 2 with 1930–45, and vol. 3 with 1945–65 (vol. 3 deals extensively with the influence of German technology on the Soviet Union and technological ties between the USSR and East Germany). See also Ronald Amann and Julian Cooper, eds., *Industrial Innovation in the Soviet Union* (New Haven: Yale University Press, 1982); R. Amann, J. Cooper, and R. W. Davies, eds., *The Technological Level of Soviet Industry* (New Haven: Yale University Press, 1977); Bruce Parrott, ed., *Trade, Technology, and Soviet-American Relations* (Bloomington: Indiana University Press, 1985); Thane Gustafson, *Selling the Russians the Rope? Soviet Technology Policy and U.S. Export Controls* (Santa Monica, Calif.: RAND Corp., 1991). Gustafson's title refers to a remark made by Lenin to the effect that the capitalists would sell the communists the rope to enable them eventually to return to hang capitalism; but the conclusions allude to a different and more common saying: "Give them enough rope and they'll hang themselves."

11. On Japan see, for instance, Tessa Morris-Suzuki, *The Technological Transformation of Japan* (Cambridge: Cambridge University Press, 1994); on British scientific and technological capability after World War II, see David Edgerton, *Science, Technology, and British Industrial 'Decline,' 1870–1970* (Cambridge: Cambridge University Press, 1996).

12. Bentley, *Research and Technology in the Former German Democratic Republic,* 142–43 (quotation on 143).

Chapter 1: Technology in the Soviet Zone, 1945–1949

1. For an overview of political, social, and economic aspects of the Soviet occupation, see Norman Naimark, *The Russians in Germany: A History of the Soviet Zone of Occupation, 1945–1949* (Cambridge, Mass.: Belknap Press of Harvard University Press, 1995).

2. See Gary Herrigel, *Industrial Constructions* (Cambridge: Cambridge University Press, 1996), especially the map on 468.

3. Erich Sobeslavsky and Nikolaus Joachim Lehmann, *Zur Geschichte von Rechentechnik und Datenverarbeitung in der DDR 1946–1968* (Dresden: Hannah-Arendt-Institut, 1996), 13.

4. Peter Hayes, *Industry and Ideology: I. G. Farben in the Nazi Era* (Cambridge: Cambridge University Press, 1986); Raymond G. Stokes, *Divide and Prosper: The Heirs of I. G. Farben under Allied Authority, 1945–1951* (Berkeley: University of California Press, 1988).

5. Roland Kowalski, "Die Integration der Elektronik in den wissenschaftlichen Gerätebau—eine Fallstudie, dargestellt in einer vergleichenden Betrachtung von Carl Zeiss Jena und Carl Zeiss Oberkochen während der sechziger Jahre," 191, in Bähr and Petzina, eds., *Innovationsverhalten und Entscheidungsstrukturen*, 191.

6. U.S. Strategic Bombing Survey (USSBS), *Summary Report (European War)* (Washington, D.C.: U.S. Government Printing Office, 30 September 1945), 4, 6, 8–10, 12–13. See also USSBS, *Aircraft Division: Industry Report*, Final Report 84 (Washington, D.C.: U.S. Government Printing Office, January 1947); quoted in Sutton, *Western Technology and Soviet Economic Development 1945–1965*, 20.

7. Rainer Karlsch, *Allein bezahlt? Die Reparationsleistungen der SBZ/DDR 1945–1953* (Berlin: Christoph Links, 1993), 36–54, especially 44–46. Karlsch cites a publication from the late 1960s in the GDR as symptomatic of the very high (and completely undependable) figures on war damages, which clearly had entered GDR mythology. See Hans Müller and Karl Reißig, *Wirtschaftswunder DDR* (Berlin: Dietz, 1968), 15.

8. Karlsch, *Allein bezahlt?* 46 (quotation).

9. Ibid., 9, 46, 282.

10. USSBS, *Optical and Precision Instrument Industry Report*, Report 50, 2d ed. (Washington, D.C.: U.S. Government Printing Office, 1947), 22.

11. Karlsch, *Allein bezahlt?* 37, 88.

12. For more on this see, for instance, Matthias Judt and Burghard Ciesla, eds., *Technology Transfer Out of Germany after 1945* (Amsterdam: Harwood, 1996); Ulrich Albrecht, Andreas Heinemann-Grüder, and Arend Wellmann, *Die Spezialisten: Deutsche Naturwissenschaftler und Techniker in der Sowjetunion nach 1945* (Berlin: Dietz, 1992); Karlsch, *Allein bezahlt?*; Sutton, *Western Technology and Soviet Economic Development, 1945–1965*.

13. Karlsch, *Allein bezahlt?* 282.

14. See, for instance, Raymond G. Stokes, "Assessing the Damages: Forced Technology Transfer and the German Chemical Industry," in Judt and Ciesla, eds., *Technology Transfer Out of Germany after 1945*, 81–92.

15. This concept is explored (although not with specific regard to technology) in Konrad Jarausch and Hannes Siegrist, eds., *Amerikanisierung und Sowjetisierung in Deutschland, 1945–1970* (Frankfurt: Campus, 1997).

16. Sutton, *Western Technology and Soviet Economic Development, 1945–65*, 21–25 (quotation on 21).

17. Ibid., 325.

18. Ulrich Albrecht and Randolph Nikutta, *Die sowjetische Rüstungsindustrie* (Opladen: Westdeutscher Verlag, 1989), for instance, note the impact of German technology on the armaments industry, although they also insist that the Soviets did much of the development on their own.

19. More on this notion can be found in Raymond Stokes, "Americanized, Sovietized, and Still German: Theses on the History of German Technology after 1945," paper presented at conference on Americanization and Sovietization, Berlin, 24 June 1995.

20. The American effort is the only one that has been studied in great detail, most prominently by John Gimbel, *Science, Technology and Reparations: Exploitation and Plunder in Post-war Germany* (Stanford, Calif.: Stanford University Press,

1991). But there are some indications of the French and British efforts in Judt and Ciesla, eds., *Technology Transfer Out of Germany after 1945*; Marie-France Ludmann-Obier, "Le contrôle de la recherche scientifique en zone française d'Occupation en Allemagne (1945–1949)," *Revue d'Allemagne* 20 (1988): 397–414; Ludmann-Obier, "Un aspect de la chasse aux cerveaux: Les transferts de techniciens allemands en France: 1945–1949," *Relations internationales* 46 (1986): 195–208.

21. See, for instance, the popular and sometimes exaggerated treatment in Tom Bower, *The Paperclip Conspiracy* (Boston: Little, Brown, 1987); a more balanced, if somewhat older, account is in Clarence Lasby, *Project Paperclip* (New York: Athenaeum, 1971).

22. On the internment of German atomic scientists at Farm Hall, see Dieter Hoffmann's introduction to his edition of *Operation Epsilon: Die Farm-Hall-Protokolle oder Die Angst der Alliierten vor der deutschen Atombombe* (Berlin: Rowohlt, 1993). On the use of German aeronautical engineers and scientists see, for instance, Frederick Ordway III and Mitchell R. Sharpe, *The Rocket Team: From the V-2 to the Saturn Moon Rocket* (Cambridge, Mass.: MIT Press, 1982).

23. Albrecht, Heinemann-Grüder, and Wellmann, *Die Spezialisten*, 171–76.

24. Ibid., 15.

25. See Karlsch, *Allein bezahlt?* 155–66.

26. Ibid., 166.

27. Albrecht, Heinemann-Grüder, and Wellmann, *Die Spezialisten*, 23–24, 171–76 (quotations on 24, 176).

28. Naimark, *The Russians in Germany*, 189–93; German Institute for Economic Research, *Handbook of the Economy of the German Democratic Republic*, 3–5. The figure of 25–30 percent of total industrial production in the SBZ/early GDR being undertaken by the SAGs has long been accepted, but it is likely that new work using previously unavailable archival materials will begin to revise those earlier estimates upward.

29. Naimark, *The Russians in Germany*, 191.

30. Joachim Radkau, "Revoltierten die Produktivkräfte gegen den real existierenden Sozialismus? Technikhistorische Anmerkung zum Zerfall der DDR," *1999* (1990): 13–42 (quotations on 27).

31. Ibid., 27.

32. Jörg Roesler, *Die Herausbildung der sozialistischen Planwirtschaft in der DDR* (Berlin: Akademie-Verlag, 1978).

33. German Institute for Economic Research, *Handbook of the Economy of the German Democratic Republic*, 4–6.

34. Eckart Förtsch, "Wissenschafts- und Technologiepolitik in der DDR," in *Naturwissenschaft und Technik in der DDR*, edited by Dieter Hoffmann and Kristie Macrakis (Berlin: Academie-Verlag, 1997), 17–33, especially 19–20.

35. This section employs the concept of national systems of innovation as used in the collection edited by Richard R. Nelson, *National Innovation Systems* (Oxford: Oxford University Press, 1993).

36. See, for instance, Peter Nötzoldt, "Der Weg zur 'sozialistischen Forschungsakademie': Der Wandel des Akademiegedankens zwischen 1945 und 1968," in Hoffmann and Macrakis, eds., *Naturwissenschaft und Technik in der DDR*, 125–46, especially 125–30.

37. See, for instance, Alan Beyerchen, "On the Stimulation of Excellence in Wilhelmine Science," in *Another Germany: A Reconsideration of the Imperial Era,* edited by Jack Dukes and Joachim Remak (Boulder, Colo.: Westview Press, 1988), 139–68.

38. See Jeffrey Kopstein, *The Politics of Economic Decline in East Germany, 1945–1989* (Chapel Hill: University of North Carolina Press, 1997), 25–35.

39. Bähr and Petzina, "Innovationsverhalten und Entscheidungsstrukturen in der Wirtschaft der Bundesrepublik und der DDR—Fragestellung und Bilanz."

40. Karlsch, *Allein bezahlt?* 44.

Chapter 2: Technology Planning and Practice through 1958

1. This concept is based on the work of Richard Nelson and others—for instance, Nelson, ed., *National Innovation Systems.* Although she does not use this concept, Agnes Tandler provides the most detailed overview of the establishment of the GDR national system of innovation, and in particular of the development of science policy, in "Geplante Zukunft. Wissenschaftler und Wissenschaftspolitik in der DDR, 1955–1971" (Ph.D. diss., European University Institute, Florence, 1997). My thanks to Dr. Tandler for providing me with a copy of this fine work.

2. For some of these traditions see, for instance, Alan D. Beyerchen, "On the Stimulation of Excellence in Wilhelminian Science," in *Another Germany: A Reconsideration of the Imperial Era,* edited by Jack R. Dukes and Joachim Remak (Boulder, Colo.: Westview Press, 1988), 139–68.

3. Wolfgang Mühlfriedel and Klaus Wießner, *Die Geschichte der Industrie der DDR bis 1965* (Berlin: Akademie-Verlag, 1989), 100; Bundesministerium für innerdeutsche Beziehungen, *DDR Handbuch,* 3d ed. (Cologne: Verlag Wissenschaft und Politik, 1985), 436. The figures reported for 1950 in the latter source are two-thirds again as high as those reported in the former, although the reasons for the discrepancy are not clear. One possible explanation is that Mühlfriedel and Wießner's figures represent planned expenditures, while those of the *DDR Handbuch* are for actual expenditures. In any case, one-half to one percent of national income should be seen as a maximum.

4. Figures from Reinhold Geimer and Hildegard Geimer, *Science in the Federal Republic of Germany: Organization and Promotion,* 4th ed., revised and enlarged (Bonn: DAAD, 1971), table on 59.

5. Mühlfriedel and Wießner, *Die Geschichte der Industrie der DDR bis 1965,* 98–99.

6. Ibid., table on 98. There is no indication here of the size of each of the establishments, whether in terms of personnel or of funding.

7. Arlt (Amt für Erfindungs- und Patentwesen), "Rechtslage der deutschen Patente im Ausland," 7 June 1951, Bundesarchiv Berlin, formerly Potsdam (hereafter BAP), DE1/17, 109; the text of the Allied agreement is reprinted in "Accord on Treatment of German-Owned Patents," 27 July 1946, U.S. Department of State, *Treaties and Other International Acts,* Series 2415, 1–3.

8. Precisely how valuable they were is a matter of considerable uncertainty. For some thoughts on this, see Stokes, "Assessing the Damages."

9. *Jahrbuch der DDR 1958* (Berlin: Verlag Die Wirtschaft, 1958), 225.

10. Mühlfriedel and Wießner, *Die Geschichte der Industrie der DDR bis 1965*, 99.

11. Stokes, *Opting for Oil*.

12. Mühlfriedel and Wießner, *Die Geschichte der Industrie der DDR bis 1965*, 96.

13. Ibid., 100–102.

14. Rainer Karlsch, "Rekonstruktion und Strukturwandel in der sächsichen Industrie von 1945 bis Anfang der sechziger Jahre," in *Wirtschaft und Gesellschaft in Sachsen im 20. Jahrhundert*, edited by Werner Bramke and Ulrich Hess (Leipzig: Leipziger Universitätsverlag, 1998), 89–132. My thanks to Dr. Karlsch for providing me with a manuscript copy of this article.

15. Memo from ZK der SED, Abt. Maschinenbau, to Gen. Otto Schön, "Betr.: Bericht an das Sekretariat über die Lage der Kamera-Werkstätten Niedersedlitz," 4 September 1953, 1, Stiftung Archiv der Parteien und Massenorganisationen der DDR im Bundesarchiv, Berlin (hereafter SAPMO), DY 30 IV 2/604/84.

16. "Zusammenfassung nutzbarer Ergebnisse abgeschlossener Forschungs- und Entwicklungsarbeiten, die nicht in die Produktion eingeführt wurden, im Zeitraum 1950–1958," n.d. (ca. 1959), 5, BAP DE1/2299. Ideally, it would be very useful to be able to establish the value of the projects by reason for abandonment, but although the value of the projects is reported in the tables from which these figures are taken, it is not possible to link expenditure for a particular project with its reason for failing.

17. "Protokoll über die Besprechung vom 17. April 1952 betr. Technische Entwicklungspläne des Ministeriums für Maschinenbau," 21 April 1952, 1–2, BAP DE1/13292. Even Zeiss Jena did not have a long-term plan for either production or research until 1957. Carl Zeiss Jena, "Perspektivplan des VEB Carl Zeiss Jena 1958 bis 1965," September 1957, SAPMO DY 30 IV 2/604/96.

18. Eckart Förtsch and Clemens Burrichter, "Technik und Staat in der Deutschen Demokratischen Republik (1949–89/90)," in *Technik und Staat*, edited by Armin Hermann and Hans-Peter Sang (Düsseldorf: VDI-Verlag, 1992), 208–9.

19. Tandler, "Geplante Zukunft," 194.

20. Mary Fulbrook, *The Divided Nation: A History of Germany 1918–1990* (Oxford: Oxford University Press, 1991), 195–96.

21. SPK (Heckel, Leiter der Kaderabteilung), "Bericht über die Republikabgänge aus der chemischen Industrie," 23 April 1959, BAP DE1/14320.

22. Ibid.; various reports from the late 1950s from the VVB Allgemeine Maschinenbau in BAP DE1/7847.

23. "Republikflucht," *DDR Handbuch*, 1124–25.

24. Förtsch and Burrichter, "Technik und Staat in der Deutschen Demokratischen Republik," 208–9.

25. Wolfgang Mühlfriedel makes this point in "Zur technischen Entwicklung in der Industrie der DDR in den 50er Jahren," in *Modernisierung im Wiederaufbau. Die westdeutsche Gesellschaft der 50er Jahre*, edited by Axel Schildt and Arnold Sywottek (Bonn: Dietz, 1993), 159.

26. See, for instance, Jörg Roesler, "The Rise and Fall of the Planned Economy in

the German Democratic Republic, 1945–1989," *German History* 9 (1991): 46–61; Roesler, "Zum Strukturwandel in der Industrie der DDR während der fünfziger Jahre," *Zeitschrift für Geschichtswissenschaft* 35 (1987): 138–49.

27. See various essays in Rosmarie Beier, ed., *Aufbau West, Aufbau Ost: Die Planstädte Wolfsburg und Eisenhüttenstadt in der Nachkriegszeit* (Berlin: DHM, 1997).

28. *Jahrbuch der DDR 1958*, 187–88.

29. *Protokoll der Verhandlungen der 3 Parteikonferenz der Sozialistischen Einheitspartei Deutschlands*, 2 vols. (Berlin: Dietz, 1956), 76, 281, 606, 614, 1022–1113.

30. Jörg Roesler, Renate Schwärzel, and Veronika Siedt, *Produktionswachstum und Effektivität in Industriezweigen der DDR 1950–1970* (Berlin: Akademie-Verlag, 1983), 47, 82–83, 86–87.

31. For an assessment of the implications of Sputnik for the history of the Cold War and space technology, see Walter A. McDougall, . . . *The Heavens and the Earth: A Political History of the Space Race* (New York: Basic Books, 1984).

32. *Jahrbuch der DDR 1958*, essays on "Wissenschaft" and "Forschung und Entwicklung," 185–238.

33. Ibid., 187. Tandler points out that contract research was far less important than official GDR publicity claimed at first, but it nonetheless became a key means of financing research, especially at the universities and colleges, and less so at the Academy of Sciences, by the late 1950s and early 1960s. Tandler, "Geplante Zukunft," 123–24, 148.

34. Gerhard Kosel, *Produktivkraft Wissenschaft* (Berlin: Verlag Die Wirtschaft, 1957); *Jahrbuch der DDR 1958*, 187; Martin McCauley, *The German Democratic Republic since 1945* (New York: St. Martin's Press, 1983), 125.

35. *Chemie gibt Brot—Wohlstand—Schönheit Chemiekonferenz des Zentralkomitees der SED und der Staatlichen Plankommission in Leuna am 3. und 4. November 1958* (Berlin, 1958), 35 (emphasis in original).

36. For more on this, see Raymond G. Stokes, "Autarky, Ideology, and Technological Lag: The Case of the East German Chemical Industry, 1945–1964," *Central European History* 28 (1995): 29–45, especially 39–41.

37. "Grundsätze für die künftige Arbeit des Forschungsrates der DDR entsprechend den Forderungen des 12 Plenums des ZK zur Erhöhung seiner Rechte und Verantwortlichkeiten bei der Planung und Leitung der wissenschaftlich-technischen Arbeit," n.d. (ca. November 1961), 1, SAPMO DY30 IV 2/607/30. The best overview of the establishment of the Forschungsrat in its political, economic, and scientific context is Tandler, "Geplante Zukunft."

38. See Matthias Wagner, "Der Forschungsrat der DDR. Im Spannungsfeld von Sachkompetenz und Ideologieanspruch" (Ph.D. diss., Humboldt University, 1992); Tandler, "Geplante Zukunft."

39. SPK, "Programm zur Verbesserung der Versorgung der Bevölkerung mit den tausend kleinen Dingen des täglichen Bedarfs, mit Reparaturen und Dienstleistungen," 12 December 1959, 1, SAPMO DY30 IV 2/2029/95. The designation "tausend kleinen Dingen des täglichen Bedarfs" was used frequently in official GDR correspondence and speeches around this time.

Chapter 3: Technological Tourism and Display

1. Information on the study trip to the Hannover Trade Fair in 1959 is compiled from reports submitted by participants working on behalf of the office-machines, electronics, regulation-technology, and optics sections of the SPK, BAP DE1/2629, DE1/2631, DE1/2632.

2. On tourism, its definition, and its economic and social significance, see A. J. Burkart and S. Medlik, *Tourism: Past, Present, and Future*, 2d ed. (London: Heinemann, 1981), 41–42, 59.

3. VEB Carl Zeiss Jena (Söldner), "Bericht über den Besuch der Industriemesse Hannover v 26.4.–30.4.59," n.d., 1, BAP DE1/2629.

4. Ibid. (emphasis added).

5. VEB Werk für Signal- und Sicherungstechnik Berlin (Promnitz), "Politische Einschätzung," 20 Mai 1959, BAP DE1/2632.

6. Abt. Elektrotechnik, "Auswertung der Industrie-Messe Hannover 1959, Bd. I: Gesamteindruck der Messe," n.d., 3, BAP DE1/6850.

7. Ibid., 4–5.

8. VVB Büromaschinen, Forschung und Entwicklung, "Bericht über den Besuch der "Industrie-Messe Hannover" vom 26.–30 April. 1959," 4 June 1959, 6, BAP DE1/2631.

9. Matthias Judt, "Zur Geschichte des Büro- und Datenverarbeitungsmaschinenbaus in der SBZ/DDR," in *Unternehmen zwischen Markt und Macht: Aspekte deutscher Unternehmens- und Industriegeschichte im 20. Jahrhundert*, edited by Werner Plumpe and Christian Kleinschmidt (Essen: Klartext, 1992), 137–53. Judt claims that in the 1950s and 1960s there were for this industrial sector "reale Chancen vorhanden, im internationalen Wettbewerb mitzuhalten bzw. damals geringe Rückstände noch aufholen zu können" (153).

10. Deutsches Amt für Material- und Warenprüfung der Deutschen Demokratischen Republik, Fachabteilung Metallurgie-Maschinenbau, Prüfdienststelle Magdeburg, "Messebericht über die Industriemesse 1959 in Hannover" (Vertrauliche Dienstsache), 1, BAP DE1/14418.

11. See, for instance, some of the literature in science and technology studies, such as Bruno Latour, *Science in Action: How to Follow Scientists and Engineers through Society* (Milton Keynes: Open University Press, 1987); John Law, *Organizing Modernity* (Oxford: Blackwell, 1994); Law, ed., *A Sociology of Monsters* (London: Routledge, 1991).

12. See, for instance, Paul Greenhalgh, *Ephemeral Vistas: The Expositions Universelles, Great Exhibitions and World Fairs, 1851–1939* (Manchester: Manchester University Press, 1988); and Robert Rydell, *World of Fairs: The Century of Progress Exhibitions* (Chicago: University of Chicago Press, 1993); Sophie Forgan, "Festivals of Science and the Two Cultures: Science, Design and Display in the Festival of Britain, 1951," *British Journal for the History of Science* 31 (1998): 217–40.

13. VEB INTRON Leipzig, Werk für industrielle Elektronik, VVB Regelungstechnik (Ing. A. Krumpe), ["Report on visit to Hannover"], 14. Mai 1959, 8, BAP DE1/2632. There is a line and a very large question mark in blue pen in the margin next to the second passage quoted, concerning travel in private cars.

14. For instance, VEB Geräte- und Reglerwerke Teltow (Dr. Ing. W. Britall), "Zusammendfassender Bericht über den INTERNATIONALEN KONGRESS MIT AUSSTELLUNG FUER MESSTECHNIK UND AUTOMATIK INTERKAMA 1960 in Düsseldorf vom 19.–26.Oktober 1960," 28 November 1960 (mimeo), SAPMO IV 2/607/21; VVB Büromaschinen, Abt. Technik (Hanf, Abt.-Leiter), "Bericht über den Besuch der Messe in Brünn vom 21.–24.9.1960," 15.10.1960, BAP DE1/2621. Other relevant documents are in BAP DE1/699, DE1/2621, DE1/13390, DE1/6962, DE1/6847–50, DE1/15218.

15. For discussion of a similar phenomenon during an earlier period of German history, see Christian Kleinschmidt and Thomas Welskopp, "Amerika aus deutschen Perspektiven: Reiseeindrücke deutscher Ingenieure über die Eisen- und Stahlindustrie der USA, 1900–1930," *Zeitschrift für Unternehmensgeschichte* 39 (1994): 73–103.

16. Heinrich Rau, *Leipziger Messe Leistungsschau des sozialistischen Weltwirtschaftslagers* (Berlin: Deutscher Zentralverlag, 1952), 7–8.

17. *Vom Jahrmarkt zur Weltmesse. Ein Streifzug durch die Geschichte der Leipziger Messe* (Leipzig: Urania-Verlag, 1958), 219–35.

18. Rolf Kießling, "Markets and Marketing, Town and Country," in *Germany: A New Social and Economic History, Vol. 1: 1450–1630*, edited by Bob Scribner (London: Arnold, 1996), 167–72; Alan Milward and S. B. Saul, *The Economic Development of Continental Europe, 1780–1870* (London: George Allen and Unwin, 1973), 113.

19. Much of the preceding paragraph and the following are based on a reading of organizers' and participants' reports on the Leipzig Trade and Technical Fairs of the 1950s and early 1960s in SAPMO and BAP. The quotation is from HA Wissenschaft und Technik, Abt. Physik (Weidlich), "Reisebericht. Betr.: Technische Messe in Hannover 1950," 24 May 1950, BAP DF4/41136.

20. SPK Abt. Maschinenbau, Sektor Elektronik (Hegner), "Bericht über die Messe in Mailand," n.d. (1957), 2, BAP DE1/13390.

21. Zentralamt für Forschung und Technik bei der SPK (Witt) to Prof. Stanek, "Betr.: Industriemesse Hannover," 15 April 1957, BAP DF4/41141.

22. VEB Carl Zeiss Jena (Beyer), "Bericht über den Besuch der Industriemesse Hannover v 26.4–30.4.1959," n.d., BAP DE1/2629.

23. H. Werner, "Was ist Weltniveau?" *Maschinenbautechnik* 6 (1957): 288–89. Werner concludes his article on a curious note, indicating that for developing countries that are deficient in technologically trained talent (such as Vietnam), different types of machine tools were necessary. These should not simply be outmoded technologies, but rather simple yet well-designed machines to aid in their further technological development.

24. Rudolf Model, "Weltniveau in Wissenschaft und Technik," *Einheit* 15 (June 1960): 833–46 (quotation on 836, emphasis in original).

25. SPK, Abt. Investitionen, Forschung und Technik (H. Grosse), "Information für den Forschungsrat zur Auswertung der Leipziger Messe und über die Durchführung von technischen Studien auf der Messe," 14 August 1958, SAPMO DY30 IV/2/607/19; SPK Abt. Investitionen, Forschung und Technik, "Bericht über die Arbeit, die

Ergebnisse und weiteren Aufgaben auf dem Gebiet Forschung und Technik," 28 November 1959, 23, SAPMO DY30 IV/2/607/63.

26. SPK, Abt. Maschinenbau, "Auswertung der Leipziger Frühjahrsmesse 1959 durch die Abteilung Maschinenbau," 18 March 1959, 2–3, BAP DE1/14419. I have not been able to locate figures indicating the total number involved in 1959, but based on other evidence, it appears safe to assume that the number of specialists was about the same as in 1960, when 1,867 specialists participated in the assessment exercise. SPK, Abt. Investitionen, Forschung und Technik, "Bericht über die Leipziger Frühjahrsmesse 1960," 18 May 1960, 3, BAP DE1/14420.

27. Wirtschaftskommission des Politbüros, Arbeitsgruppe Forschung, technische Entwicklung, Investitionspolitik, "Bericht über die Ergebnisse unseres Kampfes um die Erreichung des wissenschaftlich-technischen Höchststandes an Hand der Exponate der Leipziger Frühjahrsmesse 1959," BAP DE1/6808.

28. Ibid., 6–17.

29. Ibid.

30. The following analysis is based on figures and calculations from figures in *Statistisches Jahrbuch der DDR* 10 (1965): 401; and 15 (1970): 319.

31. SPK, "Bericht über die Durchführung und Auswertung der Leipziger Frühjahrsmesse, 4 Entwurf," 26 March 1959, 2–3, SAPMO DY30 IV/2/607/19. In response to the first comment, concerning the "continuously rising" technical level of the Leipzig fair, one reader, probably Erich Apel, the head of the SED's Economics Commission, wrote "!?!" and *"formulate differently"* in red.

32. Gruppe Hochspannungsgeräte, Fachgebiet Transformatoren, "Exponatenvergleich Leipziger Frühjahrsmesse 1959," 1, n.d., BAP DE1/13385. The other reports of this group, as well as those from the electrical industry in general, are in this file.

33. Wirtschaftskommission des Politbüros, Abt. Investitionen, Forschung und Technik, "Bericht über die Leipziger Frühjahrsmesse 1960," 1 (my emphasis), SAPMO DY30 IV/2/607/20.

34. SPK, Abt. Investitionen, Forschung und Technik, "Bericht über die Leipziger Herbstmesse 1960," 3 October 1960, 3–4, BAP DE1/1332.

35. SPK, Abt. Forschung und Entwicklung, "Information," 15 March 1962, 11 (my emphasis), SAPMO DY30 IV/2/607/10.

Chapter 4: The High-Tech Hardware of Socialism

1. The concept of Sovietization is explored most extensively (and compared to the more frequently deployed concept of Americanization) in Konrad Jarausch and Hannes Siegrist, eds., *Amerikanisierung und Sowjetisierung in Deutschland 1945–1970* (Frankfurt: Campus, 1997), although technology is neglected. I have explored both concepts as applied to technology in my unpublished manuscript, "Amerikanisiert, sowjetisiert doch deutsch geblieben."

2. John Beer, *The Emergence of the German Dye Industry* (Urbana: University of Illinois Press, 1959); L. F. Haber, *The Chemical Industry during the Nineteenth Century* (Oxford: Clarendon Press, 1969); Haber, *The Chemical Industry 1900–1930* (Oxford: Clarendon Press, 1971); Kathryn Steen, "Wartime Catalyst and Post-

war Reaction: The Making of the U.S. Synthetic Organic Chemicals Industry, 1910–1930" (Ph.D. diss., University of Delaware, 1995); David Hounshell and John Smith, *Science and Corporate Strategy* (Cambridge: Cambridge University Press, 1988).

3. Hayes, *Industry and Ideology*; Gottfried Plumpe, *Die I. G. Farbenindustrie A. G.* (Berlin: Duncker & Humblot, 1990); Peter Morris, "The Development of Acetylene Chemistry and Synthetic Rubber by I. G. Farbenindustrie AG, 1926–1945" (Ph.D. diss., Oxford University, 1982); Stokes, *Divide and Prosper*; Rainer Karlsch, "Capacity Losses, Reconstruction and Unfinished Modernization: The Chemical Industry in the Soviet Zone of Occupation/GDR, 1945–1965," in *The German Chemical Industry in the Twentieth Century*, edited by Gerald Feldman and John Lesch (Amsterdam: Kluwer, in press).

4. The most complete discussion of this for the western zones of occupation in postwar Germany is in Stokes, *Divide and Prosper.*

5. See, for instance, Karlsch, *Allein bezahlt?*; Albrecht, Heinemann-Grüder, and Wellmann, *Die Spezialisten.*

6. The following discussion draws heavily upon my previous articles: Stokes, "Autarky, Ideology and Technological Lag"; and Stokes, "Chemistry and the Chemical Industry under Socialism," in *Science under Socialism*, edited by Dieter Hoffmann and Kristie Macrakis (Cambridge, Mass.: Harvard University Press, 1999), 199–211.

7. Leuna Werke, Büro der Werksleitung, "Besprechungsbericht," 28 November 1947, Leuna-Werke-Archiv 6026; Dr. Reitz, "Neuere amerikanische Arbeiten über Erdölchemie," 11 December 1946, BASF Unternehmensarchiv, Ludwigshafen, F9/66.

8. Rainer Karlsch, "Der Traum von Oel—zu den Hintergründen der Erdölversuche in der DDR," *Vierteljahrsschrift für Sozial- und Wirtschaftsgeschichte* 80 (1993): 63–87.

9. Leuna-Werke, "Zur Entwicklung von 'Leuna II' (1958–1986)," *Zahlen und Fakten zur Betriebsgeschichte* 54 (1986): 4; *Chemie gibt Brot - Wohlstand - Schönheit. Chemiekonferenz des Zentralkomittes der SED und der Staatlichen Plankommission in Leuna am 3. und 4. November 1958* (Berlin, 1958).

10. *Chemie gibt Brot - Wohlstand - Schönheit*, 28 (emphasis in original).

11. There seems to be some doubt as to whether the pipeline was in fact finished in December 1963. There were and are some who contend that the pipeline was not completed until sometime in 1964. Ulbricht insisted on the earlier date, so the official opening ceremony took place as scheduled, but with supplies coming from tank trucks located not very far away from Schwedt rather than from the Soviet end of the pipeline. I have not been able to locate any documentary evidence to either support or refute this contention.

12. A. Steiniger, "Der VEB Erdölverarbeitungswerk Schwedt (Oder)—ein neues Chemiekombinat der DDR," *Die Technik* 16 (October 1961): 693.

13. Percentage increases in imports and percentage of imports of oil from the USSR calculated from figures in *Statistisches Jahrbuch der DDR* 9 (1964): 387; 11 (1966): 393; 15 (1970): 309, 315. The percentage of total oil imports coming from the USSR is only available from 1960 onward, but it is fair to assume that they ac-

counted for a similar proportion of total imports in the late 1950s. Since virtually no petroleum was produced domestically in East Germany, imported petroleum was, practically speaking, the only petroleum available to the economy.

14. Girndt, attaché, "Aktenvermerk über Gespräche auf dem SPK-Abend der Botschaft am 232.[1962]," n.d., 2, SAPMO DY30 IV/2/607/16.

15. The following summarizes and analyzes G. Wyschofsky, "Niederschrift," 6 March 1964, SAPMO DY30 IV/2/202/41.

16. Willem Molle and Egbert Wever, *Oil Refineries and Petrochemical Industries in Western Europe* (Aldershot: Gower, 1984), 45.

17. "Stenographische Niederschrift der Aussprache des Gen. W. Ulbricht mit einer sowjetischen Expertendelegation im Hause des Zentralkomitees, Politbüro-saal, am Donnerstag, dem 30. Januar 1964 (Beginn 11.00 Uhr)," 22 (quotation), SAPMO DY30 IV/2/201/703.

18. Ibid., 46 (quotation).

19. Ulbricht to Khrushchev, 10 October 1964, SAPMO DY30 IV/2/202/41.

20. "Information über die Verhandlungen mit dem Vorsitzenden des Staatlichen Plankomitees der UdSSR, Genossen Lomako," n.d. (ca. December 1965), 1 (emphasis in original), SAPMO DY30 IV/2/202/34.

21. Rainer Karlsch, "'Wie Phoenix aus der Asche?' Rekonstruktion und Struktur-wandel in der chemischen Industrie in beiden deutschen Staaten bis Mitte der sechziger Jahre," to appear in *Deutsch-Deutsche Wirtschaft, 1945–1990. Struktur-veränderung, Innovationen und regionaler Wandel*, edited by Lothar Baar and Diet-mar Petzina (St. Katharinen: Scripta Mercaturae, 1999). My thanks to Dr. Karlsch for providng me with a copy of the manuscript of his article.

22. Percentage increases in imports and percentage of imports of oil from the USSR calculated from figures in *Statistisches Jahrbuch der DDR* 9 (1964): 387; 11 (1966): 393; 15 (1970): 309, 315; 17 (1972): 317, 323.

23. Raymond G. Stokes, "Energy," in *Modern Germany*, edited by Dieter Buse and Juergen Doerr (New York: Garland, 1998), 276–77.

24. Staatliche Plankommission, Abt. Chemie, "Bilanzbetrachtung zur Entwick-lung der Petrolchemie 1966–1975," 29 November 1965, 1–2 (quotations), Leuna Werksarchiv, Merseburg 13132. It is not clear from the tables in this source if the 35 percent includes all petroleum-based starting materials, since coal-based raw mate-rials and imported raw materials (which potentially were based on petroleum) are combined in the figures and contrasted with materials "aus Erdöl in der DDR hergestellt" ("produced in the GDR from petroleum"). But it appears likely that at most a tiny percentage of the combined coal-based and imported starting materials was based on petroleum.

25. Verband der chemischen Industrie (VCI), *Chemiewirtschaft in Zahlen*, 6th ed. (Düsseldorf, 1964), 83; Verband der Chemischen Industrie, "Petrochemie," n.d. (late 1960), 3 (one of a series of monographs prepared by the VCI and sent to the European Center of Federations of Industrial Chemistry (CEFIC) in a letter of 31 January 1961), Bayerwerksarchiv, Leverkusen, 271/1.1.52.15.

26. "Zusammenfassung Wünsche der DDR für technische Hilfe und Ausrüstung aus der UdSSR bis 1975," 8 January 1960, 10, BAP DE1/21411.

27. Steiniger, "Der VEB Erdölverarbeitungswerk Schwedt (Oder)," 692 (quota-

tion); S. Unger and K. Gerstenberger, "Das Erdölverarbeitungswerk Schwedt, Aufbauschwerpunkt der chemischen Industrie in der DDR," *Die Technik* 18 (11 November 1963): 716–20.

28. "Forschungsrat und Chemieprogramm, Referat von Prof. Dr. Winkler," 29 January 1959, SAPMO DY30 IV/2/607/31; Unger and Gerstenberger, "Das Erdölverarbeitungswerk Schwedt," 716–20.

29. In 1964 Wyschofsky, the minister for the chemical industry, pointed out that the yield of fractions deployed in the chemical industry was a maximum of 3.5–4 percent in the capitalist countries, while the GDR needed to obtain yields of 10–12 percent of such fractions through more intensive refining techniques. "Stenographische Niederschrift der Aussprache des Gen. W. Ulbricht mit einer sowjetisischen Expertendelegation im Hause des Zentralkomitees, Politbürosaal, am Donnerstag, dem 30. Januar 1964 (Beginn 11.00 Uhr)," 37, SAPMO DY30 IV/2/201/703.

30. "Forschungsrat und Chemieprogramm, Referat von Prof. Dr. Winkler," 29 January 1959, SAPMO DY30 IV/2/607/31; Unger and Gerstenberger, "Das Erdölverarbeitungswerk Schwedt," 716–20.

31. "Zusammenfassung Wünsche der DDR für technische Hilfe und Ausrüstung aus der UdSSR bis 1975," 8 January 1960, 10, BAP DE1/21411; Mühlfriedel and Wießner, *Die Geschichte der Industrie der DDR bis 1965*, 242.

32. Steiniger, "Der VEB Erdölverarbeitungswerk Schwedt (Oder)," 695. See, for instance, Paul R. Josephson, "'Projects of the Century' in Soviet History: Large-Scale Technologies from Lenin to Gorbachev," *Technology and Culture* 36 (1995): 519–59.

33. Steiniger, "Der VEB Erdölverarbeitungswerk Schwedt (Oder)," 695.

34. "Jahresanalyse 1959," 26 January 1960, 3 (quotation), BAP DE1/21411.

35. On talks with the French, see SPK, Abt. Chemie, Fachgebiet Internationale Oekonomische Beziehungen, "Aktennotiz über eine am 13.1.1959 durchgeführte Besprechung," 14 January 1959, BAP DE1/15277. On negotiations with the British on transfer of chemical technology, "Unterlagen des Außenhandels für Gespräche mit englischen Messebesuchern anläßlich der Leipziger Frühjahrsmesse 1961," 21 February 1961, 1–2, 6, SAPMO DY30 IV/2/607/20; Selbmann to Winkler, 9 January 1961, BAP DE1/14195. Both these documents refer to earlier, intensive negotiations with the British.

36. Selbmann to Winkler, 9 January 1961, 1, BAP DE1/14195.

37. Leuna-Werke, "Zur Entwicklung von 'Leuna II' (1958–1986)," 5, 9–10.

38. Stokes, *Opting for Oil*, 247–48.

39. Ernest Braun and Stuart Macdonald, *Revolution in Miniature: The History and Impact of Semiconductor Electronics*, 2d ed (Cambridge: Cambridge University Press, 1982). The authors make the point about the initial difficulties with transistors on 50.

40. Ibid., chaps. 4–7; Christopher Freeman, *The Economics of Industrial Innovation* (Harmondsworth, Middlesex, England: Penguin, 1974), 138–52.

41. Abt. Maschinenbau und Metallurgie, "Stellungnahme zur Entwicklung der Halbleiterfertigung," 26 July 1958, SAPMO DY30 IV/2/607/76.

42. SPK, Büro des Beauftragten für Halbleitertechnik (Gen. Bernicke), "Bericht und Maßnahmen zur kurzfristigen Überwindung des Rückstandes auf dem Gebiet

der Halbleiterentwicklung und -produktion (Germanium und Sizilium)," 20 January 1960, 1, BAP DE1/13967.

43. Braun and Macdonald, *Revolution in Miniature*, 33.

44. Abt. Maschinenbau und Metallurgie, "Stellungnahme zur Entwicklung der Halbleiterfertigung," 26 July 1958, SAPMO DY30 IV/2/607/76.

45. SPK, Abt. Investitionen, Forschung und Technik, Sektor Forschung und Technik, "Bericht über die Dienstreise . . . nach Teltow," 1 December 1958, 2, SAPMO DY30 IV/2/607/62.

46. Figures based on a chart in J. Albrecht, "Die Entwicklung des Halbleiterwerkes Frankfurt (Oder)," *Die Technik* 18 (10 October 1963): 662. In making these calculations, I assume that the relationship in production output among the three types of semiconductor components that existed in 1958 remained the same during the subsequent period. I also assume that the Frankfurt figures reported in Albrecht's article were included in the report on the visit to Teltow, and that virtually all the production was at Frankfurt. This seems reasonable given that the Frankfurt plant was at that time a subsidiary of Teltow. Finally, it is important to note that the figures say nothing about quality.

47. Braun and Macdonald, *Revolution in Miniature*, 77.

48. Sektor Forschung und Technik (Dr. Schwarz), "Stellungnahme zur Beschlußvorschlag für das Politbüro des Zentralkomitees des Sozialistischen Einheitspartei Deutschlands über Sorfortmaßnahmen zur kurzfristigen Ueberwindung des Rückstandes auf dem Gebiet der Halbleiterentwicklung und -produktion," 19 August 1959, 1, BAP DE1/13967.

49. SPK, Abt. Investitionen, Forschung und Technik, Sektor Forschung und Technik, "Bericht über die Dienstreise . . . nach Teltow," 1 December 1958, SAPMO DY 30 IV/2/607/62.

50. *Protokoll der Verhandlungen der 3 Parteikonferenz der Sozialistischen Einheitspartei Deutschlands* (Berlin: Dietz, 1956), 2 vols. The directive is on 1022–1113; quotation from Ulbricht, 76; other statements of this sort are on 281, 606, 614.

51. Bernicke, a party functionary who was eventually placed in charge of semiconductors within the State Planning Commission, noted in a presentation to the SED Economics Committee in 1960 that criticism of the existing semiconductor industry, which began at the Third Party Conference in 1956, was reinforced in the Fifth Party Conference, the Fifth Plenum, and the Ninth Plenum. "Wirtschaftskommission TOP 3," 47, SAPMO DY 30 IV/2/2101/18.

52. Abt. Maschinenbau und Metallurgie, "Stellungnahme zur Entwicklung der Halbleiterfertigung," 26 July 1958, SAPMO DY30 IV/2/607/76.

53. Arbeitsgruppe Forschung, technische Entwicklung und Investitionspolitik, "Information für Genosse Apel," 19 July 1958, SAPMO DY 30 IV/2/607/31.

54. Albrecht, "Die Entwicklung des Halbleiterwerkes Frankfurt (Oder)," 662.

55. Abt. Maschinenbau und Metallurgie, "Stellungnahme zur Entwicklung der Halbleiterfertigung," 26 July 1958, SAPMO DY30 IV/2/607/76.

56. Apel to Leuschner, 30 April 1959, SAPMO DY30 IV/2/607/63.

57. Arbeitsgruppe Forschung, technische Entwicklung und Investitionspolitik, "Information für Genosse Apel," 19 July 1958, 8–9, SAPMO DY30 IV/2/607/31.

58. Apel to Leuschner, 30 April 1959, SAPMO DY30 IV/2/607/63.

59. Sektor Forschung und Technik (Boese), "Aktennotiz über die Halbleiterbesprechung in Frankfurt/O am 7.12.1959," 9 December 1959, BAP DE1/13967.

60. SPK, Büro des Beauftragten für Halbleitertechnik (Bernicke), "Bericht und Maßnahmen zur kurzfristigen Ueberwindung des Rückstandes auf dem Gebiet der Halbleiterentwicklung und -produktion," 20 January 1960, BAP DE1/13967.

61. Wirtschaftskommission, transcript of meeting, 26 August 1960, 48–49 (quotations), SAPMO DY30 IV/2/2101/18.

62. Franco Malerba, *The Semiconductor Business: The Economics of Rapid Growth and Decline* (London: Frances Pinter, 1985), 59.

63. SPK, Abt. Elektrotechnik, "Bericht und Maßnahmen zur kurzfristigen Ueberwindung des Rückstandes auf dem Gebiet der Halbleiterentwicklung und -produktion," 16 October 1959, BAP DE1/13967.

64. "Auszug aus der Niederschrift über die Sitzung der Mitarbeiter des Arbeitskreises 52, Halbleiter," 27 May 1959, BAP DE1/6719.

65. Abt. Maschinenbau und Metallurie (F. Zeiler) to Leuschner, "Bermerkungen zur Vorlage 'Halbleitertechnik'—Ausarbeitung vom 1510.1959," 22 October 1959, SAPMO DY30 IV/2/2029/82. Information on yields in the U.S. transistor industry is from Freeman, *Economics of Industrial Innovation*, 150.

66. Mühlfriedel and Wießner, *Die Geschichte der Industrie der DDR bis 1965*, 291. SPK, Büro des Beauftragten für Halbleitertechnik (Bernicke), "Bericht über die Maßnahmen zur kurzfristigen Überwindung des Rückstandes auf dem Gebiet der Halbleiterentwicklung und -produktion," 20 January 1960, 4, BAP DE1/13967.

67. Arbeitsgruppe Forschung und technische Entwicklung, "1 Entwurf. Gesamtbericht über den gegenwärtigen Stand und die zu lösenden Probleme auf dem Gebiet der Halbleitertechnik," 22 October 1962, 5, SAPMO IV/2/607/73.

68. P. Görlich, report on Internationaler Kongress über Transistoren- und Halbleiteranordnungen, 2 June 1959, 3, BAP DF4/41143.

69. Abt. Maschinenbau und Metallurgie, "Stellungnahme zur Entwicklung der Halbleiter-Fertigung," 26 July 1958, 10, SAPMO DY30 IV/2/2029/82.

70. P. Görlich, report on Internationaler Kongress über Transistoren- und Halbleiteranordnungen, 2 June 1959, 3, BAP DF4/41143; "Bericht über die Entwicklung und Fertigung von Halbleiterbauelementen," 22 July 1959, 9, SAPMO DY30 IV/2/604/161.

71. Abt. Maschinenbau und Metallurgie, "Stellungnahme zur Vorlage für das Politbüro über die Entwicklung der Halbleitertechnik bis 1965 in der DDR," 13 August 1959, 4, SAPMO DY30 IV/2/604/161. The report was anticipated by a lower level one, which similarly suggested intervention by the Politburo: "Bericht über die Entwicklung und Fertigung von Halbleiterbauelementen," 22 July 1959, 9, SAPMO DY30 IV/2/604/161.

72. Ulbricht to Khrushchev, 15 August 1959, SAPMO DY30 IV/2/202/29.

73. Abt. Elektrotechnik, Fachgebiet Internationaler Zusammenarbeit, "Aktenvermerk über die Abschlussbesprechung zum TWZ-Beschluss 10/3/X 'Sowjetische Hilfeleistung beim Aufbau der Halbleitertechnik' am 20.12.1959 im Hotel 'Johannishof'," 20 December 1959, BAP DE1/8221; copies of the report are also in this file and in SAPMO DY 30 IV/2/604/161.

74. Sektor Forschung und Technik (Boese), "Aktennotiz zur Halbleiterbesprechung am 9.11.1959 im Werk für Fernmeldewesen, Berlin-Oberschöneweide," 2 December 1959, BAP DE1/13967.

75. On copying in general and the importance of obtaining licenses for goods to be exported, "Information über den Nachbau von Erzeugnissen des kapitalistischen Auslandes," n.d. (ca. early 1963), SAPMO DY30 IV/2/604/141. A specific example of licenses purchased from the West (in this case IBM) in the area of electronics and semiconductors is in Mitteilung von Rechtsabteilung (Linden) an Koll. Otte, "Betr.: Lizenzverträge," 26 May 1959, BAP DE1/14195.

76. Falter, "Bericht über Londoner Tagung und Ausstellung für Halbleiter vom 21 Bis 27.5.1959," 1 June 1959, BAP DE1/6719.

77. This is implied in many documents discussing the relative weakness and backwardness of GDR semiconductor technology and production, including, for instance, Dr. Raabe, "Reisebericht über den Besuch englischer Firmen, die Einrichtungen für die Produktion von Halbleiterbauelementen herstellen," 10 December 1959, SPMO DY 30 IV/2/603/161.

78. P. Görlich, report on Internationaler Kongress über Transistoren- und Halbleiteranordnungen, 2/6/1959, BAP DF4/41143. On Japan as a model for the GDR see, for instance, P. Görlich's speech at the Forschungsrat on 12 November 1962, in "Stenographische Niederschrift der 2. Plenartagung des Forschungsrates der DDR am 12. November 1962 in Berlin," n.d., 29–30, SAPMO DY 30 IV/2/607/33.

79. Dr. Raabe, "Reisebericht über Dienstreise nach Köln zur Firma Leybold," 26 August 1959, SAPMO DY 30 IV/2/604/161; SPK, Abt. Investitionen, Forschung und Technik, Sektor Forschung und Technik (Busse), "Aktennotiz betr. Reisebericht vom 2.11. und 3.11.1959," 5 November 1959, BAP DE1/13967. Contacts with Leybold were extremely important for the development of electronics in the GDR from the 1960s through the end of the regime, and especially in the 1980s. Leybold frequently provided embargoed equipment to the GDR. MfS Hauptabteilung XVIII/8, "Information. Gespräch zwischen dem Gen. Prof. Biermann, Generaldirektor des Kombinates Carl Zeiss Jena, und dem Geschäftsführer der BRD-Firma Leybold-Heraeus, am 22. April 1987," 27 April 1987, 2, Bundesbeauftragte für die Unterlagen des Staatssicherheitsdienstes der ehemaligen Deutschen Demokratischen Republik, Zentralarchiv, Berlin, MfS-HA XVIII Nr 10843.

80. On British R&D capability in the postwar period generally, see David Edgerton, *Science, Technology, and the British Industrial "Decline," 1870–1970* (Cambridge: Cambridge University Press, 1996).

81. The following is taken largely from Bernicke, "Zusammenfassung der Informationsberichte über die Reise nach Großbritannien," 14 December 1959, BAP DF4/41150. All direct quotations are from this summary. The reports themselves, accompanied by some photographs of what had been seen (mostly taken from books or brochures), are in SAPMO DY30 IV/2/604/161.

82. SPK, "Vorlage für die Staatliche Plankommission, Bericht und Maßnahmen zur kurzfristigen Überwindung des Rückstandes auf dem Gebiet der Halbleiterentwicklung und -produktion (Germanium und Silizium)," 25 February 1960, 39.

83. SPK, Büro des Beauftragten für Halbleitertechnik (Bernicke), "Bericht über die

Maßnahmen zur kurzfristigen Überwindung des Rückstandes auf dem Gebiet der Halbleiterentwicklung und -produktion," 20 January 1960, 6, BAP DE1/13967.

84. H. Grosse to Berater des Botschafters der UdSSR in der DDR in Wirtschaftsfragen (Bobyrew), 29 March 1960, BAP DE1/8221; Mühlfriedel and Wießner, *Die Geschichte der Industrie der DDR bis 1965*, 291–92. On continued and expanded Soviet influence after the construction of the Berlin Wall, see Leuschner to W. Nowikow, Stellv. des Vors. des Ministerrates der UdSSR, 17 November 1962, Anlage 5–8, SAPMO DY30 IV/2/607/16.

85. SPK, Abt. Elektrotechnik, Sektor Halbleitertechnik, Bauelemente und Vakuumtechnik, "Konzeption zum Stand sowie der technisch-ökonomischen Entwicklung der Mikro-Modul-Technik und der Molekular-Elektronik," 2 September 1960, BAP DE1/13914, as well as the collection of journal and newspaper articles in this file.

Chapter 5: The Software of Socialism

1. See, for instance, Peter Schneider, *The Wall Jumper: A Berlin Story* (New York: Random House, 1983); Brian Ladd, *The Ghosts of Berlin: Confronting German History in the Urban Landscape* (Chicago: University of Chicago Press, 1997).

2. This section is based heavily on Raymond G. Stokes, "In Search of the Socialist Artefact: Technology and Ideology in East Germany, 1945–1962," *German History* 15 (1997): 223–39. My thanks to the editors and publishers for permission to use extended extracts.

3. Bruce Parrott, *Politics and Technology in the Soviet Union* (Cambridge, Mass.: MIT Press, 1983), 5.

4. Heinrich Rau, *Die führende Rolle der Industrie beim Aufbau des Sozialismus und der neue Kurs in der Deutschen Demokratischen Republik* (Berlin: Tribune, 1953).

5. Ibid., 74–75 (quotations on 74).

6. Ibid., 74.

7. Ibid., 74–79.

8. John L. Burbidge, *The Introduction of Group Technology* (London: Heinemann, 1975). Burbidge points out that the term *Group Technology* "came into the English language in translations from Russian works dealing with the technological aspects of machining families of parts. Group Technology is now more important as a managerial break-through than as a technological revolution" (23).

9. On Group Technology in general, see Sergei P. Mitrofanov, *Wissenschaftliche Grundlage der Gruppenbearbeitung* (Berlin: Verlag Technik, 1960); John Grayson, "Innovation at the Soviet Plant Level: The Case of Group Technology (1950–1970)," in Amann and Cooper, eds., *Industrial Innovation in the Soviet Union*, 101–26.

10. VEB Zeiss Jena (Haupttechnologe Gen. Blume), "Die Mitrofanow-Methode und ihre Einführung im VEB Carl Zeiss Jena," 30 September 1960, 2–3, SAPMO DY30/IV 2/604/41.

11. Various documents in SAPMO DY30/IV 2/604/42, which deal with the "Einführung und Durchsetzung der Gruppenbearbeitung nach der Mitrofanow-Methode in der DDR, 1960–1962." Quotation in "Einladung zum Leserforum über

die Mitrofanow-Methode: 'Es geht um eine Milliarde! Welchen Beitrag leistet der Bezirk Suhl?' Am Freitag, dem 28.April 1961 (Suhl)," 26.

12. Sektor Werkzeugmaschinen und Automatisierung, "Einschätzung des Standes der Durchsetzung der Gruppenbearbeitung nach Mitrofanow in der DDR und Information über Maßnahmen zur Verbesserung ihrer Einführung," 21 February 1961, SAPMO DY30/IV 2/604/41.

13. "Plan für Erfahrungsaustausch mit Gennossen Mitrofanow und Genossen Professor Matalin," 22 February 1961, SAPMO DY30/IV 2/604/41.

14. See VEB Industriewerke Karl-Marx-Stadt, "Vortragsdisposition für die Vortragsreihe 'Einführung der Mitrofanow-Methode' beim Deutschen Fernsehfunk," 16 February 1961, SAPMO DY30/IV 2/604/42, which outlined twenty-five, twenty-minute television programs on the subject. This same file also contains a large number of clippings from newspapers and professional journals from August 1960 through April 1961.

15. Stenografische Niederschrift, "Beratung mit dem Genossen Mitrofanow am 1 März 1961 im Hause des Zentralkomitees der SED," n.d., 9 (quotation), SAPMO DY30/IV 2/604/40.

16. Burbidge, *The Introduction of Group Technology*, v, 260.

17. Stokes, "Chemistry and the Chemical Industry under Socialism."

18. See, for instance, Merritt Roe Smith, *Harpers Ferry and the New Technology: The Challenge of Change* (Ithaca, N.Y.: Cornell University Press, 1977); David Hounshell, *From the American System to Mass Production, 1800–1932* (Baltimore: Johns Hopkins University Press, 1984).

19. Gary Herrigel, *Industrial Constructions: The Sources of German Industrial Power* (Cambridge: Cambridge University Press, 1996).

20. Ronald Shearer, "Talking about Efficiency: Politics and the Industrial Rationalization Movement in the Weimar Republic," *Central European History* 28 (1995): 483–506.

21. Richard Kiencke, *Die deutsche Normung. Geschichte. Wesen. Organisation* (Berlin: Beuth, 1949); Bruno Holm, *50 Jahre Deutscher Normenausschuß* (Cologne: Beuth, 1967); Deutscher Normenausschuss, *Die deutsche Normung 1917–1957* (Berlin: Zack, 1957).

22. Robert McWilliam, "Business Standards and Government: The Formation of British Standards from the Day Queen Victoria Died," presentation at Glasgow-Reading Colloquium, University of Glasgow, 11 July 1998.

23. "Beschluß über die internationale Zusammenarbeit der sozialistischen Laender in Fragen der Standardisierung," 15 July 1957, 2, BAP DE1/495.

24. Otto Franke, *Neue Wege in die Normung* (Berlin: Beuth, 1948), 4–5.

25. Michael Wolff, *Die Währungsreform in Berlin 1948/49* (Berlin: de Gruyter, 1991), notes the continuity of cooperation in Allied air-traffic control even during the First Berlin Crisis. See also Kristie Macrakis, "Einheit der Wissenschaft versus deutsche Teilung: Die Leopoldina und das Machtdreieck in Ostdeustschland," in Hoffmann and Macrakis, eds., *Naturwissenschaft und Technik in der DDR*, 147–69. See also Sybille Gerstengarbe, "The All-German Character of the Leopoldina and the Importance of the Academy to the Scientists in Germany Divided," paper

presented at colloquium, "Science and Technology in the GDR," at the Twentieth International Congress of the History of Science, Liège, 21 July 1997.

26. Deutscher Normenausschuss, *Die deutsche Normung 1917–1957*, 84.

27. Ibid., 95.

28. SPK, Zentralamt für Forschung und Technik, Abt. Normung und Gütesicherung, "Mitarbeit im Deutschen Normenausschuß," 17 June 1952, BAP DE1/10916.

29. "Über die Mitarbeit im Deutschen Normenausschuß (DNA)," 22 June 1953, BAP DE1/10916.

30. Amt für Standardisierung, Der Leiter (Meister), "Analyse über den ersten Fünfjahrplan–Planteil Standardisierung," 22 July 1955, 4, BAP DE1/5010.

31. Ibid., 5.

32. "Beschluß über die internationale Zusammenarbeit der sozialistischen Laender in Fragen der Standardisierung," 15 July 1957, 4–6, BAP DE1/495.

33. Reports on these conferences during the second half of the 1950s are available in SAPMO DY 30 IV/2/607/18.

34. "Beschluß über die internationale Zusammenarbeit der sozialistischen Laender in Fragen der Standardisierung," 15 July 1957, 6, BAP DE1/495.

35. Stokes, "Autarky, Ideology and Technological Lag."

36. TOP 6, n.d. (ca. July 1958), SAPMO DY IV 2/607/65.

37. Abt. Planung und Finanzen, "Beschlussvorlage" (mimeo), 11 April 1958, SAPMO IV 2/607/65.

38. TOP 6, n.d. (ca. July 1958), SAPMO DY IV 2/607/65.

39. Abt. Planung und Finanzen, Beschlussvorlage (mimeo), 11 April 1958, SAPMO IV 2/607/65.

40. Arbeitsgruppe Forschung und technische Entwicklung (Pöschel), "Stellungnahme zur Vorlage des Politbüros über den 'Entwurf des Gesetzes über die Standardisierung in der Deutschen Demokratischen Republik,'" 3 November 1959, SAPMO IV 2/607/65.

41. Amt für Standardisierung, Entwurf, "Gesetz über die Standardisierung in der Deutschen Demokratischen Republik von ..." (mimeo), 6 October 1958, SAPMO IV 2/607/65.

42. "Diskussionsbeitrag auf der 4 Hauptauschußsitzung über die Fragen der Standardisierung," 16 June 1960, 1–2, SAPMO IV 2/607/66.

43. *DDR. Werden und Wachsen. Zur Geschichte der Deutschen Demokratischen Republik* (Berlin: Dietz, 1974), 379–81.

44. Amt für Standardisierung, "Bericht über die Lehren und Schlußfolgerungen bei der Durchführung des Standardisierungsplanes 1960 und zur Herstellung einer engen Zusammenarbeit mit der UdSSR auf dem Gebiet des internationalen Standardisierung," 27 March 1961, BAP DE1/14402; SPK, Stellvertreter des Vorsitzenden Maschinenbau, "Anweisung zur Realisierung des Beschlusses der SPK über die Sicherung der Wirtschaft der DDR gegen willkürliche Störmaßnahmen militarischer Kreise Westdeutschlands vom 41.1961," 2 February 1961, BAP DE1/10241; Richtenbach, Sektor Elektrotechnik, "Disposition für die Erarbeitung eines einheitlichen Vorschriftenwerkes der Elektroindustrie der DDR und zur Lösung der dabei auftretenden Probleme," 7 February 1961, SAPMO DY30 IV/2/604/162.

45. *Anlage* to letter, H. Grosse to Leuschner, 27 March 1961, 4 (quotation, emphasis added), BAP DE1/11826. A slightly altered version of this was indeed published in "Interview zu aktuellen Fragen der Standardisierung," *Einheit* 16 (April 1961): 601–4 (quotation on 603).

46. "Vorschlag über die Stellung der DDR zum Deutschen Normenausschuß und über die Verstärkung der Standardisierungsarbeit in der DDR" (Vorlage für das Politbüro des ZK), 9 June 1961, BAP DE1/1297. Ulbricht had already informed members of the Politburo in April 1961 that the GDR's official policy was to have separate members of the ISO for the two German successor states. Ulbricht to Members and Candidates of the Politburo, 25 April 1961, SAPMO DY30 IV/2/607/11.

47. "Einstellung der Mitarbeit im Deutschen Normenausschuß," n.d. (September 1961), SAPMO DY 30 IV/2/607/66.

48. Holm, *50 Jahre Deutscher Normenausschuß*, 72.

49. Amt für Standardisierung, "Die Entwicklung der Standardisierung in der DDR im Jahre 1962," 5 February 1963, 6, SAPMO DY 30 IV/2/607/41.

50. Joachim Radkau, "Revoltierten die Produktivkräfte gegen den real existierenden Sozialismus? Technikhistorische Anmerkungen zum Zerfall der DDR," *1999* (1990): 27.

51. For more on Soviet-bloc technological culture see, for instance, C. C. Gallagher, "The Influence of Different Economic Systems on Detailed Technology," *Soviet Studies* 26 (1974): 604–9; Josephson, "'Projects of the Century' in Soviet History," 520 (quotations), 559.

Chapter 6: Technology in the New Economic System

1. See Horst Mendershausen, "Dependence of East Germany on Western Exports," U.S. Air Force Project RAND Research Memorandum, 17 July 1959.

2. "Informationsbericht des Volkswirtschaftsrates an das Politbüro über Probleme der Störfreimachung," 29 January 1962, SAPMO DY30 IV 2/202/31 (emphasis in original).

3. "Fragen der Arbeitsteilung in der Industrie, insbesondere im Maschinenbau und der Elektrotechnik," n.d. (ca. April 1962), SAPMO DY 30 IV/2/604/37.

4. "1 Information über die Verhandlungsergebnisse der Maschinenbau-Delegation in Moskau vom 25. bis 27. April 1962," 27 April 1962, 1, SAPMO DY 30 IV/2/604/37.

5. "4 Information über die Wirtschaftsverhandlungen DDR/UdSSR auf dem Gebiet der Spezialisierung des Maschinenbaus," 4 May 1962, SAPMO DY 30 IV/2/604/37.

6. "10 Information über die Wirtschaftsverhandlungen DDR/UdSSR, Betr.: Maschinenbau und Metallurgie," 18 May 1962, 6, SAPMO DY30 IV/2/604/37.

7. Arbeitsgruppe Maschinenbau, "Einige grundsätzliche Fragen der Entwicklung und Profilierung des Maschinenbaus der DDR 1963–1965," 30 May 1962, 9, SAPMO DY 30 IV/2/604/37.

8. W. Liebig, "Auswertung der Arbeit der deutschen Delegation während der Wirtschaftsverhandlungen UdSSR/DDR in Moskau auf dem Gebiet des Maschinenbaus (25.4.–31.5.1962)," 13 June 1962, 5, SAPMO DY 30 IV/2/604/37.

9. Sobeslavsky and Lehmann, *Zur Geschichte von Rechentechnik*, 100–110.

10. Burghard Ciesla, "Die Transferfalle: Zum DDR-Flugzeugbau in den fünfziger Jahren," in Hoffmann and Macrakis, eds., *Naturwissenschaft und Technik in der DDR*, 193–211; Hans-Liudger Dienel, "'Das wahre Wirtschaftswunder'—Flugzeug-produktion, Fluggesellschaften und innerdeutscher Flugverkehr im West-Ost-Vergleich 1955–1980," in Bähr and Petzina, eds., *Innovationsverhalten und Ent-scheidungsstrukturen*, 341–71 (quotation on 348).

11. Ciesla, "Die Transfer-Falle," 208–9 (quotation on 208).

12. Ibid.

13. Friedrich Naumann, "Vom Tastenfeld zum Mikrochip—Computerindustrie und Informatik im 'Schrittmaß' des Sozialismus," in Hoffmann and Macrakis, eds., *Naturwissenschaft und Technik in der DDR*, 261–81, especially 265; Judt, "Zur Geschichte des Büro- und Datenverarbeitungsmaschinenbaus." For an overview coauthored by one of the key actors of the period, but based on documents seen after 1989, see Sobeslavsky and Lehmann, *Zur Geschichte von Rechentechnik*.

14. *Protokoll der Verhandlungen der 3 Parteikonferenz der Sozialistischen Ein-heitspartei Deutschlands*. The directive for the second Five-Year Plan is on 1022–1113; the quotations are from a speech by Ulbricht, 76.

15. Wunderlich (SPK, Abt. Maschinenbau), "Protokoll über die Besprechung mit Dr Kortum (VEB Carl Zeiss Jena) über den Aufbau des Instituts für Automatisierung in Jena am 20.8.59," n.d. (ca. late August 1959), 1, 3–4, BAP DE1/809.

16. Ibid., 3; SPK, Abt. Werkzeugmaschinen und Automatisierung, "Diskussions-grundlage für das Dokument 'Zentralinstitut für Automatisierung,'" 10, 18 June 1960, BAP DE1/13903; Belitz (SPK, Abt. Werkzeugmaschinen und Automatisier-ung), "Bericht vor der Wirtschaftskommission des Politbüros beim ZK der SED über Rolle, Aufgaben und Stand des Aufbaues des Zentralinstitutes für Automatisierung in Jena," 18 August 1960, 9 (quotations), BAP DE1/1287.

17. Wunderlich (SPK, Abt. Maschinenbau), "Protokoll über die Besprechung mit Dr Kortum (VEB Carl Zeiss Jena) über den Aufbau des Instituts für Automatisierung in Jena am 20.8.59," n.d. (ca. late August 1959), 4, BAP DE1/809; Belitz, "Stand des Aufbaues des Zentralinstitutes für Automatisierung, Jena, und Probleme, die dabei bestehen," 17 June 1960, 3–4, BAP DE1/13833; Belitz, "Bericht vor der Wirtschafts-kommission des Politbüros beim ZK der SED über Rolle, Aufgaben und Stand des Aufbaues des Zentralinstitutes für Automatisierung in Jena," 18 August 1960, 9, 10–11, BAP DE1/1287; Gen. Helmut Schmidt, Betriebsparteiorganisation des VEB Carl Zeiss, "Information," 22 August 1959, SAPMO DY 30/IV 2/604/123.

18. Belitz, "Stand des Aufbaues des Zentralinstitutes für Automatisierung, Jena, und Probleme, die dabei bestehen," 17 June 1960, 3–4, BAP DE1/13833; Erich Apel to 1. Sekretär der Bezirksleitung Gera, Gen. Paul Roscher, 29 July 1960, 1–2, BAP DE1/13903.

19. Apel to Roscher, 29 July 1960, 1–2 (quotation on 1), BAP DE1/13903.

20. Judt, "Zur Geschichte des Büro- und Datenverarbeitungsmaschinenbaus"; "Aufgaben des Zentralinstituts für Automatisierung," 11 April 1962, SAPMO DY30 IV/2/607/38.

21. Judt, "Zur Geschichte des Büro- und Datenverarbeitungsmaschinenbaus," 146.

22. VVB Bauelemente und Vakuumtechnik, "Bericht über die Entwicklung der Halbleitertechnik in der DDR," 24 September 1962, SAPMO DY 30 IV/2/607/74; Arbeitsgruppe Forschung und technische Entwicklung, "Gesamtbericht über den gegenwärtigen Stand und die zu lösenden Probleme auf dem Gebiet der Halbleitertechnik," 22 October 1962, SAPMO DY 30 IV/2/607/73 (quotation on 5); "Auswertung der Halbleiterratstagung vom 6. Juli 1962," n.d., SAPMO DY 30 IV/2/604/161.

23. Zentrale Kommission für staatliche Kontrolle, "Bericht über die Ergebnisse der Überprüfung des Lizenzhandels unter besonderer Beachtung der Tätigkeit des Außenhandelsunternehmens LIMEX GmbH," 15 October 1962, SAPMO DY30 IV/2/607/29.

24. Stokes, "Autarky, Ideology, and Technological Lag."

25. VVB Werkzeugmaschine to ZK der SED, Abt. Maschinenbau und Metallurgie, "Bericht über die Führung der Plandiskussion und die Ausarbeitung des Planes 1963," 29 September 1962, 2, SAPMO DY30 IV/2/604/83.

26. E.g., Robert Rompe, "Probleme der Überführung wissenschaftlicher Forschungsergebnisse in die Produktion," *Einheit* 16, no. 6 (June 1962): 23–32.

27. For an early, pessimistic assessment of the NES's potential for success, see Karl Thalheim, *Die Wirtschaft der Sowjetzone in Krise und Umbau* (Berlin: Duncker & Humblot, 1964), 90. See in addition McCauley, *The German Democratic Republic since 1945*, 107–25; Michael Keren, "The New Economic System in the GDR: An Obituary," *Soviet Studies* 24 (1973): 554–87; Jörg Roesler, *Zwischen Plan und Markt: Die Wirtschaftsreform in der DDR zwischen 1963 und 1970* (Berlin: Haufe, 1990). The most recent treatment is the most comprehensive and far-reaching: André Steiner, *Die DDR-Wirtschaftsreform der sechziger Jahre. Konflikt zwischen Effizienz- und Machtkalkül* (Berlin: Akademie-Verlag, 1999).

28. See Thalheim, *Die Wirtschaft der Sowjetzone*; Keren, "The New Economic System," 557–69.

29. Keren, "The New Economic System," 569.

30. McCauley, *The German Democratic Republic since 1945*, 125–26.

31. On planning for science and technology, see Roesler, *Die Herausbildung*, 192–217. Information on the organizational structure of research and technology in the GDR comes from Bundesarchiv Berlin, Findbuch DF4 Ministerium für Wissenschaft und Technik.

32. Roesler, *Die Herausbildung*, 215.

33. Eckart Förtsch, "Wissenschafts- und Technologiepolitik in der DDR," in Hoffmann and Macrakis, eds., *Naturwissenschaft und Technik in der DDR*, 26; Bentley, *Research and Technology in the Former German Democratic Republic*, 19. See also Tandler, "Geplante Zukunft," 123–24, 148.

34. Forschungsrat der DDR, Ministerium für Wissenschaft und Technik, "Prognose Organische hochpolymere Werkstoffe und ihr effectiver Einsatz in der Volkswirtscahft," December 1967, Bundesarchiv Außenstelle Hoppegarten, DF4/19860; see also Raymond G. Stokes, "Plastics and the New Society," in *State and Socialism: Modernity and Material Culture in Postwar Eastern Europe*, edited by David Crowley and Susan Reid (Oxford: Berg, forthcoming).

35. *Statistisches Jahrbuch der DDR* 17 (1972): 131.

36. Cited by André Steiner, "Zwischen Frustration und Verschwendung," in

Wunderwirtschaft. DDR-Konsumkultur in den 60er Jahren, edited by Neue Gesellschaft für Bildende Kunst (Cologne: Böhlau, 1996), 33.

37. Axel Schildt, "Gesellschaftliche Entwicklung," *Deutschland in den fünfziger Jahren, Information zur politischen Bildung* 256 (1997): 8.

38. See, for instance, David Noble, *America by Design* (Oxford: Oxford University Press, 1977); Guy Alchon, *The Invisible Hand of Planning: Capitalism, Social Science, and the State in the 1920s* (Princeton: Princeton University Press, 1985).

39. Keren, "The New Economic System," 574. Keren refers to those who wished to reform the bureaucracy through technological measures as "computopians" (555).

40. McCauley, *The German Democratic Republic since 1945,* 126; Jerome Segal, "Cybernetics in the German Democratic Republic: From Bourgeois Science to Panacea," in Severyns, Hoffmann, and Stokes, eds., *Science, Technology, and Political Change.*

41. Sobeslavsky and Lehmann, *Zur Geschichte von Rechentechnik,* 17–18.

42. Alan H. Smith, *The Planned Economies of Eastern Europe* (London: Croom Helm, 1983), 40–41.

43. Förtsch, "Wissenschafts- und Technologiepolitik in der DDR," in Hoffmann and Macrakis, eds., *Naturwissenschaft und Technik in der DDR,* 26.

44. Steiner, "Zwischen Frustration und Verschwendung."

45. Sobeslavsky and Lehmann, *Zur Geschichte von Rechentechnik,* 100–110.

Chapter 7: Substituting for Success, 1970–1989

1. Jörg Roesler, "Industrieinnovation und Industriespionage in der DDR. Der Staatssicherheit in der Innovationsgeschichte der DDR," *Deutschland-Archiv* 27 (1994): 1031. Roesler cites his book *Die Herausbildung* to support this contention.

2. For more on this, see one of the earliest and still one of the best books on the Stasi, Karl-Wilhelm Fricke, *Die DDR Staatssicherheit,* 3d ed. (Cologne: Verlag Wissenschaft und Politik, 1989), especially 166–68. The first edition of his book appeared in 1982, while the third edition preceded the fall of the wall.

3. See Rainer Karlsch and Harm Schröter, eds., *"Strahlende Vergangenheit." Studien zur Geschichte des Uranbergbaus der Wismut* (St. Katharinen: Scripta Mercaturae Verlag, 1996).

4. Karlsch, "Der Traum von Oel."

5. Abt. Planung und Finanzen, "Information über die 1. Rationalisierungskonferenz des Wirtschaftszweiges 'Altrohstoffe,'" 5 June 1972, SAPMO DY30/vorl. SED 11655; "Statut des Ministeriums für Materialwirtschaft vom 22. Januar 1976," *Gesetzblatt der Deutschen Demokratischen Republik* 1, no. 4 (6 February 1976): 49–52; "Ministerium für Materialwirtschaft," in *DDR Handbuch,* 907–8.

6. Eberhard Garbe and Dieter Graichen, *Sekundärrohstoffe Begriffe, Fakten, Perspektiven* (Berlin: Verlag Die Wirtschaft, 1985), 160.

7. "Zum Bericht der Arbeitsgruppe für Organisation und Inspektion beim Ministerrat über die Erfassung und Nutzung von Sekundärrohstoffen," 3 December 1982, 1, SAPMO DY30/vorl. SED 30156.

8. Wolfgang Rauchfuss to Mittag, 1 October 1981, 1, SAPMO DY30/vorl. SED 30156.

9. "Zum Bericht der Arbeitsgruppe für Organisation und Inspektion beim Ministerrat über die Erfassung und Nutzung von Sekundärrohstoffen," 3 December 1982, 1–3, SAPMO DY30/vorl. SED 30156.

10. Ibid.

11. Wolfgang Rauchfuss to Mittag, 29 April 1983, SAPMO DY30/vorl. SED 38523.

12. The phrases are from "Statut des Ministeriums für Materialwirtschaft vom 22 Januar 1976," *Gesetzblatt der Deutschen Demokratischen Republik* 1, no. 4 (6 February 1976): 49.

13. Ibid., 50.

14. MfS, "Information über wesentliche Erkenntnisse zu feindlichen Plänen, Absichten und Maßnahmen gegen die Volkswirtschaft der DDR und die sozialistische ökonomische Integration," 8 December 1979, especially 33–34, BStU Zentralarchiv (ZA), Berlin.

15. "Ende für Emmy," *Spiegel* 44 (4 June 1990): 55, 58; "Wie uff 'ner Kippe," *Spiegel* 44 (15 October 1990): 74, 77.

16. See, for instance, Manfred Schell, *Stasi und kein Ende* (Frankfurt: Ullstein, 1992); David Childs and Richard Popplewell, *The Stasi* (Basingstoke: Macmillan, 1996); Timothy Garten Ash, *The File: A Personal History* (New York: Vintage, 1997).

17. File of IMS "Hans Müller," BstU, ZA, Erfurt AIM 1701/89, Teile 1, 2, especially T 2.

18. Kristie Macrakis, "Das Ringen um wissenschaftlich-technischen Höchststand: Spionage und Technologietransfer in der DDR," in Hoffmann and Macrakis, eds., *Naturwissenschaft und Technik in der DDR*, 59–88.

19. "Wissenschafts- und Wirtschaftsspionage in der Bundesrepublik Deutschland," *Innere Sicherheit* 54 (15 August 1980), seen in BStU ZA ZAIG/1, 9666, 114–17; Macrakis, "Das Ringen um wissenschaftlich-technischen Höchststand," 64–69.

20. For a detailed overview of the tasks and personnel of these sections in 1989, see Klaus-Dietmar Henke and others, eds., *Anatomie der Staatssicherheit. Geschichte, Struktur und Methoden. MfS Handbuch* (Berlin: BStU, 1995), 172–85, 364–67 (quotation on 366).

21. This is evident from a list of "informational priorities" (*Informationsschwerpunkte*) that the HVA put together in 1985. There is a very heavy emphasis on the acquisition of *firmeninterne* documentation in areas such as business organization; capacity; plants slated for expansion, for construction, or for closure; research and development plans; and so on. HVA, Stellvertreter (Vogel), "Informationsschwerpunkte zum Komplex Wirtschaftsaufklärung," October 1985, 2–10, BStU ZA, MfS ZAIG, no. 14484.

22. Roesler, "Industrieinnovation und Industriespionage in der DDR," 1026–40.

23. Macrakis, "Das Ringen um wissenschaftlich-technischen Höchststand," 59–88.

24. Items are on 24, 26, 28–29 of BStU ZA, MfS-HA XVIII, no. 10297.

25. Roesler, "Industrieinnovation und Industriespionage in der DDR," 1026; "Wissenschafts- und Wirtschaftsspionage in der Bundesrepublik Deutschland."

26. This practice is discussed with regard to Robotron's copying of other VAX computers in a memorandum from Stasi HA XVIII, 11 May 1987, 1–3, BStU ZA MfS-HA XVIII, no. 9553; and in HA XVIII, 8 January 1986, 2–3, and Leiter, HA XVIII, to Bezirksverwaltung für Staatssicherheit, Dresden, 28 April 1986, 4–5, BStU ZA MfS-HA XVIII, no. 10207.

27. Calculated on the basis of the exchange rate for 1 June 1988 listed at the U.S. Federal Reserve's web site: ⟨http://www.federalreserve.gov/releases/H10/hist/dat89__ge.txt⟩. The rate was DM 1.73/$1.00.

28. Leiter, HA XVIII, "Information zum Import eines VAX-Rechners 8800 der Firma Digital Equipment Corporation (DEC)," 15 August 1988, 4–5, BStU ZA, MfS-HA XVIII, no. 10974.

29. The awareness of this problem and a large number of ways of keeping such information secure are outlined in MfS, Stellvertreter des Ministers, "Politisch-operative Sicherung der Auswertung und Nutzung politisch-operativ beschaffter wissenschaftlich-technischer Erkenntnisse in der Volkswirtschaft der DDR," 1 January 1983, 1–15, BStU ZA, 6. Durchführungsbestimmung zur Dienstanweisung no. 1/82.

30. See generally John Tirman, ed., *Empty Promise: The Growing Case against Star Wars* (Boston: Beacon Press, 1986). For material on the Soviet (and eastern bloc) response, see Richard L. Garwin, "The Soviet Response: New Missiles and Countermeasures," in Tirman, ed., *Empty Promise*, 129–46.

31. "Preisaufschläge auf Basis Preislisten," *Anlage* 3 to report by IMS Hans, "Bewertungskriterien zu derzeit genutzten Embargolieferlinien," n.d. (ca. 1986), 6, BStu ZA MfS-HA XVIII, no. 10329.

32. MfS, HVA, SWT, Leiter (Oberst Weiberg), "Kurzbericht über wichtige Arbeitsergebnisse der wissenschaftlich-technischen Aufklärung im 1 Halbjahr 1971," 12 August 1971, 14–22 (quotation at 8, 21), BStU ZA, MfS-Sekretariat des Ministers 355.

33. Fricke, *Die DDR Staatssicherheit*, 166–68; "Wissenschafts- und Wirtschaftsspionage in der Bundesrepublik Deutschland," 115–16; MfS, HVA, SWT, Leiter, "Kurzbericht über wichtige Arbeitsergebnisse der wissenschaftlich-technischen Aufklärung im 1. Halbjahr 1971," 14–22, BStU ZA, MfS-Sekretariat des Ministers 355. By the 1980s biotechnology and environmental technology had been added to this list of priority projects, as indicated in HVA, Stellvertreter (Vogel), "Informationsschwerpunkte zum Komplex Wirtschaftsaufklärung," 13, 15, 9–10, BStU ZA, MfS ZAIG, no. 14484.

34. MfS, HVA, SWT, Leiter, "Kurzbericht über wichtige Arbeitsergebnisse der wissenschaftlich-technischen Aufklärung im 1 Halbjahr 1971," 8, 21, BStU ZA, MfS-Sekretariat des Ministers 355.

35. HVA, Stellvertreter (Vogel), "Informationsschwerpunkte zum Komplex Wirtschaftsaufklärung," 1–16, 3–10, BStU ZA, MfS ZAIG, no. 14484.

36. MfS, Leiter, HA XVIII to Bezirksverwaltung für Staatssicherheit, Dresden, 28 April 1986, BStU ZA MfS-HA XVIII, no. 10207, 4–6; HA XVIII, "Memo," 11 May 1987, BStU ZA, MfS-HA XVIII, no. 9553, 1–3.

37. MfS, Leiter, HA XVIII to Bezirksverwaltung für Staatssicherheit, Dresden, 28 April 1986, 4, 7, BStU ZA MfS-HA XVIII, no. 10207.

38. MfS, HVA, SWT, Leiter, "Kurzbericht über wichtige Arbeitsergebnisse der wissenschaftlich-technischen Aufklärung im 1 Halbjahr 1971," 6, 19, BStU ZA, MfS-Sekretariat des Ministers 355.

39. MfS, HVA, SWT, Leiter, "Kurzbericht über wichtige Arbeitsergebnisse der wissenschaftlich-technischen Aufklärung im 1 Halbjahr 1971," 6, 19, BStU ZA, MfS-Sekretariat des Ministers 355.

40. Roesler, "Industrieinnovation und Industriespionage in der DDR," 1038. Roesler mentions cases from the machine-tool industry in which the companies' products were of such an internationally advanced standard that they could easily withstand the shock of the exchange of GDR currency to the DM at 1:1.

41. For a discussion of these terms with regard to the West German economy and technology, see Gerd Junne, "Competitiveness and the Impact of Change: Applications of 'High Technologies'," in *Industry and Politics in West Germany*, edited by Peter Katzenstein (Ithaca, N.Y.: Cornell University Press, 1989), 249–74.

Chapter 8: Technological Tactics in the Endgame

1. Bentley, *Research and Technology in the Former German Democratic Republic*, 142.

2. Sutton, *Western Technology and Soviet Economic Development 1945–1965*, xxvi, 40, 57, 304, 381.

3. Joseph Berliner, *The Innovation Decision in Soviet Industry* (Cambridge, Mass.: MIT Press, 1976), 517. See also Amos Jordan, foreword, in Parrott, ed., *Trade, Technology, and Soviet-American Relations*.

4. W. R. Lee and Nigel Swain, "The New Technology That Failed: Information Technology and Computing in the GDR and Hungary," in *The System of Centrally Planned Economies in Central-Eastern and South-Eastern Europe after World War II and the Causes of Its Decay* (Prague: University of Economics, 1994), 305. My thanks to Dr. Swain for permission to use this quotation.

5. K. Biener, "Nachruf für Konrad Zuse," Internet document, URL: ⟨http://www13.informatik.tu-muenchen.de/gi/gi-html/info/fokus/geschichte/zuse.nachruf.html⟩. A recent history of computing in the GDR indicates that the program to develop a mechanical rather than an electronic computer continued in the GDR through 1960. See Sobeslavsky and Lehmann, *Zur Geschichte von Rechentechnik*, 18–19.

6. Judt, "Zur Geschichte des Büro- und Datenverarbeitungsmaschinenbaus," 138, 142.

7. *Protokoll der Verhandlungen der 3 Parteikonferenz der Sozialistischen Einheits-Partei Deutschlands*, 76.

8. Matthias Judt, "Der Innovationsprozess. Automatisierte Informationsverarbeitung in der DDR von den Anfang der fünfziger bis Anfang der siebziger Jahre" (Ph.D. diss., Humboldt University, 1989).

9. MfS, HA XVIII, Leiter (Kleine), to Bezirksverwaltung Dresden, "Standpunkt zu den Entwicklungsvorhaben 0023 des VEB Kombinat Robotron," 28 April 1986, 3,

BStU ZA MfS-HA XVIII/10207; Lee and Swain, "The New Technology That Failed," 277–88.

10. See *Protokoll des IX Parteitages der Sozialistischen Einheitspartei Deutschlands, 18. Bis 22. Mai 1976*, 2 vols. (Berlin: Dietz, 1976), 2:331–57, especially 342–45; VEB Robotron-Elektronik Zella-Mehlis, *In eigener Sache* (Berlin: Verlag Tribune, 1977), 185 (quotation).

11. Bentley, *Research and Technology in the Former German Democratic Republic*, 76, 79, 181, 195.

12. Ibid., 50, 78.

13. *Statistisches Jahrbuch der DDR* 29 (1984): 140; 34 (1989): 142.

14. OECD, *Gaps in Technology: Electronic Components* (Paris: OECD, 1968), 15.

15. In the source, the GDR's Statistical Yearbook for 1989, the production of integrated circuits is listed as being in "1,000 Stück" units, although it appears that this is a typographical error and should simply read "Stück." *Statistisches Jahrbuch der DDR* 34 (1989): 148.

16. For an initial assessment of the need for "eine Kooperation, besonders mit der UdSSR" in the area of data processing, "Erste Abschätzung des Entwicklungstrends der Datenverarbeitungstechnik . . . im Zeitraum 1970–1980," 25 November 1967, 17, SAPMO DY30 IV/2/202/430. The desire for cooperation continued throughout the GDR's existence, but there were many practical difficulties: Trautenhahn, "Diskussionsmaterial zur Ausarbeitung der Vorlage für die Wirtschaftskommission . . . über 'Die Durchführung der Beschlüsse des IX. Parteitages der SED auf dem Gebiet der Elektrotechnik und Elektronik,'" 3 January 1977, SAPMO DY30/vorl. SED 17791; "Zu Problemen der Entwicklung der Mikroelektronik," 25 March 1977, 1, SAPMO DY30/vorl. SED 17691.

17. "Information über den Stand der Durchführung der Festlegungen über den Import von Ausrüstungen für die Mikroelektronik im Rahmen des Abschlusses von Kompensastionsgeschäften," 21 September 1979, SAPMO DY30/vorl. SED 22168; entries on Beil and Schalck-Golodowski, in *Wer war Wer in der DDR*, 3d ed. (Frankfurt: Fischer Taschenbuch Verlag, 1995), 52–53 and 628.

18. K. Hermann (Stellvertreter des Ministers für Wissenschaft und Technik), "Bericht über die Teilnahme an der Reise der Staatsdelegation der DDR nach Japan unter Leitung . . . Gen. Dr. Günter Mittag," 20 November 1977, 5, SAPMO DY30/vorl. SED 22352; VEB Mikroelektronik, "Information über den Besuch des Präsidenten der Toshiba Corporation, Tokyo,, am 15.3.1981," 16 March 1981, SAPMO DY30/vorl. SED 29978; AHB Elektronik Export-Import, "Verhandlungsbericht über die Beratung mit Mitsubishi Electric Corporation . . . ," 17 March 1982, SAPMO DY30/vorl. SED 29978.

19. K. Hermann (Stellvertreter des Ministers für Wissenschaft und Technik), "Bericht über die Teilnahme an der Reise der Staatsdelegation der DDR nach Japan unter Leitung . . . Gen. Dr. Günter Mittag," 20 November 1977, 5, SAPMO DY30/vorl. SED 22352.

20. VEB Mikroelektronik, "Information über den Besuch des Präsidenten der Toshiba Corporation, Tokyo, am 153.1981," 16 March 1981, SAPMO DY30/vorl. SED 29978. The facility refers to machines developed by Perkin Elmer and Bell

Laboratories that use x-rays to etch circuits onto chips using sophisticated masks made of plastic and metal. See Braun and Macdonald, *Revolution in Miniature*, 118.

21. MfS HA XVIII/8, "Auszug aus einem IM-Bericht," 15 April 1982, BStU ZA, MfS-HA XVIII/8255.

22. Bentley, *Research and Technology in the Former German Democratic Republic*, 176.

23. "Zu Problemen der Entwicklung der Mikroelektronik," 25 March 1977, 1, SAPMO DY30/vorl. SED 17691.

24. MfS, Verwaltung Rückwärtige Dienste, Abt. Planung, Leiter (Kraus) to Stellvertreter des Ministers (Geisler), "Information zur Liefersituation für Erzeugnisse der Elektrotechnik/Elektronik aus dem NSW," 18 July 1980, BStU ZA, MfS-AGM/263.

25. MfS, Verwaltung Rückwärtige Dienste, Abt. Planung, Leiter (Sommer) to Hauptabteilung IX, Leiter, "Information zur Entwicklung der Liefersituation auf den kapitalistischen Märkten für Embargo- un genehmigungspflichtige Erzeugnisse, besonders auf den Gebieten der Elektrotechnik/Elektronik und Datenverarbeitung," 22 February 1982, BStU ZA, MfS-HA IX/562. The continuation of this policy, and its deleterious effects on the GDR economy and technology, are described in MfS, HA XVIII/8, "Zu aktuellen Erscheinungen und Tendenzen der gegnerischen Embargopolitik im Bereich Mikroelektronik," 11 May 1987, BStU ZA, MfS-HA XVIII/10329.

26. Braun and Macdonald, *Revolution in Miniature*, 103–20.

27. An account of this controversy can be found in Siegfried Wenzel, *Plan und Wirklichkeit. Zur DDR Oekonomie. Dokumentation und Erinnerungen* (St. Katharinen: Scripta Mercaturae Verlag, 1998).

28. MfS HA XVIII (Kleine), "1 Maßnahmeplan zur politisch-operativen Sicherung der Zielstellung des Beschlusses 'Höchstintegration,'" 26 February 1987, and addenda, especially 4–7, in BStU ZA, MfS-HA XVIII/638.

29. MfS HA XVIII (Kleine), "1 Maßnahmeplan zur politisch-operativen Sicherung der Zielstellung des Beschlusses 'Höchstintegration,'" 26 February 1987, and addenda, especially 8–14, in BStU ZA, MfS-HA XVIII/638.

30. MfS, HVA, SWT, and HA XVIII/8, "Bericht über den Arbeitsbesuch des Generalsekretärs der SED, Genossen Erich Honecker, vom 22.23.5.1986 in Betrieben der Kombinate Mikroelektronik, Robotron und Carl Zeiss Jena," 24 May 1986, 2, in BStU ZA, MfS-HA XVIII/9505.

31. MfS, HA XVIII/8, "Information zum Stand der Realisierung höchstintegrierter mikroelektronischer Schaltkreise in der DDR," 30 March 1988, in BstU ZA, MfS-HA XVIII/10215.

32. Ibid.

33. As was the case with the Friendship oil pipeline, rumors about which are reported in chapter 4, there are rumors about the GDR's one-megabit chip: that it was not developed there at all but was simply stolen from the West. Again, documentary evidence to support this contention, not surprisingly, does not seem to be available, although Macrakis, "Das Ringen um wissenschaftlich-technischen Höchststand," cites an interview with a former Stasi officer. Whether the chip was made in the GDR or not, the key point seems to be that the country spent a huge

amount of money developing it, but was most definitely *not* in the position of mass-producing it in 1988 or anytime soon.

34. K. Nendel, "Sorfortbericht über den Besuch der CeBit-Messe in Hannover vom 18.–20.3.1988," 21 March 1988, 1, SAPMO DY30/vorl. SED 41817.

35. MfS, HA XVIII, "Information," 9 January 1989, BStU ZA, MfS-HA XVIII/ 10222.

36. MfS, HA XVIII/8, "Information: Gespräch zwischem dem Gen Prof. Biermann, Generaldirektor des Kombinates Carl-Zeiss Jena und dem Geschäftsführer der BRD-Firma Leybold-Heraeus am 22. April 1987," 27 April 1987, BStU ZA, MfS-HA XVIII/10843. For prior contact between Leybold and the GDR, see chapter 5.

37. MfS, "Information," 22 February 1989, p 3, BStU ZA, MfS ZAIG Z3742.

38. Braun and Macdonald, *Revolution in Miniature*, 108, 119.

Conclusion

1. Sigrid Meuschel, *Legitimation und Parteiherrschaft. Zum Paradox von Stabilität und Revolution in der DDR 1945–1989* (Frankfurt: Suhrkamp, 1992).

2. Kopstein, *The Politics of Economic Decline in East Germany, 1945–1989*, 18 (quotation).

3. Georg C. Bertsch, Ernst Hedler, and Matthias Dietz, *SED: Schönes Einheits-Design; Stunning Eastern Design; Savoir Eviter le Design* (Cologne: Taschen, 1994), 7.

4. For a detailed and readable survey of the collapse of the GDR, which takes into consideration economic and technological factors, see Charles S. Maier, *Dissolution: The Crisis of Communism and the End of East Germany* (Princeton: Princeton University Press, 1997).

5. Alan Purkiss, "Industrial Revolution in East Germany," *Business* (June 1990): 62–67 (quotations on 62).

Bibliographic Essay

Source material for the history of the German Democratic Republic (GDR) is almost unimaginably rich and growing by the day. Therefore, this brief essay cannot pretend to be exhaustive in detailing and analyzing it, but can only outline some of the major primary and secondary sources available for particular topics related to the history of technology in the GDR.

Primary Sources

Archival sources are abundant and highly centralized. They are also not subject to the usual thirty-year rule for official archival holdings: every piece of paper produced between 1945 and 1990 that was deemed of historical value is available in principle. There are, however, some restrictions on some items, in particular the materials produced by and for the East German secret service, mainly owing to West German personal-protection laws.

The bulk of the holdings is available at or through the Bundesarchiv branch in Berlin Lichterfelde. There researchers can obtain materials previously separated into at least two separate archives. The records of the Socialist Unity Party (Sozialistische Einheitspartei, or SED), previously located in central Berlin, are now accessible in Lichterfelde. Held under the auspices of the Stiftung Bundesarchiv der Parteien und Massenorganisationen der DDR (SAPMO), these records include materials by and for the Politburo, the so-called *Handakten* (files that needed to be easily accessible) of key party figures such as Ulbricht and Honecker, and the records of various party organizations.

Party and state were, of course, organizationally separate in East Germany, and the state records are held separately, though also now available under the same roof in Lichterfelde. Previously located in Potsdam at the East German Central Archives, and after 1990 under the control of the Bundesarchiv Potsdam (BAP), they include the records of most key ministries, as well as those of the State Planning Commission (Staatliche Plankommission, or SPK). Because these records are so voluminous, some of them are stored physically in other locations around Berlin, but the archivists who control the records as well as the finding aids for locating them are available for consultation in Lichterfelde.

The other major archival source used in this study is the records of the so-called Gauck-Behörde, or Gauck Authority. The authority is named after Joachim Gauck, who for most of the period after 1990 has been the head of the organization controlling the records of the State Security Service (Ministerium für Staatssicherheit, or Ministry of State Security, normally known as the Stasi) of the GDR. The records are also located in Berlin, but in the center of the city. They are officially available through the Bundesbeauftragte für die Unterlagen des Staatssicherheitsdienstes der ehemaligen Deutschen Demokratischen Republik (Federal Deputy for the Documents of the State Security Service of the Former German Democratic Republic, or BStU), and scholars must make a detailed statement of their research topic before gaining admission. Once admitted, they will find that it takes a considerable amount of time to get access to the actual documents, which must first be scrutinized by an archivist in order to remove potentially harmful personal details (under West German personal-protection legislation).

For this study, the records of the Stasi Hauptverwaltung Aufklärung (Main Administrative Unit for Espionage) would have been most useful, but they were unfortunately largely destroyed in conjunction with the collapse of the GDR: apparently those most tuned in to the West through autumn 1989 were also most tuned in to the likely implications of a paper trail of their actions. Nevertheless, the records of the Stasi's Hauptabteilung XVIII (Main Section XVIII), which was responsible for domestic economic security, are voluminous and very useful, not least because members of the section sometimes construed domestic security very broadly. In the course of investigating these records, one frequently comes across the names of informal and formal agents, and it is possible, too, to see some of their personnel files. This is, however, a complicated procedure, since one must establish not only the cover name of the agent, but also the officer in charge of him or her in order to gain access to files.

Owing to limitations of time and because this is meant to be a general study, I have not made extensive use of two other sets of archival sources. The first includes regional and local archives, which, by the nature of the state in which they were located, are generally less useful than for, say, West Germany. The second is "firm" archives, which existed in the GDR as they do elsewhere, although the firm was a very different animal from that in the capitalist West. The GDR "combine" controlled not just production facilities (sometimes far apart from one another), but also housing stock, sports facilities, and a variety of subsidiary functions in its surrounding communities. These are a more important source than the regional and local archives, and I have used them occasionally, but most often indirectly. In any case, these archives vary widely in quality and availability, not least owing to the actions of the market and of the privatization agency set up in conjunction with the end of the GDR, the Treuhandanstalt. So, for instance, the records of the Buna chemical combine in Schkopau remain largely intact, owing to the engagement of key employees and the Schkopau facility's takeover in toto (together with sites in Böhlen and a small part of Leuna) by the Dow Chemical Corporation in 1995. The records of the nearby, but much larger, Leuna combine from the GDR period were transferred by and large to the control of the major regional archive in the German state of Sachsen-Anhalt, the Merseburg State Archive, largely because Leuna was privatized piecemeal rather than as a whole. In portions of this book I have relied heavily on some of the secondary literature listed below for details about particular combines, and this scholarship in turn has frequently been based upon holdings of various firm archives.

Primary printed materials have also been very useful in producing this history of East German technology. Key journals include *Die Technik, Die Standardisierung,* and *Der Maschinenbau* as well as the *Statistisches Jahrbuch der DDR.* Also of interest is the main party ideological journal, *Einheit.* The journals are available in some British and American research libraries, but the best collections remain in Germany, in particular at the Deutsches Museum in Munich. The *Statistisches Jahrbuch,* on the other hand, is frequently available in major research libraries.

The SED produced detailed documentation of virtually every meeting it sponsored, some of which were major party conferences, but some of which were relatively small and unimportant. Many of the proceedings are available in major research libraries around the world.

Finally, a large number of often very small books printed in the 1950s and 1960s and beyond proved very valuable. They are available piecemeal in various holdings, generally in Germany, but a very large collection related to technology in particular is in the Deutsches Museum.

Secondary Sources

In terms of secondary literature, the GDR has always been a source of fascination for the West, not least because of the extensive research efforts undertaken in the other German state. Some of this literature spans the gap between primary and secondary sources, including much produced under the auspices of the West German Ministry for Inner German Relations during the 1950s and 1960s. Such sources must be used with some caution, partly because they were written without access to official documentary sources or unpublished statistics, and partly because they were conditioned by political agendas of the day to portray the GDR as worse—or sometimes better—than it actually was. One of the best sources for overviews of key topics with regard to the GDR, however, remains the various editions of the *DDR Handbuch.* I relied extensively at times, for background information on a variety of subjects, on the third edition (2 vols. [Cologne: Verlag Wissenschaft und Politik, 1985]).

Other materials belong more clearly in the secondary-literature camp, not least the raft of articles and books appearing practically on a daily basis, and some of which I review here. The availability of vast quantities of archival sources for the GDR, some of which are very recent in vintage, has only one historical precedent that I know of: the post-1945 period in Germany. Even more than the 1950s, the 1990s have witnessed the production of enormous numbers of studies of aspects of GDR politics, economy, and society. Given that the GDR was a much smaller and much less significant state than the Third Reich, many detailed studies are of very narrow interest indeed. To appeal more broadly, the best of the emergent literature places the country's history into context, either by comparing the GDR with other countries, or by emphasizing the international dimensions of the GDR experience, or both.

I have found some of the literature from Soviet studies produced in vast quantities during the Cold War particularly helpful in providing context, although it rarely deals with the GDR directly. Technology was clearly a key concern of policymakers in that era, especially in the late 1970s and 1980s, and some fascinating scholarship was produced. One of the first, and certainly the most detailed, of these studies, and one based almost entirely on sources held at the Hoover Institution, is Anthony Sutton's three-volume study of technology in the Soviet Union, *Western Technology and Soviet Economic Development* (Stanford, Calif.: Hoover Institution Press, 1968–73). The final volume, published in 1973, covers the period from 1945 to 1965, and is both informative and suggestive about the impact of German technology (through reparations, removals, and relocation of personnel) on Soviet development. In a trilogy as long as this, there are no doubt many errors, and the source base is not always the most reliable, since much of it was produced by Soviet émigrés or by obviously engaged Cold Warriors. But Sutton gives a huge amount of detail, provides interesting hypotheses for further research, and offers a huge bibliography. Slightly later, Raymond Hutchings, in *Soviet Science, Technology, Design: Interaction and Convergence* (London: Oxford University Press, 1976), provided a superb overview of the linkages between scientific and technological development, on the one hand, and the design of Soviet artifacts, on the other. Joseph S. Berliner's *Innovation Decision in Soviet Industry* (Cambridge, Mass.: MIT Press, 1976) is an economic study that stresses the impact of social factors on innovation policy.

One key collection of articles in the field of studies of Soviet technology was compiled by Frederic J. Fleron Jr., *Technology and Communist Culture: The Socio-Cultural Impact of Technology under Socialism* (New York: Praeger, 1977). More valuable collections still appear in two volumes edited by members of the Soviet studies group at the University of Birmingham in England: Ronald Amann, Julian Cooper, and R. W. Davies, eds., *The Technological Level of Soviet Industry* (New Haven: Yale University Press, 1977); and the less quantitative volume edited by Ronald Amann and Julian Cooper, *Industrial Innovation in the Soviet Union* (New Haven: Yale University Press, 1982). Later studies include Bruce

Parrott, *Politics and Technology in the Soviet Union* (Cambridge, Mass.: MIT Press, 1983), which provides a very good overview of Soviet politics (and in particular foreign policy) and technology policy between the 1920s and the 1970s. Bruce Parrott, ed., *Trade, Technology, and Soviet-American Relations* (Bloomington: Indiana University Press, 1985), compiles articles related specifically to trade in technology. Thane Gustafson, in *Selling the Russians the Rope? Soviet Technology Policy and U.S. Export Controls* (Santa Monica, Calif.: RAND Corp., 1991), continues the study of trade and technological development, which was clearly of major importance in the waning days of the Cold War.

Literature on Soviet technological development helped place East German technology in an eastern-bloc context, but it does not usually deal explicitly with the German Democratic Republic. What is more, East Germany, which was at once much more highly industrialized, had more highly developed traditions of technological excellence, and was much smaller than the Soviet Union, shared many characteristics of the larger country but developed very differently.

The other major strand of work useful for placing developments in the GDR in comparative context is more recent and explicitly comparative. It emphasizes comparisons between the two heirs of German technological traditions, the Federal Republic of Germany and the German Democratic Republic. Such studies now abound, not least because of intensive work over the course of years by a team of researchers funded by the Deutsche Forschungsgemeinschaft. A vast number of articles and some books have now appeared as a result of this project, which compares innovation systems in East and West Germany. Many of the individual case studies of particular industries or technologies are summarized in an excellent overview volume edited by Johannes Bähr and Dietmar Petzina, *Innovationsverhalten und Entscheidungsstrukturen. Vergleichende Studien zur wirtschaftlichen Entwicklung im geteilten Deutschland 1945–1990* (Berlin: Duncker und Humblot, 1996). A second volume based on some of the project's case studies is soon to appear (Lothar Baar and Dietmar Petzina, eds., *Deutsch-Deutsche Wirtschaft 1945–1990. Strukturveränderung, Innovationen und regionaler Wandel* [St. Katharinen: Scripta Mercaturae, 1999]). A similar comparative approach is followed in a separate project undertaken by a team of American and German researchers, which emphasizes science much more but also deals with technology and other issues. The project's main findings are reported in a volume edited by Dieter Hoffmann and Kristie Macrakis, *Naturwissenschaft und Technik in der DDR* (Berlin: Akademie, 1997). The volume has now appeared in somewhat different form in English (with some different contributions and different introductory material) as *Science under Socialism* (Cambridge, Mass.: Harvard University Press, 1999).

Although a comparison of technological developments in the GDR with those in the Federal Republic is valuable, it is also somewhat problematic. As detailed in my study, the two countries, although emerging from similar traditions, grew apart over time, in part because of their very different social and economic systems, and in part because of demographic differences, differences in resource endowments, and so on. For all these reasons, it is also necessary to study the GDR on its own terms, although some of the best of this literature, too, is at least implicitly comparative.

Because of the centrality of technology to the development of GDR economy and society, even general treatments contain some references to it, and some go well beyond that. Standard reference works in this regard include the *DDR Handbuch*, mentioned above, as well as more recent works: Klaus Schröder (with cooperation of Steffen Alisch), *Der SED-Staat. Partei, Spaat und Gesellschaft 1949–1990* (Munich: Carl Hanser Verlag, 1998); and Matthias Judt, ed., *DDR Geschichte in Dokumenten* (Berlin: Christoph Links, 1998). *Wer war Wer in der DDR. Ein biographisches Handbuch*, 3d ed. (Frankfurt: Fischer Taschenbuchverlag, 1996), provides short biographical entries on key figures in GDR politics, economy, and society.

In terms of general historical overviews, David Childs, *The GDR: Moscow's German Ally* (London: George Allen and Unwin, 1983), remains a standard treatment of political, economic, and social development in the GDR; Martin McCauley, *The German Democratic Republic since 1945* (New York: St. Martin's Press, 1983), is useful as well. More recently, Sigrid Meuschel's sociohistorical study, *Legitimation und Parteiherrschaft. Zum Paradox von Stabilität und Revolution in der DDR 1945–1989* (Frankfurt: Suhrkamp, 1992), places technology and technocrats at the center of her interpretation without going into detail on specific technologies or technology policy. Norman Naimark, *The Russians in Germany: A History of the Soviet Zone of Occupation, 1945–1949* (Cambridge, Mass.: Belknap Press of Harvard University Press, 1995), details politics and economics in the formative years of the GDR just after World War II, on the basis of archival materials in both the former East Germany and Russia. Stefan Wolle, *Die heile Welt der Diktatur. Alltag und Herrschaft in der DDR 1971–1989* (Berlin: Christoph Links, 1998), is concerned with the later decades of East German social history, but includes some telling and often highly entertaining material on economy and technology. Essays by André Steiner and Ina Merkel in *Getting and Spending: European and American Consumer Societies in the Twentieth Century*, edited by Susan Strasser, Charles McGovern, and Matthias Judt (Cambridge: Cambridge University Press, 1998), also deal with the social history of consumption in the GDR, at times touching directly on, and always with implications for, the history of technology and innovation in the GDR. *Wunderwirtschaft: DDR-Konsumkultur in den 60er Jahren* (Weimar: Böhlau, 1996) also includes several essays—and some excellent photographs—relating to the history of technology and innovation in the GDR.

Studies of the GDR economy are more likely still to provide useful information on technological development. Some of them were produced in East Germany before 1989 and are withstanding the test of time (and of a completely different ideological environment) reasonably well. These include several studies in which Jörg Roesler was involved, especially Roesler, Renate Schwärzel, and Veronika Siedt, *Produktionswachstum und Effektivität in Industriezweigen der DDR, 1950–1970* (Berlin: Akademie-Verlag, 1983); and Roesler, Veronika Siedt, and Michael Elle, *Wirtschaftswachstum in der Industrie der DDR 1945–1970* (Berlin: Akademie-Verlag, 1986). Also very useful is Wolfgang Mühlfriedel and Klaus Wießner, *Die Geschichte der Industrie der DDR bis 1965* (Berlin: Akademie-Verlag, 1989). After the fall of the Wall, a new wave of studies of the GDR appeared. In German, one such study is Falk Küchler, *Die Wirtschaft der DDR. Wirtschaftspolitk und industrielle Rahmenbedingungen 1949 bis 1989* (Berlin: FIDES, 1997); another, which includes reflections by a former actor in the GDR system, is Siegfried Wenzel, *Plan und Wirklichkeit. Zur DDR Oekonomie. Dokumentation und Erinnerungen* (St. Katharinen: Scripta Mercaturae, 1998). One of the earliest and most useful overviews of GDR economic history is in English: Jeffrey Kopstein, *The Politics of Economic Decline in East Germany, 1945–1989* (Chapel Hill: University of North Carolina Press, 1997). Charles S. Maier, *Dissolution: The Crisis of Communism and the End of East Germany* (Princeton: Princeton University Press, 1997), is heavily oriented toward the end of the GDR, and contains as much about politics as about economics or technology, but it includes an excellent chapter giving a historical overview of the economy and its problems. Ulrich Voskamp and Volker Wittke, "Industrial Restructuring in the Former German Democratic Republic (GDR): Barriers to Adaptive Reform Become Downward Development Spirals," *Politics and Society* 19 (1991): 341–71, look mostly at the perspectives for the former GDR in the period after 1990, but offer a stimulating interpretation of some dimensions of the economic history and technological culture of East Germany.

Other economic historians deal with specific issues or periods. Rainer Karlsch, *Allein bezahlt? Die Reparationsleistungen der SBZ/DDR1 1945–1953* (Berlin: Christoph Links, 1993), has produced the definitive work on the reparations issue; Ulrich Albrecht, Andreas Heinemann-Grüder, and Arend Wellmann, *Die Spezialisten. Deutsche Naturwissenschaftler und Techniker in der Sowjetunion nach 1945* (Berlin: Dietz, 1992), deal with the seizure of technical and scientific personnel from the GDR and their deployment in the late 1940s and early 1950s in the Soviet Union. Some of the essays in *Technology Transfer Out of Germany after 1945*, edited by Matthias Judt and Burghard Ciesla (Amsterdam: Harwood, 1996), deal with aspects of human and material reparations from the GDR as well. The GDR's experiment in economic planning in the 1960s after the construction of the wall, the New Economic System (NES), has been getting some of the most extensive treatment by scholars. Jörg Roesler, *Zwischen Plan und Markt. Die Wirtschaftsreform der DDR zwischen 1963 und 1970* (Berlin: Haufe, 1990), argues that the NES had considerable potential for making the GDR more viable economically but was sabotaged by political interests. André Steiner's more recent consideration of the period, *Die DDR-Wirtschaftsreform der sechziger Jahre.*

Konflikt zwischen Effizienz- und Machtkalkül (Berlin: Akademie-Verlag, 1999), appeared too late for full inclusion in this book, but offers a very different interpretation of the NES. Steiner's work is based on extensive archival research and deals in part with innovation and technological development during the period.

The literature more specifically on GDR technology and innovation is often of high quality, and new additions to it are appearing at a fast and furious pace. Some of the best current research appears in editions of the journals *Deutschland-Archiv*, *Jahrbuch für Wirtschaftsgeschichte*, and *Technikgeschichte*. Raymond Bentley provided an overview, *Research and Technology in the Former German Democratic Republic* (Boulder, Colo.: Westview Press, 1992), not long after the fall of the wall. The book is mainly oriented toward economic analysis of research and development spending and performance in the latter years of the regime, although it does give an interpretive historical overview. More dependable, because based on extensive archival research, although somewhat more limited in temporal coverage, is Agnes Tandler's Ph.D. dissertation, "Geplante Zukunft. Wissenschaftler und Wissenschaftspolitik in der DDR 1955–1971" (European University Institute, Florence, 1997). There is also a short overview of GDR technological development in the 1950s in Wolfgang Mühlfriedel, "Zur technischen Entwicklung in der Industrie der DDR in den 50er Jahren," in *Modernisierung im Wiederaufbau: Die westdeutsche Gesellschaft der 50er Jahre*, edited by Axel Schildt and Arnold Sywottek (Bonn: Dietz, 1993), 155–69. More general, but still useful, is the brief overview written by two longtime West German GDR specialists, Eckart Förtsch and Clemens Burrichter, "Technik und Staat in der Deutschen Demokratischen Republik (1949–89/90)," in *Technik und Staat*, edited by Armin Hermann and Hans-Peter Sang (Düsseldorf: VDI-Verlag, 1992), 205–28. Last but not least among the overview treatments is Joachim Radkau's highly stimulating and suggestive immediate response to the collapse of the GDR, "Revoltierten die Produktivkräfte gegen den real existierenden Sozialismus? Technikhistorische Anmerkung zum Zerfall der DDR," *1999* (1990): 13–42.

Detailed studies of individual industries and technology appear in some of the collections noted above, most notably those of Bähr and Petzina, and there are also special issues of *Technikgeschichte* (63, no. 4 [1996], and 64, no. 1 [1997]) that do the same. There are also essays on various scientific and technological areas in *Science, Technology, and Political Change*, edited by Benoit Severyns, Dieter Hoffmann, and Raymond Stokes (Turnhout: Brepols, 1999). For additional material on the electronics industry, a study cowritten by one of the most prominent actors in the GDR is fascinating, although it is sometimes weak on the linkages between technology and politics. See Erich Sobeslavsky and Nikolaus Joachim Lehmann, *Zur Geschichte von Rechentechnik und Datenverarbeitung in der DDR 1946–1968* (Dresden: Hannah-Arendt-Institut, 1996). Matthias Judt deals with the office-equipment and data-processing industries in "Zur Geschichte des Büro- und Datenverarbeitungsmaschinenbaus in der SBZ/DDR," in *Unternehmen zwischen Markt und Macht: Aspekte deutscher Unternehmens- und Indus-*

triegeschichte im 20. Jahrhundert, edited by Werner Plumpe and Christian Kleinschmidt (Essen: Klartext, 1992), 137–53.

Jörg Roesler continued his pre-1990 work through a series of articles on various aspects of innovation in the GDR. His work on the machine-tool industry is particularly insightful. See, for instance, his article on numerical control, "Einholen wollen und Aufholen müssen. Zum Innovationsverlauf bei numerischen Steuerungen im Werkzeugmaschinenbau der DDR vor dem Hintergrund der bundesrepublikansichen Entwicklung," in *Historische DDR Forschung,* edited by Jürgen Kocka (Berlin: Akademie-Verlag, 1993), 263–85. Chemicals are treated in English in Raymond G. Stokes, "Autarky, Ideology, and Technological Lag: The Case of the East German Chemical Industry, 1945–1964," *Central European History* 28 (1995): 29–45, and in essays by Rainer Karlsch and Harm Schröter in the compilation edited by Bähr and Petzina. The ill-fated aviation industry in the GDR is dealt with in Gerhard Barkleit and Heinz Hartlepp, *Zur Geschichte der Luftfahrtindustrie in der DDR 1952–1961,* 2d corrected ed. (Dresden: Hannah-Arendt-Institut, 1995). The uranium-mining and nuclear-power industries of the GDR are covered by essays in *"Strahlende Vergangenheit." Studien zur Geschichte des Uranbergbaus der Wismuth,* edited by Rainer Karlsch and Harm Schröter (St. Katharinen: Scripta Mercuratae, 1996).

The fascinating connection between spying and technological change is being investigated by scholars on the basis of materials available in the BStU. Kristie Macrakis's essay in the compilation by Hoffmann and Macrakis is the most extensive treatment in English. Jörg Roesler's "Industrieinnovation und Industriespionage in der DDR. Der Staatssicherheit in der Innovationsgeschichte der DDR," *Deutschland-Archiv* 27 (1994): 1026–40, provides an early and very suggestive interpretation. See also Gerhard Barkleit, *Die Rolle des MfS beim Aufbau der Luftfahrtindustrie der DDR,* 2d corrected ed. (Dresden: Hannah-Arendt-Insitut, 1996).

Finally, the history of industrial design in the GDR touches on crucial issues related to technology. A general treatment of issues related to politics, ideology, and design in the 1950s and 1960s is Raymond Stokes, "In Search of the Socialist Artefact: Technology and Ideology in East Germany, 1945–1962," *German History* 15 (1997): 221–39. The connection between industry, technology, and design in the 1950s and 1960s is also explored briefly in Stokes, "Plastics and the New Society," which will appear in a collection edited by David Crowley and Susan Reid, *Style and Socialism: Modernity and Material Culture in Postwar Eastern Europe* (Oxford: Berg, forthcoming). A more detailed treatment by a design historian is available in Heinz Hirdina's fascinating study, *Gestalten für die Serie. Design in der DDR 1949–1985* (Dresden: VEB Verlag der Kunst, 1988), which was published before the fall of the Berlin Wall and contains a mass of illustrations. A suggestive illustrated study of design in the GDR is also available in Georg C. Bertsch, Ernst Hedler, and Matthias Dietz, *SED* (Cologne: Taschen, 1994).

Index

Page numbers in *italics* denote illustrations; those in **boldface** denote tables. GDR, German Democratic Republic.

acetylene chemistry, 11–12, 50, 85, 89, 151, 203
aeronautical engineering, 25, 26, 27, 195; end to in GDR, 136–37
Agfa, 40
Albrecht, Ulrich, 27–28
Allied occupation of Germany, 17, 18, 30; as applied to Berlin, 110, 119; general policy, 15, 21, 43; restrictions on R&D, 27, 136; seizure of intellectual reparations, 25–26
Apel, Erich, 87, 88, 99–100, 115–16, 136, 139–40
atomic bomb, Soviet, 26, 27, 51
atomic energy. *See* nuclear power
autarky, 81, 111, 156–57; in chemical industry, 82; continuity into GDR period, 39–40; impact on technological development, 11–12, 17, 18, 132, 151, 203
automation, 48, 53, 72, 137–40, 171–72, 181, 195
aviation. *See* aeronautical engineering

Bähr, Johannes, 5
BASF AG, 83, 84
Baumbach, Alfred, 51
Beil, Gerhard, 185
Bell Labs, 94–95, 189
benchmarking, 80. *See also Weltniveau*
Bentley, Raymond, 4–5, 12, 177
Berlin Crisis, First, 34
Berlin Crisis, Second, 9, 53, 58, 76, 125, 139,

156, 196, 198, 201; and Group Technology, 116; and oil and chemical industry, 85–86, 92–93; and semiconductor industry, 102, 107, 108; and standardization, 121–25
Berlin Wall: construction of, 9, 10, 43, 57, 65; as factor in East German technological development, 10–11, 76, 110, 125, 131, 132–34, 136, 141, 144, 152, 196, 201; fall of, 1, 160, 161, 204; and Group Technology, 116; and oil and chemical industry, 86; *Republikflucht* of science and technology personnel and, 44–45; and semiconductor industry, 99–100; and technical standards, 119, 122, 123–24
Berliner, Joseph, 178
Bernicke, Eberhard (Special Deputy for Semiconductor Industry), 100, 101–2, 103–7
Bitterfeld, 16, 17, 44
BRABAG (Braunkohlenbenzin AG), 39
British Philips, 106
British-Thomson-Houston, 106
BSL Olefinverbund GmbH, 206
buna. *See* synthetic rubber
Buna Works, 85, 141, 206
Burrichter, Clemens, 46
BVS (Bundesministerium für vereinigungsbedingte Sonderaufgaben), 204

CAD/CAM (computer-aided design/computer-aided manufacturing), 171–88
camera industry, 17, 40–41, 72
capitalism, critique of by visitors to Hannover Trade Fair, 59–60, 61, 66

capitalist technology, 113, 122, 195
Carl Zeiss Jena. *See* Zeiss
Central Committee, 50, 112, 123, 139, 157, 181. *See also* SED
Central Institute for Automation, 137–41, 180
Central Office for Science and Technology, 69, 71, 95, 119–20, 144
centralization, 32, 37, 140
Chamber of Technology, 71
chemical industry, 4, 5, 12, 16–17, 53, 76, 107, 195; after 1990, 205–8; concentration into SAGs, 28; destruction in war, 19–20; under Honecker, 153, 169–70, 173; labs in, 38; in NES, 141, 150; pace of technological change in, 131–32; reparations and removals and, **20**, 22; *Republikflucht* and, 44–45; Soviet seizures of personnel from, 26; traditions of coal-based chemistry, 40, 156. *See also* chemicalization program; petrochemicals; plastics
chemicalization program, 50, 84–85, 86, 92, 205
Chemnitz, 16, 115, 137, 206
coal, 7, 87, 89, 155, 156
coal-based chemistry, 40, 50, 82, 85, 89, 156
COCOM (Coordinating Committee [for East-West trade]), 11, 78, 104–5, 107, 188, 192–93; evasion of restrictions of, 163, 164, 167–68, 171–72, 186–87
Cold War, 3, 7, 25, 46, 77, 85, 118, 133, 156, 162; and aeronautical engineering, 137; and semiconductor industry, 102
COMECON (Council for Mutual Economic Cooperation), 47, 134, 135, 180, 184
Commercial Coordination Agency (KoKo), 186
computers, 25, 136, 151, 181, 184, 188, 195, 196, 200; beginnings in GDR, 138, 179–80; impact of NES on, 149; and Stasi, 166–67, 170–74, 185, 187. *See also* microelectronics
consumer goods, 12, 61, 72, 76, 145–46, 151, 202, 203; under Honecker, 153–54
contract research, 49, 144, 152

control instrumentation, 25, 76
copying, 107, 171–72, 178, 185, 191–92
cybernetics, 148, 196
Czechoslovakia, 7, 76, 88, 115, 167

Degussa AG, 193
design, industrial, 17, 29, 48, 70, 113, 124, 128, 203; deficiencies in 1950s, 61; over-reliance on pre-1945 during fifties, 48; plastics and impact on, 145
destruction, 36; in chemical industry, 82; estimates of by USSBS, 18–19; in GDR literature, 19; levels of owing to war, 15, 17, 18–21, **20**
Deutsche Akademie der Wissenschaften (DAW, or AdW). *See* German Academy of Sciences
Deutsche Industrie-Normen (DIN; German Industrial Norms), 112, 117, 118, 125, 126–27
Deutsche Normen-Ausschuss (German Norms Committee), 118–25, 126–27
Digital Equipment Corporation (DEC), 166, 167, 168, 171–72, 181, 185
diodes. *See* semiconductor industry
dismantling: in chemical industry, 82; impact on USSR, 24–25; in Soviet zone of occupation, 19, **20**, 21–24, 28
Dow Chemical Company, The, 206, 207
Dresden, 16, 48, 119, 137, 140, 180
dyes, 80, 82

Economics Commission, 71, 101, 171
education, scientific and technical, 34, 43, 207
Edwards, Vincent, 4
Einheit (SED ideological journal), 70, 124
Eisenhüttenstadt, 16, 47, 90
EKO Combine (steel manufacturer), 47
electrical goods and electronics, 1, 4, 5, 11, 12, 48, 53, 195; capacity increases in war, 20; and chemical industry, 82; and cooperation with Japan, 105; at Hannover Trade Fair, 60–61; impact of Soviet seizures of on GDR technology, 24–25;

impact of war and dismantling on, **20**, 22; labs in, 38; at Leipzig Trade Fair, 72, 76; in 1960s, 145–46, 150; problems of innovation in, 41–43. *See also* computers; microelectronics; semiconductor industry

embargo. *See* COCOM

England. *See* United Kingdom

environmental problems, 96, 100, 207

espionage, industrial and technological, 67, 69, 122, 159, 203. *See also* Stasi

"failure," 3, 5–6, 33–35, 128; first system, 9

Falter, Martin, 94, 100–101, 104

Federal Republic of Germany. *See* West Germany

fine mechanics industry. *See* precision mechanics industry

Five-Year Plans, 181; First, 30, 42–43, 48; Second, 47–48, 138

foreign exchange, 64–65, 66, 78, 106, 154, 201; and oil and chemical industry, 84, 86, 88, 93; and Stasi, 169, 172, 185–86, 187

Forschungsrat. *See* Research Council

Förtsch, Eckart, 46

Frankfurt (Oder), 90, 100, 105; development of semiconductor works at, 97, 97–99, 145–46, 180; Soviet aid and, 103

"Friendship" pipeline, 86, 90

Gauck Authority, 161, 164

German Academy of Sciences, 52, 190; establishment and initial tasks, 31–32; as part of innovation system, 49

German Economics Commission, 30, 34, 38

"Germanization" of Soviet technology, 24–25, 28

Germany, division of: impact on traditional regional relationships, 17–18, 21, 33, 36, 156; as process of cultural divison, 57, 65–67

Gorbachev, Mikhail, 191, 198

Görlich, Paul, 103

GOST norms (Soviet state standards), 117, 121–122, 124, 127, 134. *See also* standardization

Great Britain. *See* United Kingdom

Group Technology, 111, 114–17, 126, 201

Halle, 16

Hannover Trade Fair, 9, 57–66, 68, 69, 75, 77, 79, 188

Hennecke, Adolf, 32–33

Hennecke movement, 32–33, 34, 46, 114

Herrigel, Gary, 16

Honecker, Erich, 11, 151, 153, 154, 157, 176, 198, 202, 204; and GDR in 1980s, 177, 179, 181, 182, 184, 190–91; and Stasi, 163, 168

Hoover Institution, 25

Humboldt University, 51

Hungary, 86, 167, 179

IBM, 181

ideology, 69, 127, 195; change of technology's place in, 49–50, 52–53, 77–78, 143–44; impact of on technological development, 1, 4, 102, 111–17, 131. *See also* socialist technology

I.G. Farben, 17, 44, 80–81, 92, 205; successors of, 6

Imperial Board for Economic Efficiency, 117–18

Imperial Chemical Industries (ICI), 93, 106

innovation, 8; reasons for poor record of in early GDR, 4, 5; shortcomings in, 39–43. *See also* system of innovation

Institute for Machine Tools, 72

Institute for Nuclear Physics, 48

Institute for Physical Chemistry, 51

Institute for Semiconductor Technology, 94, 100

integrated circuits. *See* semiconductor industry

Intel, 193

intelligentsia, 44–46, 52, 196

International Federation of Standardizing Associations (ISA), 118, 119, 121
International Standards Organization (ISO), 36, 112, 119, 121, 122, 124, 134

Japan, 7–8, 102, 105, 119, 186–88, 194
Jena, 17, 140
jet engine technology, 28

Kaiser Wilhelm Society and Institutes, 17, 31, 51
Karl-Marx-Stadt. *See* Chemnitz
Karlsch, Rainer, 19, **20**, 27, 34
Khruschev, Nikita, 88, 103
know-how, 132, 169, 184; acquired from western firms, 11, 106, 125, 201; impact of Soviet seizures of, 23
Kombinat Mikroelektronik Erfurt (KME; Erfurt Microelectronics Combine), 165, 181–82, 187–88, 190–91
Kopstein, Jeffrey, 199
Kortum, Herbert, 72, 138–40, 180
Kosel, Gerhard, 49

laser technology, 5
Lawrence, Peter, 4
Lee, W. R., 179
Lehmann, Nikolaus Joachim, 138, 149, 180
Leipzig, 16
Leipzig Trade Fair, 10, 59, 60, 77–79, 188; attempt to use for benchmarking, 66–76; decline in significance in late 1950s and 1960s, 72–76; history of through 1950s, 67–68; oil industry and, 86–87
Lenin, 1
Leuna Works, 83, 85, 91, 141, 145, 205–7
Lewis, Arthur, 106
Leybold AG, 105, 193

machine-building industry, 16, 18, 48, 71, 75, 112, 126, 175–76, *178*; chemical industry and, 88; complacency in, 141–42; Group Technology and, 114; labs in, 38; problems with innovation in early

GDR, 41–43; and recycling, 203; specialization in, 134–36; war damages to, 20
machine tools, 1, 4, 5, 10, 16, 48, 53, 112, 153, 200; after 1990, 206; assessment of technological development at Leipzig Trade Fair, 69–72; complacency in, 141–42; concentration into SAGs, 28; under Honecker, 153, 169–70; labs in, 38; in Soviet occupation period, 18
Macrakis, Kristie, 164
Magdeburg, 16
Maschinenbautechnik (journal for machine-building technology), 69
Mauer im Kopf (Wall in the Head), 10, 65
Max Planck Society and Institutes, 17
mechanization, 48, 96, 113, 138, 180
Merseburg, 16, 17, 83
metallurgical industry, **20**, 22
Meuschel, Sigrid, 199
microelectronics, 12, 196–97, 204; GDR traditions in, 179–81; under Honecker, 177–79, 181–94. *See also* computers; electrical goods and electronics
Mielke, Erich, 190
Ministry for Electrotechnics and Electronics, 166, 185
Ministry of Finance, 95
Ministry of Foreign Trade, 186
Ministry of Justice, 45
Ministry of Machine Building, 41, 121
Ministry for the Materials Economy and Trade, 157, 175
Ministry for Science and Technology, 51, 144
Ministry for State Security. *See* Stasi
missiles, 26, 27–28, 137, 195
Mitrofanov, Sergei, 114–16
Mittag, Günter, 171–72, 189
modular system, 72
motor industry, 17, 20, 27, 195

National Socialism, 30, 51, 68, 197; effects of autarky policies on East German industry, 17; and organic chemical industry, 81; and standardization, 118; technical cooperation with USSR, 1939–41, 27

national system of innovation. *See* system of innovation
nationalization of industry, 37, 52. *See also* SAGs; VEBs
NATO, 47, 122
Nelles, Johannes, 52
New Economic System (NES), 11, 142–52, 177, 202
norms. *See* GOST norms; standardization
nuclear physics, 26
nuclear power, 1, 48, 53, 146, *147*, 170, 180

office machinery, 16, 61, 138, 180, 183, 200
Office for Standardization, 120, 121, 123
oil industry, 19, 155, 156, 170, 202; imports from USSR and, 50, 84, 85–89, 151
Operation Ossawakim, 26–28
optics industry, 1, 4, 5, 10, 17, 42, 126, 138, *178*, 200; concentration into SAGs, 28; labs in, 38; at Leipzig Trade Fair, 72, 76; in Soviet occupation period, 18, **20**, 22; Soviet seizures of personnel from, 26
Ordinance on the Increase of Salaries for Engineering and Technical Personnel, 45
Ostpolitik, 154

Passport Penal Decree, 45
patents, 46, 70, 105; creation of system in GDR, 38–39
perspective planning, 43, 51
petrochemicals, 1, 11, 50, 108–9, 113, 116–17, 125–26; development in late 1950s, 80–93; at the Leuna Works, 201, 203; and NES, 151
Petzina, Dietmar, 5
pharmaceuticals, 75, 80, 82
Physikalisch-Technische Reichsanstalt (PTR; Imperial Institute for Physics and Technology), 17
planning system, 4, 8, 9, 52, 127; changes to under Honecker, 153–54; increasing sophistication of in 1950s, 46, 47–48, 50–52; introduction by Soviets during occupation, 28, 30–31; in NES, 148–49, 151, 202; as obstacle to innovation, 5; for

science and technology, 32, 38, 40, 42–43, 46, 99–100, 131, 144, 200; technology of, 195–96
plastics, 1, 50, 82, 92, 117, 125, 146; in chemicalization program, 85, 88; poly-ethylene development in GDR, 83–84, 141, 145; PVC, 92, 145
Poland, 15, 86
Politburo, 71, 101, 124, 134
precision mechanics industry, 17, 18, 20, 22, 114; labs in, 38
productivity, 32, 46, 50, 88, 188, 196, 200
Prussian Academy of Sciences, 31
Purkiss, Alan, 206

Radkau, Joachim, 29–30, 127
rate of defects, 40, 102
rationalization, 48, 117, 195
Rau, Heinrich, 112–13, 137
recycling, 12, 154–55, 158–61, 174
regional development policies, 16, 90, 97
Reisekader (officially vetted travel cadres), 65, 67
reparations, 9, 19, 21–26; end to, 47
Republikflucht (flight from the [German Democratic] Republic), 9, 10, 18, 27, 40–41, 43–45, 50–51, 196, 200; as factor in trade fair attendance in 1950s, 65, 67, 76, 78; and high-technology industry, 103, 107, 125, 137; and standardization, 122
Research Council, 45, 51–52, 71, 91; and semiconductor industry, 98–99
research and development (R&D), 9, 150, 200; Allied restrictions on, 27, 136; in chemical industry, 81–82, 85; difficulty of translating results into production, 41–43; funding for, 32, 37–38, 48, 144; impact of SAGs on, 37; in microelectron-ics in 1980s, 181–83, 204; planning for, 32, 38, 40, 42–43, 46, 47, 99–100, 131, 144; policy on in 1950s, 51–52; in re-cycling technology, 159–60; in semicon-ductor industry, 98, 99–100; shortage of capacity in GDR owing to Germany's division, 17–18

reverse engineering. *See* copying
Robotron, 166, 171–73, 182, 190, 192
Roesler, Jörg, 153, 164, 174

Saale River, 17
sabotage, 24, 25
safety technology, 70
SAGs (Soviet Joint-Stock Companies), 28–
    29, 32, 37; R&D in, 39, 40; return of to
    GDR, 47
Schabowski, Günter, 160
Schalck-Golodowski, Alexander, 86, 190
Schkopau, 16, 17, 50, 52
Schürer, Gerhard, 189
Schwedt, 16, 50, 90–92, 97
science and technology policy, 5, 42–43, 46,
    51–53, 144; Research Council and, 51–
    52; Stasi and, 174
scientific management, 33
secret service. *See* Stasi
Secretariat for Research and Technology,
    51, 144
SED (Socialist Unity Party), 11, 47, 58, 115,
    122; Central Committee conferences:
    —11th, 123; —16th, 112; party congresses:
    —3rd, 48, 138, 180; —5th, 50, 85; —8th,
    157; records of, 3
seizures: of equipment by Soviets (*see* rep-
    arations); of scientific and technical per-
    sonnel by Soviets, 9, 21–28, 32, 36, 82;
    return of personnel after end to, 9, 36, 44,
    51
self-sufficiency. *See* autarky
semiconductor industry, 48, 72, 80, 90, 113,
    125–26, 133, 141, 188, 201; development
    in late 1950s and early 1960s, 93–109,
    180; development during 1960s, 145–46
Semiconductors Corporation, 106
Sero (Secondary Raw Materials Company),
    12, 154–61, 174–76, 177, 202–3
Seven-Year Plan, 43
Shearer, Ronald, 117
Shell, 84
Siemens AG, 105, 192–93; move from
    Berlin to Munich during World War II, 18

Siemens-Edison, 106
Silesia, 15
socialist technology, 38, 109, 113, 114–16,
    125–28, 195; critique of by visitors to
    Hannover Trade Fair in 1950s, 60–61; and
    standardization, 122–25
Soviet Control Commission in Germany, 47
Soviet Military Administration in Ger-
    many, 28
Soviet Union, 1, 7, 46, 151, 156–57, 202;
    Communist Party of, 49, 86, 103; occupa-
    tion of zone in Germany, 8, 9, 15–35, 77;
    role of in GDR technical development,
    132; support for GDR, 53, 198, 204; tech-
    nical cooperation of with GDR, 9, 52–53,
    80, 90–92, 102–4, 108, 116–17, 125–26,
    134, 178, 184–85, 201; as unsuitable
    model for GDR, 111–12
Sovietization: of design, 29; of technology,
    4, 80, 93, 108, 109, 125–26; through plan-
    ning system, 31
space optics, 5
specialization, 133–36
Sputnik, 2, 9, 49, 53, 86, 125, 201
Stakhanovite movement, 32, 114
Standard Telephone Works, 106
standardization, 60, 72, 108–9, 117–125,
    126, 133, 157, 201
Standardization, Office for, 71
Stasi (Ministry for State Security), 154–55,
    159, 161, 177, 192, 198, 202; records of, 3,
    161–62; role in GDR technological
    development, 161–76, 185–87
State Planning Commission (SPK), 30, 50,
    58, 112, 119, 124, 144; and automation,
    138, 139; and Leipzig Trade Fair, 69, 71,
    76; and semiconductor industry, 95, 99,
    101, 103, 106
Statistisches Jahrbuch der DDR (*Statistical
    Yearbook of the GDR*) 74
steel industry, 42, 47, 90
Stiller, Werner, 166
Störfreimachung (policy of "freeing from
    [economic] disturbance"), 116, 133, 134,
    135, 136

Sutton, Anthony, 24–25
Swain, Nigel, 179
synthetic fibers, 50, 88, 145
synthetic oil, 19, 81
synthetic rubber, 17, 19, 52, 81, 82
system of innovation, 200, 201–2, 207;
   in aftermath of World War II, 136–42,
   144–45; continuity and change in, 37–38;
   creation of in GDR, 1953–57, 46–52; in
   GDR, 5, 11, 31, 33, 108, 132; problems
   of in initial GDR period, 38–43; and
   Stasi, 174

tape recording, 61, 62
Taylor, Frederick Winslow, 33
technical standards. See standardization
technically determined work norms, 46
technological culture: division of German,
   110–11, 124; East German, 10; shared
   German, 6; Soviet, 28
technological display, 57, 63–64, 76–77
technological style, 25, 28, 108; of eastern
   bloc, 127–28
technological tourism, 58–66
technological traditions, 9, 10; common
   German, 4, 65, 176; continuity of in East
   Germany, 29, 52–53, 207; divergence
   between East and West Germany, 35, 65–
   66, 126, 196, 200
technology transfer, 3, 4, 9, 80, 127, 136;
   Leipzig Trade Fair as mechanism for, 10,
   69–79; during Soviet occupation, 21–29;
   by Stasi, 165–68; from USSR, 90–92, 98,
   102–4; from West, 92–93, 98, 104–7
Texas Instruments, 101, 106
tire industry, 22
Thiessen, Peter-Adolf, 51–52, 99
Toshiba Corporation, 186–88
Trabant, 1, 2, 48, 49, 175
trade, 132, 153–54, 156; foreign trade companies, 74; in oil, 50, 84, 85–89; with
   USSR, 30, 43, 47, 134–36, 151
trade fairs, 9–10. See also Hannover Trade
   Fair; Leipzig Trade Fair
transistors. See semiconductor industry

Treuhandanstalt (THA; privatization
   agency), 204, 205
Two-Year Plan, 30

Ulbricht, Walter, 9, 11, 48, 49, 148, 153,
   157, 184, 202, 205; and automation, 139–
   40; and chemicalization program, 84–85;
   and NES, 142, 146, 149–52; and oil industry, 88–89; and semiconductor industry,
   103
United Kingdom, 7–8, 116, 155, 184, 194;
   standardization in, 118, 120; technological cooperation of with GDR, 92–93, 98,
   104–7
United Nations, 36
United States, 116, 155, 194; chemical
   industry in, 82; computers in, 179, 186;
   and embargo, 168, 172, 187–88, 189, 192;
   as mission-oriented economy, 176;
   occupation of eastern Germany by, 15,
   18; seizure of German scientific and technical information and personnel by, 25–
   26; semiconductor industry in, 94–95, 98,
   101–2, 104–5, 108, 184; space program,
   25; standardization in, 117, 118, 120
U.S. Strategic Bombing Survey (USSBS), 18–
   19
uprising of 17 June 1953, 9, 46, 112, 198,
   199
uranium, 7, 156
USSR. See Soviet Union

VEBs (People's Own Enterprises), 9, 28, 32,
   47, 49; R&D in, 39, 40
"virtual wall," 10, 110, 126, 128

Warsaw Pact, 47
Weiz, Herbert, 139
Weltniveau (world class technology), 88;
   measurement of, 69–70, 76
West Germany, 16, 149–50; activities in
   former GDR after 1990, 204–7; comparison with technological development
   in, 6–8, 34, 37–38, 50, 102, 116, 133–34,
   156, 175, 177, 188, 196, 200–201; as

West Germany (*continued*)
   diffusion-oriented economy, 176; East
   Germany's absorption into, 3; estimates
   of war damage to industry in, 19; founding of, 36; and standards/norms, 119,
   123–25; technical cooperation with and
   dependence on, 98, 104, 105, 107, 133
Wolfen, 16, 17
work norms, 9, 46
World War II, 12, 15, 83, 111, 118, 195
Wyschofsky, Günter, 86–87

Zeiss, 6, 17, 40, 59, 69, 103, 104, 180, 182;
   and automation technology, 138–40;
   damage to main works in war, 20; and
   Group Technology, 115; Oberkochen
   rival, 18; one-megabit chip and, 189–92;
   research capacity in Soviet occupation,
   18
Zeiss-Ikon, 17, 40–41
Zeitz Hydrogenation Works, 39
Ziegler, Karl, 141
Zuse, Konrad, 179–80

Library of Congress Cataloging-in-Publication Data

Stokes, Raymond G.
Constructing socialism : technology and change in East Germany
1945–1990 / Raymond G. Stokes.
   p. cm.
Includes bibliographical references and index.
ISBN 0-8018-6391-0 (hc : acid-free)
1. Technological innovations—Social aspects—Germany (East)
2. Technology—Social aspects—Germany (East) 3. Socialism—
Germany (East) 4. Germany (East)—Social conditions. I. Title.
HC290.795.T4 S76 2000
303.48′3′0943109045—dc21   00-008336